Can Privatization Deliver?

Infrastructure for Latin America

Edited by
Federico Basañes
Evamaría Uribe
Robert Willig

Published by the Inter-American Development Bank
Distributed by The Johns Hopkins University Press
1999

1300 New York Avenue, N.W.
Washington, D.C. 20577

Produced by the IDB Publications Section.
Distributed by The Johns Hopkins University Press
P.O. Box 50370
Baltimore, Maryland 21211

The views and opinions expressed in this publication are those of the authors and do not necessarily reflect the official positions of the Inter-American Development Bank.

Cataloging-in-Publication data provided by the Inter-American Development Bank Felipe Herrera Library

Can privatization deliver? : infrastructure for Latin America / edited by Federico Basañes, Evamaría Uribe, Robert Willig.

p. cm.

Includes bibliographical references.

ISBN:1886938385

1. Privatization—Latin America. 2. Privatization—Law and legislation—Latin America. 3. Investments—Latin America. 4. Infrastructure (Economics)—Latin America. 5. Contracting out—Latin America. 6. Concessions—Latin America. 7. Electric utilities—Latin America. 8. Water utilities—Latin America. I. Basañes, Federico. II. Uribe, Evamaría. III. Willig, Robert D., 1947– IV Inter-American Development Bank.

338.9805 C26—dc20 99-71691

Foreword

The potential for economic growth of nations is related to the state of their infrastructure. In this connection, it has been estimated that one percent growth in GDP requires an investment of 1 percent of GDP in energy, transportation, telecommunications, and water and sanitation infrastructure. For the economies in Latin America and the Caribbean to grow at annual rates of 5 percent, that same percentage of GDP will have to be invested each year, which in average 1998 regional GDP figures translates into annual investments of nearly $70 billion. Given the dilapidated state of infrastructure in many countries of the region, investment needs may be even greater.

Private sector participation in this investment process is sorely needed. Multilateral and bilateral sources supply enough funds to meet only 10 percent of investment needs, with the private sector supplying about 15 percent and governments the remaining 75 percent. But the capacity of governments to finance these investments is limited, not only because they come on top of pressing social needs, but because growth of public expenditure is increasingly constrained by the overriding need to maintain macroeconomic stability. In turn, governments have had to curtail investments or transfer responsibility to the private sector or communities.

During the past decade, there has been a significant change in the roles of the state and the private sector. The state has been progressively getting out of the role of planner, financier and manager, and assuming that of grantor (privatization, concession, management) and regulator or overseer of the provision of services by the private sector. The private sector, in turn, has moved from constructor of public works to financier, constructor, operator and manager. This shift in roles for the private and public sectors has not been easy. The services provided—public services of critical importance for economic development and loaded with political implications—are still the responsibility of the state.

The process of the state assuming the role of grantor received a strong push in the mid-1990s. As the decade closes, a wealth of experience has been accumulated in the granting process and in the subsequent private sector operation and government oversight. This experience can provide valuable information about the process of private sector participation— how to do it, how not to do it, or how to do it better.

The Inter-American Development Bank invited infrastructure development practitioners to meet and discuss these experiences at a conference on "Private Investment, Infrastructure Reform and Governance in Latin America and the Caribbean" in September 1997. The goal was to provide countries of the region with a compendium of best practices in private sector participation in infrastructure. This volume presents core studies from the conference along with others commissioned by the Bank. The studies deal with a timely second generation of issues such as legal frameworks, post-privatization governance, and contract enforcement and renegotiation, and not with the why and how to effect private participation.

The Bank Group itself—which has financed more than $35 billion in infrastructure since it began lending in 1961—has changed its instruments over the years to adapt to evolving needs in infrastructure development. The Inter-American Investment Corporation, created in 1989 to provide direct financing to the private sector, has moved toward financing small infrastructure works. Since 1994, the Multilateral Investment Fund under administration by the Bank has provided grants to develop regulatory frameworks, facilitate privatization and concessions, and support sector restructuring. Finally, the Bank's private sector window provides direct loans and guarantees for private infrastructure without government counter guarantees. This window promotes private sector participation not only through its financing, but because of its catalytic effect in attracting outside financing through risk guarantees and the umbrella protection on perceived political risks

This book marks a continuation of the Bank's evolving efforts to contribute to more effective and efficient provision of infrastructure services, a key ingredient in the economic development of the countries of Latin America and the Caribbean.

Enrique V. Iglesias, President
Inter-American Development Bank

Table of Contents

About the Authors

Fred Aarons is General Counsel for the Venezuela Branch of Citibank. He formerly served as Legal Counsel and Investment Officer for the Private Sector Department of the Inter-American Development Bank.

Rubén Avendaño is a Water and Sanitation Specialist with the Inter-American Development Bank and has worked for the Fondo Financiero de Desarrollo Urbano, the Departamento Nacional de Planeación and the Comisión de Regulación de Agua Potable y Saneamiento Básico in Colombia.

Federico Basañes is an Economist with the Infrastructure and Financial Markets Division of the Inter-American Development Bank.

Jacques Cook is the Senior Counsel of the Legal Department of the Inter-American Development Bank. As the Head of the Project Finance Unit, he coordinates all legal work related to IDB private sector infrastructure financing.

Paul Hennemeyer is an Economist with National Economic Research Associates. His international work in the electricity sector covers industry structure and regulation, legal and regulatory design, organization and management, and financial modeling.

Charles Jenne is a Partner in the Energies and Utilities Consulting Practice of PricewaterhouseCoopers, where he advises clients on private sector participation in the power and water sectors and other issues.

Janusz A. Ordover is a Professor of Economics at New York University and has served as the Deputy Assistant Attorney General for Economics in the U.S. Department of Justice.

Hugo Palacios Mejia is Partner and Legal Representative of Estudios Palacios Lleras S.A. He has served as Deputy Finance Minister of Colombia and as an Executive Director at the Inter-American Development Bank.

María Angela Parra is an Economic Research Analyst with the Banca de Inversión de la Corporación Financiera del Valle in Colombia.

Alejandro P. Radzyminski is an Associate with Skadden, Arps, Slate, Meagher and Flom.

Gustavo Ramírez is Director of Infrastructure for the Banca de Inversión de la Corporación Financiera del Valle in Colombia.

William Savedoff is Senior Economist with the Social Programs Division of the Inter-American Development Bank.

Pablo T. Spiller is the Joe Shoog Professor of International Business and Public Policy, and Chair of the Business and Public Policy Group, at the Walter A. Haas School of Business, University of California at Berkeley.

David Stiggers is a Civil Engineer who currently serves as a Senior Water and Sanitation Specialist with the World Bank. He has worked for Severn Trent Water International (STWI), one of the world's largest private water utilities.

Richard Tomiak is the Head of Commercial Development at Eastern Group, which carries out the company's international investment strategy. He was the Electricity Purchasing Manager with Midlands Electricity following privatization of the electricity industry in England and Wales.

Evamaría Uribe is Advisor to the Minister of Mines and Energy in Colombia. She formerly served as Senior Infrastructure Specialist with the Infrastructure and Financial Markets Division of the Inter-American Development Bank.

Sylvia Wenyon is a Senior Associate in Coopers & Lybrand. She specializes in water sector regulation and institutional reform, water resource management, and water pricing and trading.

Robert Willig is Professor of Economics and Public Affairs at the Woodrow Wilson School at Princeton University. He served as Deputy Assistant Attorney General in the Antitrust Division of the U.S. Department of Justice from 1989 to 1991.

Introduction

"Can Privatization Deliver?" is a question of critical importance to the economic future of Latin America and the Caribbean as well as the rest of the world. The current configuration of this fundamental query has been shaped by the interplay among three powerful forces: high expectations for infrastructure privatization to spur growth and development; some highly visible successes of infrastructure privatization; and many examples of disappointments in the slow pace and mixed results of such reforms. This book assesses both what is known as well as the issues that need more focused attention. Can privatization indeed live up to optimistic expectations? What policies might best improve the performance of infrastructure privatization in promoting economic development?

The novel perspective that emerges from this research focuses on the roles played by Latin American legal and governmental systems and structures in the design and workings of privatization instruments and post-privatization governance mechanisms. While there are features of the economic and political environment that can constrain institutional design and performance, there are also reforms, policies and types of concession and privatization contracts that can mitigate or eliminate some of the obstacles to successful privatization. The chapters in this volume detail the successes of infrastructure privatization in Latin America, but they also point to such problems as the reluctance of private investors to accept economic and political risks; resistance of national and subnational governments to relinquishing control over infrastructure; post-privatization monopolization and regulation that is excessively protective of private operators and unresponsive to dynamic needs; and post-privatization infrastructure management unconducive to creative entrepreneurship and broad-based development.

During the past decade, some Latin American countries have accumulated extensive experience in the privatization of infrastructure and in the institutional and regulatory reforms essential to foster a suitable environment for private investment. Chile and Argentina undertook remarkable reforms that allowed them to transfer publicly-owned utilities to the private sector either by selling the assets or through concession agreements. Because of the reforms, these countries were able to attract private participation to telecommunications, transportation, energy, and potable water and sewerage. The results in most cases have been more efficient services and increased coverage.

Potable water and energy have been a particularly important part of the infrastructure reform processes throughout the region. Most countries launched extensive reorganizations of their energy and potable water sectors that, in general, included the establishment of new regulatory frameworks, comprehensive sector restructuring, and different forms of private sector participation. Cities like Buenos Aires are considered pioneers at the international level, while others are just beginning to implement reforms.

Although the reform process has been widespread in the region, some countries have been more successful in attracting private sector participation than others. Different schemes have been attempted under diverse economic, legal and institutional circumstances. Success has depended on how well countries have implemented the reforms essential to attract private investment. In some cases, private participation has been restricted to "intermediate" contracts for the management of services, without major investment commitments; in others, private participation has been limited or nonexistent. Understanding these differences in performance requires identifying the determinants of a successful reform process, particularly the regulatory, legal and institutional frameworks that favor private involvement in infrastructure services.

Experience gleaned from early initiatives with private sector participation in the construction, investment and operation of infrastructure services in Latin America has shown that the absence of a sound legal foundation constrains privatization of public services. In such cases, private investors and potential lenders will seek to mitigate risk through government guarantees, indemnities from the sponsors, political insurance, or political cover from multilateral financial institutions. This adds to the transaction costs and makes privatized infrastructure contracts riskier and therefore more expensive and cumbersome to finance. In some circumstances, these flaws may be so serious as to render private investment in the sector impractical.

The reform process is now reaching smaller, less developed economies whose institutional capacity is weak and where it may be harder to encourage low-cost private sector participation. Therefore, the emphasis should be on establishing sound and credible rules and enforcement mechanisms that foster private initiative, preserve property rights, settle disputes, and protect contracts and consumers. Cumbersome regulations coupled with inefficient government institutions will result in high transactions costs for the new private investment initiatives, increasing the perceived risk.

This book analyzes the legal, regulatory, economic and institutional issues that are key to smoothing the transition to privatized infrastructure. Distinguished analysts from the private sector, academia, the banking community and international multilateral institutions contribute their diverse perspectives and recommend reforms in these areas to promote private sector involvement in infrastructure.

The analyses focus on the problems and solutions countries have been choosing during their transition to private participation in infrastructure provision. Based on high theory as well as examples from countries and stakeholders, the studies identify the barriers to private involvement in infrastructure and offer strategies for successful reform.

Part I examines, both theoretically and empirically, the structural conditions of the legal and economic systems that may critically bear on the success of privatization. This part includes a survey of the legal systems of five Latin American countries and a comparative analysis of critical areas that affect the long-term viability of private sector participation in infrastructure. It also includes fundamental explanations in terms of legal and economic theory of the structural requirements for successful privatization.

Part II presents and analyzes case studies of reforms in Latin American and Caribbean potable water and energy sectors. These two sectors have particular characteristics that have profoundly shaped the way in which private sector participation has been introduced. Water provision is an intrinsically local service with natural monopoly conditions. Competition generally cannot play a major role. Some segments of the energy industry are more open to competition, while others often remain natural monopolies. The surveys of empirical experiences are thematic and present evidence both on successful and problematic policies in terms of private participation in infrastructure.

Chapter 1 concludes that detailed concession contracts can help to launch initial privatization efforts by mitigating certain risks that a country's legal framework has not anticipated. But for privatization to be sustainable and irreversible, more complex legal and regulatory institutions must be established in order to minimize the political and regulatory risk imbedded in a contract modality not necessarily adapted to attract private investors.

Chapter 2 examines the legal systems of Honduras, Guatemala, Panama, Colombia and Argentina. The focus is on treatment of contractual agreements for infrastructure construction, investment and operation, as well as on the potential for financing these projects in international markets. It shows that there is significant variance among jurisdictions. Some already have considerable experience with concessions for infrastructure services, while others are still in a developmental phase. The chapter identifies legal uncertainties that are obstacles to private participation in infrastructure and provides insights for possible legislative reforms to improve the legal environment.

Chapter 3 discusses the bases of legal theory involved in securing efficient enforceability of infrastructure privatization agreements. In an effort to remedy or mitigate problems identified with contract enforcement, it proposes the novel concept of a treaty for the uniform treatment of investments in infrastructure projects. The key rationale is that a widely adopted uniform body of law would generate a larger body of precedent than would the law of a small country, and so the applicable law would mature more quickly and surely to the benefit of infrastructure development.

Chapter 4 examines concession contracts in the region. These often attempt simultaneously to serve a variety of functions, including regulation and allocation of project risks between the public and private sector. The chapter shows, however, that the practice of regulation by contract, rather than through a formal statutory framework, creates such significant difficulties as lack of clarity and flexibility. The chapter concludes that sustainable infrastructure development in the region depends vitally on creating a transparent legal and regulatory framework that defines the rules of the game and enforces them fairly.

Chapter 5 explains the use of concession contracts in Latin America and how a weak evaluation and awards process, as well as the lack of a formal regulatory framework, can result in inadequate agreements that ultimately lead to a need for renegotiation. It discusses pitfalls in contract design that predictably result in costly renegotiations of the agreements. These include inaccurate tariff structures and revenue forecasts, inappropriate allocation of risks, and failure to clearly outline key elements such as causes for termination, assignment of the concession and its revenue streams, tariff adjustment mechanisms, cost overruns, force majeure, and dispute resolution.

Chapter 6 looks at the growing trend toward local and regional provision of infrastructure, and analyzes two of the most important elements of successful private participation: local financial sectors that evolve and adapt to the needs of emerging infrastructure projects, and the development and implementation of institutional and regulatory reforms. Local and regional projects with smaller investment requirements experience difficulties in obtaining foreign capital from strategic investors because they are perceived to be riskier and unable to take advantage of economies of scale.

Chapter 7 emphasizes from the standpoint of economic theory and experience that a major task of public policy is to establish commitment. That commitment is hampered by a basic governance problem inherent in infrastructure sectors—the overarching political temptation to behave opportunistically vis-à-vis infrastructure operators, triggering a downward spiral of low prices, investment, quality and coverage, along with high levels of corruption. The solution starts with development of a regulatory framework that drastically limits governmental discretion; a policy of industry fragmentation, coupled with the elimination of exclusivity so as to promote potential competition; and the privatization of the sector, with an emphasis on domestic participation.

Economic analyses in Chapter 8 show that successful privatization requires that the government in some fashion become reliably committed to appropriate limits on its power to intervene in the operations and finances of the privatized enterprise. A balance is required between commitment to reduce political and regulatory risk, and flexibility to solve problems as they arise in the public interest. The body that performs the regulatory function must be committed to reaching decisions and resolving disputes on the basis of transparent application of economic principles that are publicly articulated before the commercial investment is ever made by the private operator. These principles can be articulated within a concession or privatization agreement, so that they become part of the contractual agreement between the enterprise and the government. Or they might be contained in an overarching statute, if it is credibly stable. The chapter articulates economic principles that might be included in a statute or in a concession agreement to serve as the foundation for transparent decisionmaking and dispute resolution.

Chapter 9 studies nine cases of private sector participation in water and sewerage services in the region. Its conclusions are based on an analysis of competition, information deficiencies, benefits, financial innovations, price impacts, regulation and institutional reform. The chapter finds that, on the whole, there has been little difficulty in attracting bidders for concessions. In some cases, however, there have been problems with the small number of bidders qualifying for the final tender. Information deficiencies appear to be commonplace, particularly with regard to asset and customer bases. Price increases also appear to be common. The chapter concludes that where investment commitments are clear throughout the life of the contract, it is possible to regulate by contract, using a fixed price formula. Where investment finance is provided by the private sector and there is uncertainty regarding future investment requirements, clear principles regarding these requirements are needed, and they are better stated and enforced through separate regulatory bodies.

Chapter 10 analyzes and compares the experience of private sector participation in potable water and basic sanitation services in five cities in Colombia. The chapter describes the particular difficulties of a reform process in a highly decentralized country with a fragile regulatory environment. The case studies show that while private sector participation has generated gains, primarily in terms of systems management efficiencies, the lack of a strong regulatory environment to limit discretion and the highly decentralized structure of service provision has limited private participation to management contracts, without major commitments for additional investments.

Turning to the Caribbean, Chapter 11 examines the Interim Operating Arrangement of the Water and Sewerage Authority in Trinidad and Tobago as a means of reviewing the country's experience in introducing private participation to its water and wastewater services.

Chapter 12 compares the reform and privatization experiences of the energy sectors in Argentina, Bolivia, Brazil, Chile, Colombia, Peru and El Salvador, largely from the perspective of testing, in a preliminary way, a strong theory about the principal elements needed for effective reform. The chapter identifies and discusses major successes and flaws in design and implementation of the reform processes, and proposes avenues of further research on how reform and privatization might best be pursued in order to achieve optimal outcomes.

Chapter 13 analyzes and compares independent power projects in Central America that share a common set of contracts for the purchase of electricity. The chapter finds that power purchase agreements generally satisfy investor demands, but not those of the customer. The agreements also protect independent operators from market pressures when exactly the opposite effect would be better policy. In light of the way other markets are developing in response to demands for greater efficiency in the electricity industry, the chapter suggests that Central American countries need to move away from the concept of the power purchase agreement as a contract for the physical delivery of energy, and move instead toward financial instruments that guarantee the purchaser a fixed price for a fixed volume of energy, irrespective of the physical state of the generating plant.

PART I

Can Privatization Deliver? Legal and Institutional Issues

CHAPTER 1

Sustainable Privatization in Infrastructure: The Role of Legal and Regulatory Institutions

Janusz A. Ordover and Evamaría Uribe

The privatization of public infrastructure services in Latin America and the Caribbean has proceeded rapidly over the past decade. Although further privatization may appear inevitable and the trend irreversible, governments will continue to pursue this policy only if the results are in the broad public interest. The participation in the privatization process of private capital—financial, physical or managerial—requires certainty and continuity. Accordingly, the *rules of privatization* must be clearly defined. Governments and private parties must achieve a balance to minimize the risks stemming from continued state involvement in public infrastructure, while at the same time assuring that the privatized entities do not exert undue market power to the detriment of consumers and the economy as a whole, compromising the initial objectives of privatization.

The privatization of infrastructure and public services has required the assistance of international investors and lending institutions to promote an enabling environment. Latin American policymakers have realized that legal, institutional and economic measures are needed to sustain financing.

Infrastructure privatization raises unique challenges beyond those generally encountered in other sectors. For infrastructure privatization to be successful, effective protection is needed of the interests of all the stakeholders—government, investors and the public. A clear legal framework that assures property and other rights of all the stakeholders, backed by independent regulatory and legal institutions, is essential to the success of privatization.

Chapter 2 of this book presents the results of a survey of the basic laws that govern the concession regime in five Latin American countries—Argentina, Colombia, Honduras, Guatemala and Panama. Based on that survey, this chapter provides some insights into the specific legal, regulatory and institutional conditions in Latin America that govern concession contracts for private investment in infrastructure. It analyzes the role of the legal system and regulatory institutions in the context of economic theory, and discusses specific legal decisions, emphasizing the analysis of concession contracts. The intention is to highlight the implications of concession contracts for sustainable private sector involvement in infrastructure.

Detailed concession contracts may help to launch the initial privatization effort by expressly providing for risks that a country's legal framework may not have anticipated. But for privatization to be sustainable and irreversible, there is a need to build more complex legal and regulatory institutions that minimize the deficiencies in contracts not necessarily designed to woo private entrepreneurs. By explicitly acknowledging that certain infrastructure activities are best advanced by private participants, this chapter highlights the need to put in place the necessary legal and regulatory institutions to support and enforce a private property regime. Other activities, like transportation infrastructure and public works, fall more under the realm of governments, and modern public procurement rules are needed to reduce risk as well as the uncertainties linked to unilateral actions of governments.

The first section sets forth characteristics—unique to infrastructure privatization—that require that the process be supported by a sound legal system as well as appropriate institutions to effectively protect all stakeholders. The second section defines the scope of privatization in infrastructure activities, distinguishing transportation infrastructure from public utilities services. The legal framework required for successful privatization is also analyzed. The third section discusses features of the privatization process in Latin America and analyzes some implications of privatization by concession for the sustainability of the reform effort. The fourth section examines the Latin American regulatory experience, emphasizing complexities in the concession. The last section summarizes the conclusions and options for reform.

The Need for Advanced Legal and Regulatory Frameworks in Infrastructure

General Benefits of Privatization

Privatization can improve basic public services and infrastructure and increase economic efficiency by improving the *static allocation* of scarce social resources.

When prices are brought closer into line with underlying costs, inefficiencies in the operation of the enterprise are reduced, the quality of service is improved, and the drain on the government's resources is reduced. Moreover, privatization improves the *dynamic allocation* of resources. By rewarding investors with the required rate of return on their investments, it assures appropriate incentives for investment and sustained growth. Privatization helps boost the development of domestic capital and financial markets, secures modernization and adoption of the technologies best suited for the particular product and geographic markets, and allows the introduction of socially desirable service offerings. Finally, privatization stimulates competition by fostering the efficient entry of new providers into the market and the exit of inefficient ones.

Privatization can also be consistent with certain public objectives at the least cost to society. In particular, if the costs and the financing involved are clearly identified, privatization can help to achieve *equity* objectives in the provision of infrastructure services. Also, governments may want to minimize the fiscal drain or maximize the privatization proceeds while seeking legitimate fiscal objectives.

The attainment of those objectives and benefits from privatization imposes tradeoffs. For example, maximizing revenues from privatization can conflict with the objective to stimulate an intensive investment program; keeping prices in line with costs can pose difficulties in ensuring universal service; and short-run pressures to guarantee financially viable privatizations can conceal the long-term benefits of fostering competitive private entry into infrastructure.

Unique Characteristics of Infrastructure

Infrastructure privatization raises unique legal, economic, technological and political issues beyond those generally encountered in the privatization of other sectors or industries.

• Services delivered by these industries are often regarded as "essential" both to the public and to the effective functioning of the economy. Hence, post-privatization oversight of the sector by the government or its agencies is essential. Such oversight, however, creates the danger of intervention that is inimical to the interests of the private sector.

• Provision of some infrastructure services is often characterized by scale and scope economies, leading to highly concentrated market structures with weak competitive forces, which can compromise efficiency in pricing and investment or imperil the quality of service. In certain cases, pre-privatization contractual provisions and ongoing regulation raise the risk that the sector will not adjust to changing market conditions. There is also the danger that the private operator of a regulated infrastructure service or industry might capture the regulatory process to its advantage (Noll, 1989).

• Because the necessary investments are often long-lived and sunk, they have a low value (productivity) in uses other than those for which they were designed.[1] The more the assets are sunk, the riskier the investment, and the greater the risks of operating them.[2] Thus, the government must make a credible commitment not to behave opportunistically vis-à-vis new owners of the infrastructure assets in order not to increase the financial costs of their investment. Because infrastructure assets are generally sector specific, the government can expropriate some of the post-privatization returns for itself (or for others) without fearing that the assets will be redeployed.[3] In particular, the government may attempt to capture some of the quasi-rents—revenues in excess of opportunity costs—that the investor earns while the assets are being depreciated, without fear that the assets will be moved into an alternative use.

• The fear of expropriation creates an inefficient incentive for the investor to try to recoup the full value of the investment rapidly. A major problem of concession arrangements in public works is that investors usually want to get out of the contract by selling the rights in the company that sponsors the concession contract. This is particularly common in road concessions and BOT (build, operate and transfer) schemes. Moreover, if the investor operates a concession, it runs the risk that the government can terminate the concession rights early and expropriate the return, or that it will undercompensate the concessionaire at the end of the concession.

• The longevity of the productive assets and the expertise acquired by the owners or concessionaires in operating them create the converse problem: that the investor will behave opportunistically vis-à-vis the government, consumers and other stakeholders. For example, an investor in a concession may impose switching costs on the government and extract some additional profits

---

[1]For example, a water treatment plant has no alternative uses; neither does a local telephone network or a high-voltage electrical network.

[2]See Baumol, Panzar, and Willig (1982) for a discussion of sunk costs and Dixit and Pindyck (1994) for the analysis of investment rules when costs are sunk and future returns are uncertain.

[3]Since concession agreements involve an important commitment of investment funds from the private partner, this discussion treats concessions as a type of privatization.

when the concession is up for renewal. Also, at renewal time, the concessionaire will likely have superior information regarding the future value of the concession license, and may be able to benefit from it.

• There may be significant impediments to entry into the provision of these services, even if post-privatization entry is permitted. Hence, competition alone cannot be relied upon to constrain the post-privatization performance of the sector. However, there is also a risk that concerns regarding the recovery of investments in these long-lived and sunk assets will be used to justify extended protection from competition.

• Prior to privatization, public services are generally run by a state-owned monopoly enterprise. Privatization often entails not only a transfer of these assets into private hands, but also the break-up of the state enterprise. Such restructuring is often opposed by many interests, and these political reactions can lead to inefficient enterprise structures and governance arrangements.[4]

• Because public services are considered essential and highly visible, political considerations are likely to affect the privatization process itself and raise the risk that public sector policies could be driven by political objectives rather than more neutral public goals.[5]

• Market competition plus appropriate legislation assure pro-consumer competitive pricing behavior, but these safeguards are not always present in certain bottleneck facilities or natural monopoly activities in infrastructure.

Sound Legal and Institutional Systems

These unique characteristics of infrastructure require that the privatization process be supported by a sound legal and institutional system that effectively protects all the stakeholders, particularly consumers of the services, investors in the privatized entity, the lending community, present and future competitors of the privatized provider of the infrastructure service, and the general public. This increases the importance of stable, transparent, unbiased, comprehensive and predictable legal and regulatory regimes and the appropriate institutions. For example, the service provider may want to take out profits sooner rather

---

[4]For example, there may be restrictions on layoffs or insistence that the concessionaire or the private company continue providing services that are unnecessary or unremunerative.

[5]See Chapter 8, which discusses the economic welfare criteria pertinent to analyzing sectoral performance.

than later.[6] This leads to upward pressures on prices in the post-privatization period, which might conflict with the government's objectives to keep prices low, or even to reduce them (possibly in excess of inflation). Clear legal and regulatory rules reduce the risk of government-induced under-recovery of investment expenditures. Also, for a variety of reasons (such as national security), countries often restrict foreign participation in certain public sectors. Since political tensions may arise due to even limited foreign participation in these sectors, foreign investors may require more protection than in other sectors. Applying international norms for nonpoliticized dispute resolution would reduce the perceived investment risks and increase the likelihood of foreign participation on competitive terms.[7]

Infrastructure industries are generally protected by economic and legal barriers to entry. Changing technologies have reduced impediments to entry in many sectors, and legal impediments may continue even after entry has become an economic possibility. Hence, the owner/operator of the privatized assets faces the risk that the government will remove the legal barriers and foster competition to the detriment of the incumbent.[8] While the incumbent must be protected against such surprises (particularly when the privatization agreement assures exclusivity), the government should also have enough flexibility to promote competition when it becomes feasible and in the public interest.

Transparent and predictable legal and regulatory frameworks, including rules, regulations and procedures, facilitate the balancing of conflicting interests. In Latin America, the private sector participates, in varying degrees, as an investor in infrastructure assets and services. The challenge is to reduce further the obstacles to guaranteeing sustainable private sector participation and to improve the environment for both private investors and the international lending community to participate in these projects. The terms on which the private sector is willing to participate in privatizing a country's infrastructure or services reflect the perceived risks of privatization: the lower the perceived risks, the better the terms on which such participation will occur. The country's legal

[6]Recall that the longevity of infrastructure assets, their sunk nature, and the limitations on the scope of contracts that can be written between the government and the concessionaire create incentives for quick recovery of the investment cost.

[7]The escalation of disputes in critical sectors is not confined only to less developed countries. Consider the tensions between the United States and the European Union regarding the merger between McDonnell Douglas and Boeing, two U.S. aircraft manufacturers, as well as other airline industry disputes throughout the world.

[8]In Argentina, the government authorized international call back services even though the original concession contract apparently barred them.

and regulatory framework and institutions play a significant role in determining the magnitude of such risks.

Key Legal Aspects

Infrastructure privatization is not likely to take root, succeed and achieve its public policy objectives unless private investors can be assured that their investments in human resources and physical, organizational and other assets will generate an adequate economic return.

Because privatization of infrastructure assets creates a novel set of property rights, and with it a new set of risks for those who own or operate the property, the government must provide legal assurances that it will not act opportunistically. Clear private property rights and mechanisms to enforce those rights provide the necessary springboard for private business activity by creating a climate that fosters entrepreneurship, encourages private investment in productive assets, and increases reliance on markets to guide the static and dynamic allocation of resources.

In order to encourage and sustain efficient private sector participation in the provision of public services, a country's legal and regulatory framework should at least include several key aspects. The first is to clearly define the scope and nature of private property rights in the provision of public services.[9] The legal system must create an environment in which private property is established, protected, nourished and respected, while at the same time ensuring that the private sector makes use of its rights in a manner that serves the public interest. In this respect, freedom of entry into infrastructure and a sound system of competition and antitrust laws will provide an initial common ground to preserve those rights while creating opportunities for the efficient allocation of private and public resources.

Second, the legal and regulatory framework must encourage the efficient flow of private resources to infrastructure by removing legal and other artificial obstacles to the private provision of services. The provision of public sec-

[9] Contract and property laws are only two parts of the substantive legal framework necessary for effective private sector participation in the provision of public sector services. In Latin America, most of the substantive legal framework—such as banking sector laws—are already in place. However, that is not necessarily the case in infrastructure activities, where governments still reserve broad interventions for themselves, even in services that could be privately provided.

tor services that are not privatized outright also requires an environment for efficient contracting between the government and the private sector. In particular, the legal system should facilitate the efficient allocation of risks, and control and deter opportunistic behavior by all parties to the contract.[10]

Third, the legal and regulatory framework must also provide an efficient mechanism for resolving disputes between the parties and assure the private parties' recourse to fair and speedy dispute resolution mechanisms. Judicial and regulatory decisions must be transparent and based on precedent, and laws and regulations must be uniformly enforced.[11]

New Institutions

Regulatory institutions are needed to guarantee access to public bottleneck facilities or to protect consumers whose services are provided by a natural monopoly. Independent regulatory institutions are also needed to guarantee privatization commitments, protect new investors against unilateral expropriation, and ensure the return on investment to the new private entrants. Ultimately, this will guarantee long-term financing and sustainability of private investment in infrastructure.

The need for regulatory intervention in certain natural monopoly activities gives rise to regulatory risk, which involves government actions that lower the service provider's profits. These actions may or may not result from legitimate public policy concerns. The existence of regulatory risk increases the importance of a sound regulatory regime and it requires the design of new regulatory and public institutions. Otherwise, regulatory risk can increase through undue political influence on the service providers or because of institutional weaknesses such as lack of technical expertise. This problem is particularly acute in the provision of local services such as water and sewerage, where local and municipal governments may have regulatory authority over the privatized service.

---

[10]The fact that the government is a party to the concession contract, retains an economic interest in the assets, and may regulate the privatized services engenders contractual complexities and risks that differentiate this category of contracts from pure private contracts.

[11]The scarcity of judicial precedent in the area of infrastructure privatization in Latin America makes it doubly important that the courts and regulatory agencies explain their decisions as fully as possible so as to establish a body of precedent that reduces the uncertainties associated with private property rights and contract interpretation (see Chapter 3).

New and properly designed institutions will help to minimize this regulatory risk. The regulatory agency must enjoy independent legal status and not serve simply as a mouthpiece of the government. While it is proper for the relevant ministry or the local mayor to formulate overall policies for the sector, it is inappropriate for the government to enforce these policies on a day-to-day basis under the veil of a nominally independent regulator. A regulatory agency must be truly independent—it cannot be captured by the industry it regulates, and must be independent from the government. The task will be to identify those forces and constraints that prevent the regulator from being captured.

In summary, regulatory agencies must be independent, the regulatory procedures must guarantee transparency, and the regulatory system and institutions should be accountable to the society as a whole. The agencies must be free of political interference and their decisions must be appealable to the courts by well-defined procedures.

What Can Be Privately Owned?

Defining the Scope of Private Property Rights in Infrastructure

To define the scope of privatization in infrastructure, it helps to follow the microeconomic distinction between public and private goods: private goods are those that allow rivalry and exclusion, and public goods are those that exhibit nonrivalry and nonexclusion. Economic theory suggests that private property is more efficient whenever the cost of establishing and enforcing ownership rights is lower than the benefits (Cooter and Ulen, 1988). The costs of establishing and enforcing ownership claims is low for private goods and high for public goods.

The term "infrastructure" is misleading in this respect and for the purpose of this analysis we prefer to distinguish among the different activities in infrastructure (see Box 1.1). The distinction is important when analyzing the role of governments in the supply of infrastructure activities, the role of the legal and regulatory frameworks and institutions in guaranteeing that markets and private entrepreneurs supply the services, and the impact of concession contracts for the sustainability of the privatization effort. Accordingly, we distinguish transportation infrastructure and public works from public utilities (telecommunications, energy, water and sewerage, and rail services).

Box 1.1
Transportation Infrastructure vs. Public Utilities Services

Transportation Infrastructure and Public Works
Transportation infrastructure such as bridges and roads are usually termed impure public goods. For those goods, exclusion may be feasible but not desirable, since the marginal cost of using empty roads is zero, except in the case of congestion, which favors exclusion. Near the end of the "pure public goods" spectrum, the government will be active not only in regulation and monitoring, but also in publicly providing the good.

Public Utility Services
Public utility services such as telecommunications, rail services, energy, and water and sewerage fall into a grey area with respect to the economic definition of "public good." Although the incremental supply for some utilities services has a positive marginal cost, and the cost of exclusion could be greater than the benefit (i.e., water and sewerage), those services tend to fall more in the range of publicly-provided private goods (see Stiglitz, 1988).

Transportation Infrastructure and Public Works

Government at all levels play a major role in the supply of transportation infrastructure. In this class of service (roads, bridges, channels, etc.), sunk costs are significant and the government must play an active role in planning, coordinating and monitoring construction. Furthermore, this role could be extended to cost recovery, since this is usually highly dependent on the level of traffic and congestion. Generally, fiscal remedies are necessary to smooth out construction costs of the basic facilities.[12] The private sector can be a useful complement to government action. For example, BOT (built, operate and transfer) schemes for the construction and financing of public transportation facilities can help governments to channel private financing and operational expertise. In the near future, widespread private ownership is not expected, and the government will remain the main provider and contractor of private sector exper-

[12]In this line of argument, one can understand why governments bail out failed road concessions due to unexpected losses following foreign exchange devaluations.

tise. Modern public procurement rules will be needed to attract the private sector at competitive and low-cost terms.

Public Utility Services

In services like telecommunications, electricity, gas, and water and sewage, bottleneck facilities or networks coexist with a potentially competitive supply, markets for the service do exist, and the final service to the customer is commercially priced. The final commodity is a private good, prices and cost are clearly distinguished, and demand is clearly separable (in terms of ease of exclusion).

Among infrastructure activities, public utility services are the most suitable for privatization. Accordingly, the role of the law and, subsequently, of governments, is to ensure that markets work. For this, there is a need to put in place and maintain the legal institutions that support the private ownership of productive assets, including private property, as well as contract and business laws—the basic ingredients of a private property regime. The legal framework must also include basic banking, commercial, and bankruptcy law, an independent judiciary and independent regulatory institutions. All private entrepreneurs involved in providing utility services must be ensured a common set of rules. In addition, there must be economic regulations to prevent abuse of monopoly or dominant positions, and sound competition and antitrust laws to protect competitive private supply. Free entry into the public utilities sector will also be an important factor in guaranteeing that the most efficient private entrepreneurs participate, and to avoid protecting private legal monopolies.[13]

Finally (and importantly), the legal system should put in place institutions that enforce property rights and resolve infringement disputes. Even a regime that shows great deference toward private property is not necessarily free of government involvement or interference with the rights of property owners. Accordingly, there is always a risk that the government will modify the scope of those rights in ways that do not invariably benefit the owner. Property

[13]In this regard, the countries of Latin America differ from those of Eastern Europe, as well as Russia and China, where the rudiments of a private property regime are only now being developed and introduced. Frydman and Rapaczynski (1994) develop the concept of the "property rights regime" more fully. When the rule of law is extremely weak and protection of private property is not effective, private business activity is likely to be confined to sectors that do not require significant sunk investments (e.g., basic retail services, labor-intensive farming, and light manufacturing).

owners need protection and recourse against any opportunistic behavior by governments that substantially modifies their rights.

Features and Implications of Infrastructure Privatization in Latin America

Infrastructure privatization in the region has taken many forms, including the outright sale of assets as well as other intermediate forms such as concessions and contractual arrangements between the government and the private entity. This section focuses on intermediate forms and analyzes some distinguishable features and their implications for the sustainability of the privatization effort.

Constitutional and Legal Restrictions on Private Involvement in Infrastructure

Legal and institutional obstacles in Latin America can prevent efficient and low-cost private sector involvement in infrastructure. Some countries impose constitutional and legal restrictions on the private ownership of productive infrastructure assets. As surveys indicate, private sector participation in the provision of infrastructure services is still "subject to the will of the government authorities."

These restrictions stem from the fact that some countries consider "public services" to be the exclusive domain of the state. The scope of private involvement in providing infrastructure services is generally more circumscribed than in other types of services. Latin American legislatures and executive branches retain a great deal of discretion in the implementation of private sector participation in public infrastructure services.[14] This approach is an outgrowth of constitutional and legal notions that the provision of these services is not naturally in the purview of the private sector.

Ambiguities in the constitutional framework regarding ownership of infrastructure activities can create significant investment risks. A new government is more likely to reinterpret the constitution than to change it. Hence, investors may ask for, and the government may want to agree to, clear constitutional and legal provisions regarding infrastructure ownership. In this respect, it could be useful to go back to the distinction between public infrastructure

[14]For example, in some Central American countries the General Assembly is still in charge of approving concession contracts in infrastructure, including future changes in the conditions of the contracts (i.e., tariffs).

works and public utility services made earlier in this chapter. Arguments for public ownership of transportation infrastructure (roads, bridges) are usually better founded than those for public provision of services such as utilities.

Asymmetric Rights in Concession Contracts

One of the basic assumptions in private contracts is that there is a balance between the two parties in the contractual agreement, including a balanced resolution of disputes or disagreements over the performance of the contract and its interpretation. The two contracting parties have the same rights and status before the law and the courts. By contrast, in a concession agreement,[15] the government as signatory party reserves for itself certain powers to which the private party is not entitled (see Box 1.2). The notion attached to the public service concept changes the balance between the two parties. The implicit recognition that asymmetric rights exist has economic and financial counterbalances: the private party is allowed to claim economic compensation for damages in cases where the government resorts to early termination for reasons not attributable to the private concessionaire.[16]

In the case of unilateral amendment, some laws allow the private party the right to claim that the modified contract maintains the economic and financial equilibrium that was originally agreed when the contract was entered into. So, in practice, the private party accepts the imbalance if it is compensated properly. Obviously, this increases the risks perceived by possible investors, thus increasing the cost of privatization.

This asymmetry is a major source of regulatory and political risk, since the public authority generally uses these powers in the "public interest." In some legislation, the specific circumstances that can be invoked are not explicitly defined and there is wide room for the public authority to use its discretion to interpret the exact meaning of "public interest."

---

[15]A concession agreement is understood as a contract that grants the concessionaire the use of certain assets or the right to provide certain services on an exclusive basis. The rights and obligations of the parties concerning the use of the assets and the provision of the services are defined and protected by the concession contract.

[16]In some legislation, the process to claim compensation for damages involves a challenge before the courts, and the burden of proof falls on the concessionaire to demonstrate that performance followed the letter of the contract.

Box 1.2
Asymmetric Government Power in Concession Agreements

Early Termination
By invoking the public interest, the government can redeem unilaterally or terminate early the concession rights. In some instances, the authority has no need to express an explicit cause for redemption; this right stems from the powers of the government acting on behalf of society as a whole. The private counterpart is entitled to financial compensation.

Unilateral Amendments
Governments can unilaterally adapt the contract to new or unforeseen circumstances under the assumption that the amendment is necessary to preserve the public interest. By contrast, the private concessionaire is not entitled to unilaterally modify the contract.

No Early Termination for the Private Party
In some countries, government default is not considered grounds for early termination by the concessionaire. But the government has the right to early termination.

If the concession contract is merely conceived as an instrument in the hands of the government to provide a service indirectly (for example, to provide transportation infrastructure), and the contract's provisions are part of a public procurement contract (similar to buying supplies for the Ministry of Defense or computers for government offices), then the government (as the active party) could reasonably be allowed to act unilaterally to improve the contract or adapt the service to changing conditions. But even in this scenario some caution is necessary: the private party in public contracts to construct infrastructure is also assuming risks and undertaking substantial capital investments and financial commitments that otherwise could be put to better use.

Besides the distinction made between transportation infrastructure and public utilities services, there are also important differences in the implications of unilateral decisions of governments. In the case of transportation infrastructure, given the permanent role the public authority may have in building this infrastructure, unilateral rights in favor of the government will probably be necessary to guarantee performance, contract adaptation and the timely construction of the facility. As stated, the government can play a very active role in planning, coordinating and monitoring the construction of this type of infrastructure (roads, bridges, channels). Furthermore, this active role is also extended to the cost recovery stages, since investment recovery is usually highly dependent on the level of traffic and congestion. Generally, a combination of diverse fiscal resources is necessary to finance the expensive infrastructure.

By contrast, the use by the government of unilateral powers for public utilities services could become a major source of instability and risk, compromising sustainable privatization and increasing the cost of private involvement. These services are the primary focus of private investment in Latin America and present strategic opportunities in emerging markets in general. One can expect governments to intervene with good intentions; however, changes in political administrations could result in amendments to contracts that could jeopardize the privatization effort. This is one drawback of public concession contracts as efficient mechanisms to promote private investment and reduce the risks and costs of private provision. In practice, in services like telecommunications and energy, the dominant role of governments and its concessioning power are de facto barriers to entry and impose inefficient restrictions to private entrepreneurship.

International Arbitration to Enforce Ownership Rights

In many Latin American countries, concession agreements in infrastructure privatization forbid the use of international judicial arbitration mechanisms to enforce them or to settle disputes among the parties. In the legal tradition for concession agreements in some Latin American countries, the choice of forum to solve disputes is strictly confined to national courts and application of the country's public administration procedures. In short, the choice of forum and laws for conflict resolution may be limited by constitutional or legal restrictions that prevent any contractual choice by the parties to the agreement. This could have important implications in attracting international investors and could require a special guarantee regarding the independence of the national judiciary.

Differences between Sale of Assets and Privatization by Concession

In Latin America, the rights and obligations of the owner of assets privatized through sale, along with the use of those assets, are protected by the general rule of law, that is, the country's legislation, regulatory mechanisms and courts. In other words, after the transfer of the assets, the government's role becomes one of making laws and regulations and upholding the law. In an asset sale, the purchaser must be reassured that the law and the judicial institutions will protect him and that the pre-privatization commitments that prevented the government from behaving opportunistically will be reinforced.

In the case of privatization by concession, the government's twin roles as party to the contract and enforcer could entail conflicts of interest and interference. In other words, the government is a contracting party in charge of administering and renegotiating the contract, but it also enforces the appeal or dispute resolution process. In the latter case, the dispute mechanism should comply with the public administrative process that involves the government in most parts of the process. The difficulty in this case arises because the public contract (the concession) falls under a contractual regime with distinct characteristics. The contractual regime is part of public procurement laws and procedures that entail special provisions absent in private contracts. The traditional legal regime for public contracts in Latin America gives rise to concerns about its ability to guarantee private entrepreneurship in infrastructure.

Other Risks

The use of concession contracts for complex utility services such as water and sanitation has additional downside risks. Because the concessionaire does not own the assets, it does not have an adequate incentive to maintain them. In addition, the concessionaire has a strong bias for making operational decisions in its own favor which cannot be easily observed by the government. In a concession arrangement, the owner of the asset has a strong incentive to monitor the actions of the concessionaire. While this is not surprising, it makes it difficult for the concessionaire to make business decisions and disrupts daily operations of the business (this has been an endemic problem in the Argentine water sector, for example). Furthermore, if the government exercises its right to modify the contract, the result will be inefficiencies in management and distortions in the concessionaire's business and financing plans.

Institutional and Regulatory Aspects of Concession Agreements

A Decade of Regulatory Reform in Latin America

Regulatory reform has been the companion piece in Latin America's infrastructure reform effort. This has not only implied a new set of rules but an in-depth review of the way governments traditionally think about regulation. Creating new regulatory institutions in Latin America has not been an easy task. The legal and institutional peculiarities of the region are creating new and different challenges that must be addressed for reform to be successful and sustainable.

Government's traditional role in infrastructure gave ministries and public officials a full discretionary and active role in setting regulations. But "regulation" as such was limited to enacting administrative and legal rules and procedures, and was viewed as an administrative endeavor involving discretion and political will. The long-term sustainability of private sector arrangements, however, will depend heavily on successfully building new and appropriate regulatory institutions and reforming old administrative practices. This requires rethinking the meaning of regulation and the jurisdiction of the institutions involved. Even then, institutional reform does not exclude nor substitute for the most important task—allowing the markets to do their work, promoting and preserving competition whenever possible, deregulating previously overregulated infrastructure activities, and limiting intervention to areas that require consumer protection from abusive natural monopolies.

The extent of regulatory risk and the impact of regulatory practices in terms of sustainable private involvement in infrastructure will depend on the modalities of privatization and even the contractual arrangement chosen as the model for private involvement. The specific sector structure and the possible role of market competition will also influence the choice of regulatory instruments, the appropriate form of regulatory intervention, and the role of contracts as substitutes or complements for regulation. Finally, the institutional capacity for regulation will have a role in defining the extent of regulatory risk. Complex contracts will be difficult to deal with when the lack of institutional expertise and technical capabilities to handle the contract exacerbates the regulatory risk. This problem becomes acute in local services such as water and sewerage, where subnational levels of government play a major role.

What Is Regulation in a Concession Contract?

Latin American governments have shown a preference for concession agreements or some intermediate form of public/private contractual arrangement for the privatization of certain infrastructure services (particularly water supply and sewerage). From a political perspective, state ownership of infrastructure assets and the provision of services is assumed to guarantee that social obligations will be met. It is also believed that ownership will allow the government to intervene whenever it perceives that the service provider is not fulfilling its obligations.

Many private contracts are self-enforcing. Each party fulfills its obligations because reputation matters to both—the supplier wants future business and the buyer must be able to attract future suppliers. Even when reputation does not matter, in most cases it is so easy to verify that neither party can expect to profit from opportunistic behavior.

However, the longevity of concession contracts makes them poor candidates for self-regulation. Moreover, an independent agency must monitor the performance of the contract because the concessionaire does not necessarily have an incentive to meet contract provisions if doing so reduces its operating profits. Market forces in other sectors of the economy generally do not exist in certain areas of infrastructure (like public construction works) or are extremely weak (water and sewerage).[17] In such instances, the concessionaire is not driven by market forces to satisfy the public policy objectives that motivate privatization, but is driven exclusively by profit maximization motives.

The weaker the forces that make the concessionaire abide by the contract, the more important the role of the regulator. An independent agency must monitor the performance of the licensee/concessionaire and require it to adapt to unforeseen circumstances. However, some qualifications for the case of concession agreements are needed, as will be addressed below.

Concession Agreements and Regulatory Independence

Regulation of concession agreements is complex because governments often retain for themselves contradictory functions that can create conflicts of inter-

[17] In other public utilities like energy and telecommunications, these forces can be extremely weak because governments have elected to foreclose competitive entry, even when such entry would be feasible from a technological standpoint.

est or exacerbate the regulatory risk involved in the implementation of the concession agreement.

The government, as the owner of those assets, is a signatory party to the agreement. At the same time, it performs standard regulatory functions (the regulation of natural monopolies to protect consumer interests). Incentives involved in contract performance could be aligned with those of the private party. The higher the profitability and the expansion in investment, the higher the net present value of the assets involved. But the regulation of a natural monopoly that entails prevention of monopoly abuse to allow prices to mimic a competitive market could dictate exactly the opposite result. This is obviously a conflict of interest that is not easily solved by merely declaring the independence of the regulatory authority as a separate entity.

Because the public authority surrenders its duties as the main service provider only temporarily, the concession contract usually includes very detailed clauses to account for all the complexities of the service and to anticipate every possible circumstance in the development of the contract. The concession contract becomes the most important instrument available to the authority to guarantee compliance with its duties regarding service provision. Therefore, the government is also retaining another important function; namely, guaranteeing that the concessionaire or the private contractor complies with very detailed contract provisions and obligations, some of them involving operational or managerial requirements. Thus, contract interpretation and the need to adapt it to changing circumstances become major tasks in the concession performance and could become an important source of risk for the two parties involved, compromising the sustainability of the privatization endeavor.[18] If the private partner is not in compliance, the government retains the right to intervene unilaterally to sanction, or to declare the contract void. So, as a contracting party the government is not on an equal footing with the private counterpart.

Finally, the government acts not only as a contracting party but also retains its administrative functions in the appeal or dispute resolution process. This could entail conflicts of interest and interfere with concession commitments.

---

[18]The problem is exacerbated by the traditional bureaucratic and legalistic approach of public administration in some Latin American countries. When the government becomes a co-administrator of the contract risks, inefficiencies and perverse incentives are the result. For example, to avoid sanctions from an interventionist regulator or to prevent unilateral termination by the public partner, the concessionaire could choose to closely follow the letter of the contract, adopting inefficient and costly technologies or operational procedures.

The Granting Authority vs. the Regulatory Authority

A concession is by definition a contract between a public authority and a private firm. Therefore, the public authority that signs the contract (granting authority) is the party responsible for its performance. It keeps for itself the final say on tariffs and is the only party legally entitled to unilaterally intervene in or to terminate the contract on "public interest" grounds. As a signatory, the government alone can approve modifications to the agreed provisions, unless the law explicitly authorizes that another regulatory institution can do so.[19] Thus, in this setting, the role of the regulator is not clear and many overlaps can arise. Even if by law the contract monitoring and tariff negotiation can be delegated to the regulator, the public authority retains crucial duties with respect to the post-privatization performance of the contract.

In this setting, the regulatory authority becomes only a delegated party and there is no "independent" regulator as such. The menace of political interference is always present, adding further risks to this type of institutional arrangement. To complicate matters, in some Central American countries, the National Assembly is responsible for approving any substantial change in the concession agreement during the life of the contract.

The issue of nonindependence becomes acute when the granting authority is a single municipality, or when the regulatory functions are ascribed to the head of the municipality. As the party responsible for the service, the municipality (and the mayor or the local council on its behalf) has to guarantee the performance of the contract and take charge of monitoring it. At the same time, conflicts of interest can occur if the mayor is also in charge of crucial decisions with respect to the service or tariff regulation. This could magnify the regulatory risk, considering the political nature of the positions (see Appendix 1.1).[20]

Conclusions

Detailed concession contracts may help to launch the initial privatization effort by expressly providing for certain risks that a country's legal frame-

[19]As an example, all the water concessions contracts in Argentina refer final approval of tariffs to the provincial ministry with jurisdiction for water and sewerage services. Only Panama allows the regulatory authority to sign a concession agreement and delegates regulation of the post-privatization contract entirely to the regulatory authority.

[20]See examples in Colombia and Argentina in Chapter 8.

work has not anticipated. But for privatization to be sustainable and irreversible, there is a need to build more complex legal and regulatory institutions that minimize the deficiencies detected in a modality of contract that is not necessarily adapted to wooing private entrepreneurs. Explicitly acknowledging that certain infrastructure activities are best advanced by private entrepreneurs underpins the need to put in place the necessary legal and regulatory institutions to support and enforce a private property regime. Other infrastructure activities such as transportation infrastructure are more into the realm of governments. Here, modern public procurement rules are needed to reduce the risk involved and the uncertainties linked to unilateral actions of governments. As Chapters 2 and 3 will show, legal changes are necessary to guarantee sustainable privatization and to modernize public procurement rules in the case of government contracting with the private sector. Unilateral asymmetries like those described in this chapter maximize the political and regulatory risk involved in contract modality not necessarily adapted to attracting private entrepreneurship.

APPENDIX 1.1

Managerial, Leasing and Operational Contracts

The institutional and regulatory scenario becomes more complex when other contractual schemes are introduced, especially where the responsibility for operation, investment and financing obligations are shared between the public and private partners. That is the case of managerial, leasing and operational types of contracts.

Where investment and its financing continue to be an obligation of the public authority, there should be a public entity responsible for developing the investment and financing. The execution of both responsibilities has regulatory implications (i.e., impact of the investment plans on the tariff), but at the same time, the investment decisions have important implications for operation and management of the service. For example, if the state agency is responsible for expanding the service to new consumers or establishing new supply connections, these will have implications on contract development (i.e., they can affect the completion of the loss recovery or portfolio indicator determined with the private contractor if the newly connected users do not pay for the service or lack proof of their connections). This is why it is more complicated to clarify the interface between the private operator and the public agency in charge of the investment. The duties are interrelated and the contract is the central element of this relationship.

The contract is the most important regulatory instrument, stipulating the rights and duties of the parties, tariff formulas, available mechanisms to modify them, tariff adjustment indicators, deadlines, sanctions, grounds for amendments or termination, etc. However, given that the party that signs the contract retains basic duties regarding the service (i.e., investment), it is difficult to separate the contract handling in the administrative side (i.e., contract monitoring) of its regulatory components (i.e., renegotiation of clauses related with prices).

In terms of contract handling, some responsibilities can be termed regulatory, while others are more related to areas of service management, including the following:

- Fulfillment of the contract agreements (contract monitoring), a combination of regulatory and service management factors.
- Contract design, which includes regulations such as tariffs, quality, service standards, client and user management, and operational and managerial considerations.

• Contract renegotiation during the contract's performance, which can include regulatory clauses (i.e., tariffs, service quality, operational objectives that influence the tariffs) and operational and service management clauses (i.e., handling new connections, collection indicators, loss indicators, checking the fulfillment of operational clauses).

It can be difficult to separate the regulatory function and the agency that signs the contract. If this is not clearly defined, he who signs the contract will have full authority over it and regulate, modify and monitor it.

REFERENCES

Baumol, W.J., J. Panzar, and R.D. Willig. 1982. *Contestable Markets and the Theory of Industry Structure.* New York: Harcourt Brace Jovanovich.

Cooter, R., and T. Ulen. 1988. *Law and Economics* (1st. ed.). Glenview, Ill.: Scott, Foresman and Company.

Dixit, A., and R. Pindyck. 1994. *Investment under Uncertainty.* Princeton, NJ: Princeton University Press.

Frydman, R., and A. Rapaczynski. 1994. *Privatization in Eastern Europe: Is the State Withering Away?* Budapest: Central European University Press.

Noll, R. 1989. Economic Perspectives on the Politics of Regulation. In *Handbook of Industrial Organization,* eds. R. Schmalensse and R. D. Willig. Vol. 2. Amsterdam and New York: North Holland.

Stiglitz, J. 1988. *Economics of the Public Sector* (2nd ed.). New York and London: W.W. Norton & Company.

CHAPTER 2

Legal Obstacles and Incentives to Private Investment in Infrastructure Concessions

Alejandro P. Radzyminski

Private investment is critical in supplementing a necessarily limited amount of public resources, and has often accounted for a significant portion of total capital flows in Latin America. Private investment also transfers managerial and technical know-how and encourages creation of related industries and development of export markets. However, even in those countries where private investment is welcomed in principle, the terms and conditions on which it operates may give rise to legal uncertainties, lack of stability in the treatment afforded the investment, and potential controversies with the government or with other parties.

This chapter identifies the main obstacles and incentives to private participation in infrastructure projects by examining the results of a survey of laws and institutions related to infrastructure services in five Latin American countries: Honduras, Guatemala, Panama, Colombia and Argentina.[1] The initial purpose was to outline certain aspects of the legal systems of those countries relating to contractual arrangements for the construction, investment and operation of infrastructure projects and to the potential for financing these

[1]The survey was carried out as part of an Inter-American Development Bank program on infrastructure finance, regulation and management. A questionnaire addressing basic topics of constitutional law, concession law, general contract law and other related matters was developed with the assistance of IDB infrastructure and legal specialists. Responses to the questionnaire were provided by Bufete Gutiérrez Falla from Honduras; Rodríguez, Archilla, Castellanos, Solares & Aguilar, S.C. from Guatemala; Morgan & Morgan from Panama; Estudios Palacios Lleras S.A. from Colombia; and Carregal & Funes de Rioja from Argentina. Appendix 2.1 contains a comparative matrix based upon such responses.

projects in the international markets. It was assumed that such projects would proceed under medium- or long-term contracts subject to significant governmental regulations.

Past initiatives to improve the investment climate have included World Bank efforts to avoid or reduce risk and conflict between foreign investors and host countries. The 1965 Convention for the Settlement of Investment Disputes between States and Nationals of Other States was a tangible result of these efforts. Other initiatives resulted in bilateral arrangements between countries affording legal protection to their respective investors.

While such efforts constitute valuable contributions to the improvement of the investment climate, they have been by nature limited in scope and purpose. Accordingly, they do not encompass all the issues customarily addressed in the context of creating a favorable environment for private investment in infrastructure projects.

Rather than focusing on the establishment of international conventions or other agreements, the survey on which this chapter is based examined laws relating to infrastructure services. This survey is useful in two respects. First, it provides guidance on the operation of the laws of the selected jurisdictions and identifies the main legal barriers to private participation in infrastructure projects. All responses concur that infrastructure services can be granted in concession to private investors. However, the legal framework and implementation methodology for infrastructure services, and the related development of laws, varies from one country to the other. Further, some countries have broad experience in infrastructure service concession, while in others the process is still in a developmental phase. In this respect, the survey ultimately may also prove instrumental in supporting the enactment of legislative reforms necessary to improve the legal environment.

Second, the survey shows some of the typical issues that arise involving privatization of infrastructure. Accordingly, it may prove helpful both in identifying the obstacles to private participation in other jurisdictions and in suggesting necessary or appropriate legislative reforms.

The Bidding Process

Preparation of Documentation

The concession contract constitutes the basic document granting the concessionaire the authority to provide an infrastructure service. A concession contract is expected to specify the conditions applicable to the service provided, and more broadly the reciprocal rights and duties of the concessionaire, the government and consumers. Typically, concession agreements are medium- to long-term contracts. It may thus be impracticable to foresee within the agreement all potential situations that may arise during its term. Private investors may be discouraged from participating in infrastructure projects because the concession agreement does not regulate as comprehensively as possible the relationship between the parties, lacks clarity, or vests broad discretion in the government. The use of discretion by the government and the risks associated with it are to a large extent tied to historical features, the manner in which government has exercised similar discretion in the past, and its penchant for interfering with the activities of private investors. Governmental discretion may be regarded as a risk factor in itself, since it results in a lack of specificity in the obligations of the concessionaire and, potentially, increased costs for the concessionaire, lower revenues or other similar effects.

To create a favorable environment for private participation in infrastructure services, a concession agreement must adopt a complex architecture to fairly balance all interests potentially involved: the government, the concessionaires, the entities providing financing, and the users. Further, contractual uniformity for different infrastructure projects may also be conducive to a uniform case law regarding the interpretation of concession agreements.

The process of preparing concession agreements differs in the five countries studied here.

Honduras reports no experience on the matter, but concession agreements would probably be prepared by the government and the potential investors required to adhere to those terms. In Guatemala, concessions do not take the form of a negotiated contract but rather are embodied in a "unilateral" document in which the government sets forth the terms and conditions of the relevant concession. Panama has developed an initial concession agreement draft for all projects submitted for discussion with potential investors. The draft constitutes a model concession agreement. In Colombia, interested parties may request that a hearing be held to raise issues regarding the draft concession agreement prepared by the government. In Argentina, the government prepares initial drafts of each concession agreement, which are made available to interested parties together with the documents applicable to the bidding process. Generally, within the period granted to potential bidders to prepare and submit their respective bids, each bidder is entitled to request in written form such clarifications or amendments as it may deem necessary. The government retains discretion to accept or reject any such requests.

In general, there seems to be reasonable clarity in the provisions of concession agreements in the five countries and some sensitivity to incorporating provisions that facilitate the participation of lenders in infrastructure projects. However, in Guatemala, since concessions are awarded by means of a nonnegotiated agreement, there exists no possibility of discussing terms with the potential concessionaires.

Design

The successful concession of infrastructure projects also requires appropriate design of the bid process. The alternatives open to a government include public bidding, private negotiations and unsolicited proposals. To the extent that the process is not transparent, private investors may not be willing to undertake the costs and efforts associated with analyzing a particular project and submitting an offer.

Public bidding is mandatory in Honduras and Colombia. In Panama, public bidding processes are typically preceded by a prequalification procedure for interested bidders. In Guatemala, concessionaires are appointed either through public bidding or through open public invitations, which constitutes an alternative procedure similar to public bidding. In Argentina, the participation of private entities in infrastructure projects may be achieved through public bidding, contest of integrated projects, public auctions, or sale of shares. Infrastructure service concessions in Argentina have generally taken place through public bidding.

Post-award Approval Process

After the contract is awarded, a specific public authority must approve its entry into effect on behalf of the government. Until such approval has been issued, the concession agreement is generally not binding upon the government. This approval should be available as promptly as possible, since delays may alter the analysis by investors and confront the parties with a change in the circumstances underlying the concession.

The post-award approval process differs in the five surveyed countries. In Honduras, concessions and other contracts entered into by the government having a term exceeding the term for which the president serving at the time of the award has been appointed must be approved by Congress. In Guatemala, any contract affording a private party the right to provide public services is subject to approval by Congress. In Panama, congressional approval is required for contracts entered into by the government which grant to the concessionaire benefits in addition to those resulting from generally applicable legislation. By contrast, in Colombia and Argentina, the approval of the terms of the concession agreement is a matter reserved to the administration.

Congressional intervention in the approval of concession agreements may not only result in delays, but also in an unpredictable outcome. In countries where congressional approval is required, there seem to be no limitations on the congressional authority to review all terms of the agreement and dictate changes. The argument generally made to support congressional approval is that it provides greater legal comfort both for the government and for the concessionaire. Although this argument is reasonable, to the extent approval is given to any particular contract entered into by the government as prescribed by applicable law (which may not require congressional approval), such an agreement should be fully binding on the government.

Challenges to the Award

Private investors need to avoid delays in starting up operation of a concession. Third party challenges, the impossibility of operating the concession pending a decision as to the challenge, and the possibility that the award could be nullified all cause uncertainty to private investors. The right of third parties to pursue legal remedies and the need of certainty and predictability in the process of selecting a concessionaire must be balanced. In Honduras, a third party that submits a nonwinning bid has standing to contest the outcome of the selection process. The laws of Honduras contemplate a fast-track procedure applicable to this type of claim. Guatemala has adopted a more restrictive approach: the only grounds for a challenge to an award of a concession is that the winner did not submit the best offer. In Panama, a challenge may be brought against an award based upon noncompliance with the applicable selection procedure. The laws of Colombia vest in any third party having an interest and in the state attorney the right to challenge the appointment of a concessionaire. The challenge to the award is made by filing a complaint with a court of competent jurisdiction and may be based upon a breach of the applicable selection laws.

In Argentina, the appointment of a concessionaire can be challenged by other bidding parties for violation of the bidding process rules. Parties with an interest in submitting a bid, but which failed to do so for reasons attributable to a breach of the bidding rules, may also challenge the award. Such breaches may include a lack of appropriate publicity, amendment to the bidding terms following the award, or award to an entity that does not meet the requirements set forth in the bidding terms. The complainant must first pursue administrative remedies and thereafter may file a complaint with a court of competent jurisdiction. A claim may seek compensation for breach of the applicable regulations or an order nullifying the award. Pending a decision, the government may allow the winner to commence the operation of the concession, although the complainant can seek a temporary restraining order or other relief to maintain the status quo pending determination on the merits.

Realistic Restrictions and Availability of Necessary Permits

Expropriation. Concessionaires are not always adequately compensated in timely fashion in the case of expropriations, which in turn discourages private investors from participating in infrastructure projects. Expropriation risk can be assessed by examining the legal infrastructure of the country, its history, power structure, and neighboring countries.

The laws of all the countries surveyed give governments the right to expropriate assets. In Guatemala, Panama and Colombia, this includes the power to expropriate the right to operate a concession (as compared to the physical assets affected by the concessionaire to the operation of the concession). Assets of the concessionaire other than the concession itself may be expropriated in all five countries. Governmental actions relating to expropriation of assets are generally subject to judicial review, although in Argentina and Colombia the determination as to the existence of a "public interest" associated with an expropriation is, in principle, not subject to judicial review.

Vital to private participation in infrastructure projects is a comprehensive understanding of the scope of the compensation to which the affected party is entitled. In Honduras, compensation must meet the "fair price" of the relevant assets, determined in judicial proceedings. In Guatemala, the applicable formula refers to the current value of the assets. Under the laws of Panama, the expropriated owner is entitled to fair compensation, and parties to a concession agreement may agree as to the amounts payable by the government following an expropriation. In Colombia, compensation must take into account public and private interests. In Argentina, legislation expressly provides that the compensation cover the actual value of the expropriated assets, the damages of which are a direct consequence of the expropriation and accrued interests.

The foregoing are broad formulas that may give rise to disputes and delays in the availability of compensation. Also, in countries with expropriation power, inconsistencies may exist between compensation rights following expropriation of physical assets or early termination of a concession. For instance, in Guatemala and Panama, the government would be expected to terminate a concession before its term rather than to expropriate the right to operate the concession, although there is no controlling authority on the matter. This may lead a government to prefer expropriation to early termination based on a cost-benefit analysis. Additionally, the going concern value of the physical assets of the concessionaire decreases substantially when no longer related to the concession, and the right to operate the concession is deprived of economic value when the physical assets are expropriated. Where the laws or the concession agreements do not provide for comprehensive compensation in these situations, the concessionaire may be exposed to the risk of being left with worthless assets and without appropriate compensation.

Permits and Authorizations. The operation of a concession normally requires a number of permits and authorizations, including environmental, construction and import permits as well as other authorizations associated with the performance of obligations under the concession. The timeliness and availability of all such permits and authorizations may become crucial to meet requirements imposed by concession agreements. In all five countries surveyed, concessionaires needing permits must apply to governmental agencies sometimes different from the granting authority. In Honduras, the burden of obtaining certain permits and authorizations is placed on the government. In Panama, Colombia and Argentina, it falls on the concessionaire.

Under concession arrangements where the collection of revenues is preceded by a period when the concessionaire is required to make investments, revenue collection may be contingent upon the concessionaire obtaining approval from the appropriate governmental agency. The legislation of all five countries surveyed lacks provisions that would entitle the concessionaire to commence collecting revenues if the petition is not expressly rejected by the government within a certain period of time.

Rights-of-Way. A concessionaire (or the government) may need to acquire private property or rights with respect to private property, such as rights-of-way and easements. Private investors are generally concerned with the rules applicable to the acquisition of such rights, such as who is entitled to acquire them, whether they can be acquired in a timely manner, and what are the associated costs and who will bear them.

In Guatemala, there is specific regulation relating to rights-of-way in the electricity industry. The concessionaire is required to file an application with the Ministry of Energy and Mines. The owner of the affected property and the concessionaire are required to enter into negotiations to determine compensation, with general laws of real property being applicable. If no agreement is reached, the issue is determined by a court in a fast-track proceeding.

In Argentina, specific regulations have been adopted in relation to rights-of-way for energy transportation systems and the fossil fuels industry. The rights-of-way are granted to the concessionaire upon approval of the relevant project, and the owner of the affected property is entitled to a compensation that takes into consideration the value of the land and the occupation thereof by the relevant facilities. In addition, some infrastructure projects may require that private property be expropriated. Argentine law provides that the government may appoint a private entity to pursue an expropriation if a specific law contains a provision to that effect, and if that authority has actually been vested in private parties, for example, to conduct expropriations of private property necessary for the construction of certain highway systems.

Legal Structures in Concession Agreements

Direct Participation by Project Companies or Sponsors

The design of a concession requires that a determination be made as to the entity that will hold it. Generally, the alternatives available are either creating a separate project entity or directly awarding the concession to the sponsors.

From a government's perspective, awarding directly to project companies limits the possibility that the operation of the concession will be affected by any financial distress of the concessionaire resulting from unrelated businesses. This would ensure continued availability of the service to the public.

From the sponsor's perspective, a project entity may facilitate a more efficient use of tax benefits. Off-balance financing (or a similar credit objective, such as keeping the project off the balance sheet or off the liability side of the balance sheet) may be possible in some instances depending on the nature of the sponsor's ownership, control and contingent credit support obligations. With a project that is economically isolated in the project company, a wide variety of borrowing alternatives are available to the project entity.

From a lender's perspective, a project entity may be instrumental to implementing financing that isolates the project's revenues from liabilities incurred by the sponsors and from liabilities of the agency or entity that provided the service before the award of the concession. Direct lending to the sponsors makes available for the project all borrowing avenues usually available to the sponsors.

In Honduras, the participation of private investors in the telecommunications sector is effected through a project company whose stock is held by private sector investors and the government. In other sectors, private participation is channeled through direct sponsor investment.

In Guatemala, telecommunications services have been partially transferred to private sector investors who hold equity of the project company, which in turn owns the assets of the state-owned company that formerly provided telecommunication services. There is frequent use of project companies. The laws of Guatemala do not generally make the concessionaire responsible for the actions or omissions of the government prior to the award. Further, applicable laws do not make the sponsors, as shareholders of the project company, liable for the actions of the latter.

In Panama, private participation in the telecommunications industry came through the sale of a minority stake of the government-owned company and the awarding of a management contract to a private operator. Private participation in the electricity industry is being designed through the incorporation of at least six companies, which will later be transferred to private investors. Under the general principles of Panamanian legislation, the concessionaire may be considered a successor to the government entity providing the service, and thus be held liable for obligations incurred prior to the award of the concession, except for labor liabilities.

In Colombia, private participation in infrastructure services may be structured through project companies. Recent legal developments in the field of domiciliary public services tend to favor the use of this type of structure.

Finally, in Argentina, notwithstanding some early experiences of direct awards to sponsors, the bulk of the latest initiatives involved the use of project companies. Generally, special arrangements are made to identify which liabilities incurred prior to the award will be borne by the project company and which will be borne by the government or other third parties. A recent court decision rendered in a labor matter, however, has applied successorship theories to hold the licensee liable to a former employee for labor obligations incurred by the government prior to granting the license, despite the fact that an executive order provided that such liabilities were to be borne by the government. Such decisions, however, do not preclude the licensee from pursuing reimbursement from the government.

Structuring of Project Finance

Contractual Arrangements. Successful participation of the private sector in infrastructure projects depends also upon access to financing by the operators of concessions. Financing sources are interested in determining whether there are limitations to financing in general or to a particular financing technique inherent in any contractual structure relating to a concession and in the laws applicable to it. For example, lending institutions may seek to establish whether it would be best to effect financing through traditional loans or by issuing debt or equity instruments. Lenders may also require third party credit support or other types of contingent support from the sponsors. Also, lenders may want to impose limitations on the transfer of equity in a project company for a certain period, or establish the possibility that the sponsors will make equity contributions upon the occurrence of certain events. Further, financing may be structured with obligations of different ranking, some of which may rank senior or junior with respect to other obligations of the concessionaire.

In general, the surveyed countries do not impose any limitations or requirements relating to the manner in which financing is structured. Further, there are no laws giving the governments the ability to rescind or otherwise interfere with private financing arrangements or any particular financing structure.

Secured Lending. Lenders will explore the legal mechanisms to perfect a security interest in the concessionaire's assets and to protect such assets from other creditors' claims. Where financing is extended to a project company, ensuring priority of the security interest and availability of appropriate foreclosure mechanisms becomes particularly important, since only the assets pertaining to the concession will be available to the creditors.

Legislation regarding the place where assets are located at the time of perfection of a security interest is typically applied to perfection issues, the scope of the preference, and the foreclosure mechanisms. Accordingly, these issues will typically be governed by the laws of the host country.

The laws of Honduras use traditional mechanisms for securing indebtedness through mortgages and pledges of assets. In addition, it is feasible to perfect a floating charge on all the present and future assets of a company. Honduran legislation includes the possibility of creating trusts for security purposes, although only commercial banks may provide trustee services. However, a security interest or the assignment of the right to operate the concession or to collect tariffs from consumers is prohibited. Other than that, the assets placed in trust constitute an estate separate from the estate of the trustor and the trustee. Creditors secured by means of a first priority mortgage or pledge are granted an absolute priority to repay the secured obligations with the proceeds from the foreclosure. Such a preference is not affected by the insolvency of the concessionaire. Foreclosure of the collateral normally requires that the creditor resort to a court of competent jurisdiction.

Mortgages and pledges are typical security instruments in Guatemala. There is, however, no possibility of creating a floating charge in all the assets of a company. The laws of Guatemala set forth regulations relating to trust arrangements, and provide that the assets placed in trust constitute an estate isolated from those of the settlor and the trustee. Only banks and financial institutions authorized to operate in Guatemala may provide trustee services. Moreover, there are doubts as to whether the right to operate a concession or to collect tariffs from consumers can be assigned in trust or otherwise encumbered. Upon bankruptcy of the borrower, secured creditors are not required to file a proof of claims, and may directly proceed to foreclose upon the collateral.

The laws of Panama call for the taking of collateral through the perfection of mortgages, pledges and trust arrangements, although the income derived from trust property is subject to independent taxation. Under Panamanian law, it is possible to perfect a security interest on the concession taken as a whole, subject to prior governmental approval. Generally, secured creditors are preferred to all other creditors of the debtor except for the government and insurance companies. Following the bankruptcy of a debtor, secured creditors are required to file a proof of claims with the court before foreclosing.

Traditional collateral mechanisms such as pledges and mortgages are accepted in Colombia. These grant a preference upon the proceeds resulting from foreclosing on the encumbered assets, except with respect to certain limited obligations such as labor law obligations and tax liabilities. Security trusts are permissible. Only financial and other specially authorized entities are entitled to serve as trustees, and trust arrangements are subject to complex tax treatment. Rights deriving from a concession are susceptible to being assigned by way of security, subject to government approval. In security trusts, however, the settlor bears all tax liabilities. While foreclosure generally requires that the creditor resort to a court, bankruptcy of the debtor does not affect the continued enforceability of the rights of secured creditors.

The laws of Argentina contemplate mortgages and pledges as typical lien mechanisms. Mortgages can be created on real estate and also on all the equipment affixed to it. Concession agreements, however, generally impose constraints on the ability of concessionaires to encumber their assets. Foreclosure of mortgaged assets generally requires that the creditor resort to the courts, while chattels normally may be foreclosed in nonjudicial auctions. First priority mortgages and pledges create a security interest ranking senior to all other creditors, except for some limited exceptions. Further, recent legislative reforms have amended the rules applicable to real estate foreclosure, making such procedures more expeditious. Trust arrangements are also permissible under Argentine law and, subject only to fraudulent conveyance restrictions, segregate the assets conveyed in trust from the estate of the trustor and the trustee. Security trusts are not subject to taxation and the assets placed in trust may be disposed of in accordance with the terms of the relevant trust agreement without resorting to a court, even following the insolvency of the debtor.

The right to operate a concession may not be placed in trust by way of security without government approval, which may not be available for all industries. The right to collect tariffs may be transferred in trust to a security trustee subject to prior government approval. This mechanism has been applied in connection with financings for the construction and subsequent operation of highway systems. Any entity or individual may perform duties as security trustee in connection with private financing. However, in order to offer such services to the public and to perform trustee duties with respect to indebtedness evidenced in the form of publicly offered securities, the trustee is required to hold a banking license or otherwise be authorized by the *Comisión Nacional de Valores.*

Other Remedies for Lenders. Besides securing indebtedness by means of mortgages, pledges and security trusts, lenders in some cases may want to be able to exercise certain powers with respect to the operation of the concession that do not amount to a security interest, but which may prove instrumental to preserving the rights of lenders. For instance, to avoid termination of the concession due to events attributable to the concessionaire, lenders may want the right, but not the obligation, to prevent the concessionaire's default or to take over the operation of the concession in order to avoid or prevent defaults.

The enforceability of arrangements of this nature is doubtful under the laws of Honduras. In Guatemala, governmental consent would be necessary, while under the laws of Colombia and Panama lenders could enforce rights from such arrangements against the government. In Argentina, lenders would not be entitled to enforce against the government such contractual arrangements with the concessionaire.

Liability of Lenders. In financing infrastructure projects, lenders may also be concerned with local laws imposing liabilities related to the making of loans and the exercise of cure or control rights. For example, to the extent that lenders are entitled to operate the concession to avoid a default by the concessionaire, it is likely that they will appoint an operator rather than directly undertake such tasks. This raises the issue of whether any breach of the concession by the operator appointed by the lenders renders the lenders automatically liable, or whether the lenders' responsibility is limited to diligently appointing an operator with experience in the particular industry.

None of the surveyed countries has developed a doctrine of lender's liability in this area or its scope and implications. However, from the lack of legislation and controlling authority it does not necessarily follow that a lender exercising rights to cure or control is free from liabilities relating to the operation of a concession, even if such rights are ultimately exercised by an appointee.

Exchange Controls. Lenders will seek to ensure that the laws of the country where the investment is located allow the borrower to repay the loans in the agreed currency, and that the currency can be remitted outside of the country if the loan documentation requires that payments be made abroad. More generally, sponsors will want to have the ability to remit abroad profits from the operation of the concession.

Currently, there are no exchange controls in Honduras and Panama. In Guatemala, there are no foreign exchange restrictions for payments abroad, although an agreement to pay foreign currency between two Guatemalan entities is unenforceable. In Colombia, most foreign exchange transactions need to be made through authorized local entities, and there is a requirement that 30 percent of the proceeds of loans obtained abroad be deposited with the Central Bank of Colombia, which will make the funds available 18 months following the deposit.

Argentine pesos have been convertible into U.S. dollars at a 1:1 rate since 1991. Further, the Central Bank of Argentina is required to sell U.S. dollars at a 1:1 rate. Pesos received by the Central Bank in such transactions are taken out of circulation. The Central Bank may also purchase U.S. dollars in any market, and no inflation adjustment mechanisms are allowed. Notwithstanding (or, indeed, because of) this, there are no foreign exchange controls or restrictions in Argentina. However, it is customary that parties to financing agreements provide that if any such controls are enacted, the Argentine debtor will discharge its obligations by delivering U.S. dollar-denominated securities outside Argentina, the proceeds of which are sufficient to cancel the outstanding obligations of the Argentine debtor.

Concession Contracts

Risk Considerations and Allocation Principles

Infrastructure projects are unique in the risk allocation problems they pose because of equity participation by the government in the entity holding the concession, limitations regarding divestments and term of the investment, comprehensive regulation of the industry, and other similar factors. In addition, the involvement of the government as grantor of the concession and as indirect provider of the service makes it a key participant as well in terms of risk allocation.

As a general principle, risks underlying a project should be allocated to the party that is in the best position to assess and manage the risk. Alternatively, the traditional approach is that each risk must be allocated to the party that can better access mechanisms to mitigate (or insure against) the relevant risk. In this regard, in Argentina, for instance, a principle of allocation of risks underlying each concession contract states that the concessionaire is to bear all risks associated with conducting the business underlying the concession, while the government is to undertake all other risks. A similar principle is applicable in Colombia, but no such principle exists in Honduras and Guatemala.

Effectiveness of Contractual Arrangements Relating to Risk Allocation

Parties to a concession agreement may regard reliance on general legal principles concerning risk allocation as unsatisfactory or ambiguous, and may thus wish to make their own arrangements on the matter.

Risk allocation provisions are permitted in Colombia and Argentina. In Panama, risk allocation arrangements are permissible for purposes only of restoring the economic and financial balance underlying the concession agreement. The lack of regulations seems to make the issue doubtful in Honduras, while in Guatemala, since no actual concession agreement is customarily entered into upon the awarding of a project, it appears that no opportunity exists to agree upon risk allocations.

Force Majeure

Force majeure is a principle of contract law that excuses nonperformance under an agreement if the default is caused by events unforeseen and unforeseeable, or unavoidable, and beyond the control of the defaulting party. However, in practice, the application of this concept is uncertain. Accordingly, there always remains a risk that the concessionaire's nonperformance may not be excused on force majeure grounds.

One method for dealing with this risk is to incorporate into concession agreements an express listing of all force majeure events that may be invoked by the concessionaire to excuse nonperformance.

Such an arrangement would be valid under the laws of Honduras, Guatemala, Panama and Colombia. In Argentina, the arrangement is valid provided that the concessionaire does not undertake responsibility for events which would otherwise entitle it to pursue the restoration of the economic and financial balance of the concession contract.

Equilibrium Between the Rights and Obligations of the Government and the Concessionaire

Continental legal jurisdictions generally follow French doctrine regarding the underlying philosophy of a concession agreement. Under these theories, unlike private contracts, one of the parties to concession contracts is vested with certain powers that exceed the purely contractual framework and follow from its capacity as a public authority and the fact that the concessionaire is regarded as an instrument of the government for purposes of providing a public service. Such powers encompass, for instance, the ability of the government to impose unilateral amendments to concession agreements.

Aside from the foregoing, concession contracts or the laws governing such arrangements may asymmetrically grant rights and duties to the parties. A clear illustration is the right of the concessionaire to terminate the concession agreement upon default by the government and, when feasible, the manner in which such termination is required to be effected. As will be discussed below, in at least one of the surveyed countries, the concessionaire is not entitled to seek early termination of the concession agreement following a default by the government, or when entitled to do so, is required to resort to the courts to obtain a judicial declaration while, in the reverse situation, the government is not required to seek any judicial declaration.

Amendments to Concession Agreements

Unilateral Amendments. Concession agreements for infrastructure services are generally long-term arrangements that cannot anticipate all circumstances that can arise during the life of the concession. The provision of the service may require adjustments from time to time due to the incorporation of new technologies, changes in the population or in its habits, and changes in the general economic environment. Some of these may be considered in the best interest of the general public or otherwise called for by the public interest. As such, changes to the concession agreement may be necessary or desirable, regardless of whether or not they were anticipated in the agreement or whether the concessionaire is willing to consent to them.

In the countries surveyed, the right of the government to introduce unilateral amendments to concession agreements is generally deemed inherent in the scope of governmental authority. In Honduras, specific legislation grants the government the right to make unilateral changes to the terms pursuant to which the service is provided by a private party in the electricity industry and with respect to the operation of airports. In Guatemala, there are no legal impediments to the ability of the government to introduce unilateral amendments to the terms of the concession. Under the laws of Panama, the government may make unilateral amendments to concession agreements only to the extent that there is a danger that otherwise the provision of the service will be withheld or seriously affected. Such a determination is to be made by the regulator.

In Colombia, the government can unilaterally amend concessions if there is a risk that the service could be suspended or otherwise affected. However, if the unilateral changes mean that the "initial value" of the contract is modified by 20 percent or more, the concessionaire is granted the right to seek termination of the agreement.

Under Argentine law, the authority granting a concession has the right to impose modifications in the service at any time if the changes are for the public interest. Such changes may relate to the term of the agreement, the expansion of the service or the conditions for the performance of the concession agreement. However, amendments may not alter the substance of the concession agreement. In the case of concessions for public works, a 20 percent rule, similar to that in force in Colombia, is also applicable in Argentina.

The broad authority of governments to make unilateral changes to concession agreements introduces a degree of unpredictability. Concessionaires could be required to make new investments without appropriate financing or to postpone investments for which financing has been committed. Also, amendments may require the addition or layoff of workers. This may have a distorting effect on the plans of the concessionaire and the entities providing financing. The ability of the government to unilaterally amend the concession does not necessarily lack sound grounds. However, such power introduces an imbalance between the parties which, if used beyond its expected scope and purpose, is liable to discourage private participation in infrastructure projects. To some extent, the risk of unilateral amendments may be assessed by examining the frequency with which governments have resorted to this right and its practical implications. However, this may not always be possible, since the surveyed jurisdictions do not, in most cases, have comprehensive experience in infrastructure service concession. Further, it is generally unclear whether it would be valid or enforceable to impose express limitations on the manner, extent and frequency with which the unilateral powers may be exercised.

Consensual Amendments

The long-term nature of concession agreements may lead the concessionaire and the government to make consensual amendments to the agreement. Such amendments raise a number of issues. What is the permissible scope of the amendments? Are amendments subject to challenges by third parties? How are post-award amendments approved?

In Honduras and Guatemala, the legislation is silent on this matter and there is no experience relating to consensual amendments. Under the laws of Panama, concessionaires have the right to seek amendments under certain circumstances. For instance, the concession agreement relating to telecommunication services expressly contains a provision to that effect. Moreover, there is experience relating to renegotiation of a concession contract due to serious defects in the project designed by the government.

The laws of Colombia entitle the concessionaire to seek an amendment if there is a material change in the circumstances existing when the concession agreement was entered into.

Pursuant to Argentine law, a concessionaire may call on the government to amend the concession agreement following a change in circumstances unforeseen when the concession agreement was entered into, provided any such changes occur after the concession contract was in force, are not attributable to any of the parties, and are extraordinary and unforeseeable. For instance, for the railroad industry, renegotiations resulted in amendments to scheduled services, investment programs, term of the concession, service areas, tariffs, granting of subsidies, and the possibility of incorporating new shareholders into the project companies.

Challenges to Consensual Amendments

Flexibility in effecting consensual amendments allows the agreements to adapt to changing circumstances. In this respect, following consensual amendments, bidders who were not selected and other third parties could seek to challenge the validity of the amendments, impairing the ability of the government and the concessionaire to implement changes. Under the laws of Honduras, such a challenge would be grounded in discriminatory treatment. The laws of Guatemala do not give standing to losing bidders to challenge post-award amendments. If a renegotiation results in substantial changes to the concession contract in Panama, the amendments may be challenged by any third party on the grounds that they breach applicable law. Under the laws of Colombia and Argentina, amendments can be challenged if they alter the conditions under which the award of the contract was made. No clear legal doctrine has developed in this field. This may be due to the limited number of renegotiations and the fact that no third party claims have been made following renegotiation. Consequently, uncertainty exists as to when a renegotiation implies a substantial change to the agreement that amounts to a change of the conditions under which the contract was originally awarded. For instance, experiences in Panama and Argentina raise doubts about whether the amendments do not constitute ex post facto changes to the bid terms.

Approval Process for Amendments

In general, amendments to concession agreements are subject to the same approval process as the agreement itself. To the extent that any such approval of an amendment entails congressional action, the process may become time-consuming and even deprive the amendment of the practical effect pursued by the government and the concessionaire.

In Honduras, congressional approval is required only in the case of substantial amendments. In Guatemala, although the Congress is vested with the right to approve concessions and extensions, it is understood that amendments to concessions are subject to the same requirement. Moreover, a priori congressional approval for amendments granted at the time the concession is approved by Congress is likely to be unenforceable.

Restoration of Economic and Financial Balance

Under the legal doctrine of "preservation of economic and financial balance," when the ability of the concessionaire to obtain the expected benefit from the operation of the concession is jeopardized due to actions or omissions attributable to the government or to unexpected circumstances, the concessionaire is entitled to claim that actions be taken to ensure that its expected benefit is ultimately obtained. This doctrine is based upon the notion that at the time the concessionaire and the government enter into a concession agreement, an economic and financial balance is expressly or implicitly established by the parties and may not be subsequently altered. Under a concession contract the concessionaire is expected to assume those risks that may be deemed reasonably related to the business associated with the performance of the contract, but it is not expected nor required to undertake the risk of future actions or omission of the government or other extraordinary risks. Generally, restoration of the economic and financial balance may be achieved either by amending the terms of the concession agreement (e.g., extending the term of the concession), providing economic assistance to the concessionaire, or reviewing the applicable tariffs.

This doctrine exists in Panama, Colombia and Argentina, while it is unclear whether it applies in Honduras and Guatemala. Even in jurisdictions where this doctrine is accepted, however, it is unclear in which particular situations it applies, when the balance has been altered, which mechanisms are applicable for purposes of its restoration, and who is entitled to select the adjustment mechanism in a particular case.

Termination and Termination Payments

Scope of the Government's Right to Terminate a Concession

Most concession agreements have a fixed term. The term is determined by a number of factors, including required investments, tariffs to be collected, and expected benefits for the concessionaire. The continued enforceability of the concession agreement throughout its stated term is crucial for the private investor, since the time factor constitutes a key element in achieving the economic results envisaged by the concessionaire at the time of bidding.

Concession agreements may under certain circumstances, however, be terminated prior to their stated term. Typically, this occurs following a material default of the concessionaire, if the concessionaire becomes insolvent, or by mutual agreement of the government and the concessionaire.

In addition, in certain continental law jurisdictions the government is entitled to early termination of the concession even if there is no fault attributable to the concessionaire. The broader the powers of the government to terminate concessions before their stated term, the larger the risk for the concessionaire. Stability of the concession serves to encourage investments, while significant risk of early termination adversely impacts the potential benefits to the concessionaire, in particular when the concession is intended to provide long-term benefits.

In Honduras, the government retains authority to terminate a concession due to reasons of "national security." In Guatemala, the government can revoke concessions at any time subject only to 90 days' notice. The laws of Panama entitle the government to terminate concessions based on public interest considerations. Under Colombian law, public service and public policy considerations entitle the government to terminate concession agreements. An exception exists, however, with respect to concessions involving the construction and operation of highways: unilateral early termination may only be effected prior to completion of the construction. The laws of Argentina vest powers in the government to terminate concessions prior to stated maturity based on public interest considerations.

Concessionaire's Right to Terminate the Concession Agreement

Concession agreements may impose obligations not only on the concessionaire, but also on the government. For instance, the government may undertake, expressly or implicitly, to take such actions as may be necessary to ensure that the concessionaire is able to operate the concession during the applicable term. Also, to the extent the concession grants exclusivity rights to the concessionaire, the government is agreeing not to grant competing concessions. Further, the government may have agreed to provide credit support to the concessionaire. To the extent that the government undertakes obligations under the concession agreement, a performance risk is involved and remedies for the concessionaire should be contemplated in the event the government breaches its commitments. Generally, nonperformance of the concession agreement by the concessionaire entitles the government to terminate the concession. However, a similar right for the benefit of the concessionaire following a default of the government is not contemplated in all legislation. Where no right of termination is granted to the concessionaire following a default by the government, the concessionaire is not only confronted with a performance risk, but also with the further risk that it be required to continue performing its obligations despite the government's default. This imbalance between the government and the concessionaire is inconsistent with the creation of a favorable environment for private investment in infrastructure services.

The laws of Honduras do not give the concessionaire the right to terminate a concession following a default by the government. Guatemala entitles the concessionaire to terminate the concession if the government has breached its obligations. Under the laws of Panama, only grounds for termination by the government are set forth, but a concession contract may contemplate additional termination events. In Colombia, a concessionaire must seek a court judgment to terminate a concession agreement due to a breach attributable to the government. Finally, concession agreements in Argentina generally entitle the concessionaire to terminate the agreement following the government's default, subject to certain requirements relating to the continued provision of the service.

Determination of Amounts Payable by the Government to the Concessionaire

Provisions relating to payments to the concessionaire upon termination of the concession are important both if the concession runs its full course and if it is terminated earlier. Upon the end of the concession, a concessionaire may be entitled to payments from the government or from a subsequent operator of the concession, or may have fully amortized its investment and obtained the expected profit without being entitled to further payments. By contrast, following an early termination of the concession, the concessionaire is generally entitled to compensation from the government, although the scope of that compensation may differ depending on whether early termination is attributable to the concessionaire. A number of different formulas have been used in the past to determine compensation at termination, taking into consideration historical costs, replacement costs and market value.

Legislation in force in the surveyed countries either does not contain statutory compensation formulas or solely refers to general concepts. Typically, concession agreements would be expected to set forth the applicable provisions for the determination of the concessionaire's compensation upon termination, in particular when the laws of the jurisdiction are silent or unclear on the matter. Such provisions should clearly set forth both the calculation methodology and the procedure for making available termination payments to the concessionaire. Concession contracts in Panama and Argentina generally include provisions to that effect, although in Argentina some of them have raised construction issues. Lastly, all jurisdictions seem to deem enforceable contractual mechanisms for purposes of calculating termination payments.

Prompt Availability of Termination Payments

It is also critical that termination payments be made available promptly upon their determination. It should not be necessary to seek enforcement of the payments against a government, an undertaking fraught with difficulties. Although none of the surveyed countries restrict claims against the government, enforcement of monetary judgments is subject to limitations. For instance, in Honduras, before the private investor is entitled to enforce a judgment against the government, the government must incorporate the amounts due into the national budget. Under the laws of Guatemala and Panama, a private investor may not obtain an order of attachment over government assets. In Colombia, the government's annual budget must contain provisions for the payment of money judgments against it, but certain assets may not be attached or foreclosed. In Argentina, judgment amounts are included in the budget for the year following the year when the judgment has been rendered. Government assets may not be attached or foreclosed. However, there have been cases in which courts have compelled a government to comply with monetary judgments when it has not met its payment obligations in a reasonable period of time.

Assets of the Concessionaire

When concessions are operated through project companies, the principal source of loan repayment is the revenue from operation of the concession. However, if assets of the concessionaire generating such revenues are attached by other creditors (such as employees, or the government with respect to tax obligations), it is possible that no resources will be available to repay the financing or to support the continued provision of the service. Foreclosing on assets of the concessionaire, moreover, may not be an appropriate remedy for lenders. Continued provision of the service may constitute the only means of generating sufficient income to honor the concessionaire's obligations.

Under the laws of Honduras, creditors appears to have no impediment to reaching the assets of the concessionaire. Likewise, Guatemala and Colombia do not grant any type of immunity to the assets of the concessionaire. In Panama, as a general principle, the concessionaire's assets are not free from the claims of its creditors, although a statutory exception exists for the telecommunications industry. In Argentina, assets that are essential for continued provision of a public service are immune from the claims of creditors.

Price Setting and Tariffs

Mechanisms for Determination and Adjustment of Tariffs

Infrastructure concession agreements are inherently long-term contracts. At start-up, the concession contract is expected to set forth the initial tariffs. Long-term arrangements, however, cannot set out in detail all the factors that may have an influence on the concession and its operation. Over the life of the concession, changes may take place in the costs of operations, in the conditions imposed by the government relating to the manner in which the service is provided, and in the laws and other factors not under the direct control of the concessionaire. This may require that tariffs be revised. Fixed tariffs throughout the term of a concession may eventually hinder the concessionaire's performance or limit profits to the point where incentives for the efficient operation of the concession are nil. From the opposite perspective, tariffs that enable the concessionaire to reap excessive profits tend to remove the pressure for efficiency, new technologies and expansion of the scope of the services.

The tariff adjustment mechanism is the reflection of the risk allocation in any concession agreement. Only those risks which the concessionaire is not required to bear may constitute the basis for tariff adjustments. The occurrence and impact of tariff adjustments cannot be accurately predicted because of the variety of factors that give rise to them. Accordingly, while with respect to certain elements it is feasible to set forth an express formula for adjustments, other variables may require more flexible solutions.

Another factor is the manner in which adjustments are actually authorized and implemented. In general, it may be necessary to obtain authorization from regulatory agencies to effect any adjustments. Expeditious regulatory procedures and readiness to approve tariff requests becomes decisive. In their absence, there is a risk of mismatching required investments and operational costs against revenues.

The revision of tariffs in Honduras is subject to statutory requirements. For instance, in the electricity industry, tariffs may be subject to review if there is a change in the price of hydrocarbons or in the official rates of exchange. Although tied to specific events, tariff adjustments may not be made automatically, but only after application to the regulatory agency. In the telecommunications industry, the regulatory agency may issue regulations relating to adjustment of the tariffs during the period in which the concessionaire is granted the exclusive right to operate the service. By contrast, legislation applicable to operation of the airports provides that tariffs and their adjustment mechanisms be contained in the applicable concession agreements.

The laws of Guatemala are silent on the issue of tariff revision, although there seems to be no impediment to tariff adjustment mechanisms. In Panama, the regulator periodically determines maximum tariffs that may be collected by concessionaires. Concessionaires are entitled to apply for revision of such maximums. In Colombia, the statute provides that the concession contract have adjustment mechanisms that take into account inflation and other similar factors. The statutes vest in the regulatory authority the responsibility for developing formulas for the adjustment of tariffs. Such formulas are subject to revision from time to time.

In Argentina, the issue of tariff revision has been customarily addressed in concession contracts and the applicable regulatory frameworks, which entitle concessionaires to apply for new tariffs. In some cases, concessionaires are required to file annual applications for approval of their tariffs. Revision of tariffs is generally based on information provided by the concessionaire about changes in costs beyond its control. Argentine law expressly forbids inflation adjustments and deprives contractual arrangements of binding effect that incorporate inflation clauses. Certain concession agreements, however, contain provisions that entitle tariff adjustments to take into consideration inflation in the United States. The validity of such provisions has not been contested.

Tariffs and Economic and Financial Balance

Changing circumstances beyond the control of the concessionaire resulting in increased operational costs are attendant to any long-term arrangement. Under the doctrine of the preservation of the economic and financial balance of the concession contract, the concessionaire is generally entitled to ask the government to restore the "balance" by means of compensation payments, subsidies or other types of assistance. Alternatively, the economic and financial balance of the contract may be restored by reflecting the increased cost from changes imposed by the government or resulting from circumstances beyond the control of the concessionaire in the tariff payable by users. This transfers to the customers the increased costs for the concessionaire derived from governmental actions or other circumstances without exposing the concessionaire to the risks associated with claims against the government. This mechanism is available in Panama, Colombia and Argentina, while it is uncertain whether it is available in Guatemala.

Technical Capabilities of the Regulatory Agencies

Need for Technical Expertise

During the life of the concession, regulation and ongoing oversight are critical. For instance, it must be determined whether the investments or the services meet the specifications contained in the concession agreement. Also, decisions have to be made about tariffs, which may be subject to review from time to time or following an application made by the concessionaires. These tasks are generally the responsibility of regulatory agencies created by the government.

Such tasks necessarily require that the regulatory staff be technically qualified. Technical expertise is essential to competently address the complex technical issues that the operation of concessions raise, and, ultimately, to achieve independence of the regulator from governmental pressures.

The regulatory frameworks in Guatemala and Argentina require that individuals appointed by the government to hold senior positions at the relevant regulatory agencies be experts with technical capabilities in the industry.

Freedom from Undue Interference

Encouraging investment in infrastructure services requires stability in the treatment of long-term investments. This, in turn, requires that regulators be free from undue pressures, not only from private investors and consumers, but also from political authorities. Some of the features instrumental in ensuring such independence include vesting the power to grant concessions and the power to regulate in different governmental agencies; rendering the statutory functions of the regulatory authorities immune to political changes; making the regulatory agencies economically self-sufficient and not dependent on government funds; requiring regulators to have technical expertise; and ensuring that regulators cannot be removed at the whim of political authorities and that their appointments are not contingent upon the continuance in office of certain political authorities.

In Honduras, the granting authority and the regulator are the same agency in the telecommunications industry, but in the electricity industry the grantor is the executive branch and a separate regulator has been created.

In Guatemala, technical requirements for the appointment of officers of regulatory agencies are statutorily provided, and there are limitations on the grounds for their removal. However, there seems to be a general perception that regulators do not perform their duties independently from the government and without political interference.

In Panama, the regulator has the power to grant concessions, but the law has been designed to ensure broad independence from political authorities.

In Colombia, with respect to domiciliary public services, the regulator does not grant concessions. However, in the operation of airports, ports and highway systems, the authority granting the concession is also the regulatory authority.

The regulatory framework for infrastructure services in Argentina requires that the granting authority not be the regulator. In the gas and the electricity industry, regulatory agencies have been organized to operate independently from the authority granting the concession. Their members are appointed based on their knowledge and experience in the relevant industry, and their appointment and replacement are subject to rules that purport to make them independent from the government. For instance, the executive must inform a special committee of the Congress about any proposed appointment or removal, which may then be effected only with the consent of the committee. This procedure, however, is not applicable in the telecommunications industry, where the executive retains broad powers to appoint and remove regulators. Regulatory agencies for the gas, electricity and telecommunication sectors have some economic independence, while the regulator of postal services does not.

Timing of Regulatory Implementation

The predictable and stable regulation of infrastructure services requires effective timing in the creation and implementation of the regulatory framework and agencies. It is beneficial for regulators to be in operation at the time that an infrastructure service concession is awarded. This allows them to become familiar with the advantages and constraints of the concession process, as well as with the issues associated with start-up of the business of the concessionaire. Likewise, the private investor can have a better understanding of the operation and application of the regulatory framework if the regulators are in place at the inception of the concession.

In all surveyed countries except Argentina there seems to be a trend to ensure that regulatory agencies are in operation at the time that infrastructure services concessions are awarded. In Argentina, with respect to certain industries, the relevant regulatory agencies were created after the concessions were awarded.

Overlapping Jurisdictions

An appropriate regulatory framework for infrastructure services requires that the jurisdictions of the different agencies having authority over the concessionaire not overlap. Overlapping competence fosters uncertainty and the risk of diverging decisions on the same issues. Although mechanisms to solve potential conflicts of jurisdictions among different agencies may be designed, any potential conflicts, irrespective of the ultimate outcome, result in delays and uncertainties for the investors.

There appears to be some overlapping of jurisdictions in Colombia, and some overlapping in Argentina has been noted between the jurisdiction of regulatory agencies and other governmental agencies.

Dispute Resolution Mechanisms

The long-term nature of concession agreements and the impossibility of establishing a regulatory mechanism that covers all future eventualities may result in disputes throughout the term of the concession. From another perspective, concessions result in a number of relationships: the concessionaire and the granting authority, the concessionaire and the regulator, and the concessionaire and consumers. Consequently, disputes in the operation of a concession may, on occasion, relate to the concession contract, its construction or performance, while at other times the disputes may relate to the scope of the regulator's authority, the protection of consumers' rights, protection of the environment, or other issues not regulated by the contract.

An appropriate legal climate for private investments should include features for efficiently and promptly solving disputes relating to a concession, regardless of whether the dispute relates to matters directly subject to the concession agreement. Such features would include specialized independent and impartial courts, expedited procedures for adjudication, reasonable litigation costs and expenses, a concern for the protection of private investments, and rapid enforcement of court decisions.

When disputes relate to matters associated with the concession but not subject to the express provisions of the concession agreement, the mechanism for the settlement of disputes seems principally to be the courts of the host country. By contrast, disputes directly associated with the concession agreement may be resolved elsewhere. Although the typical procedure for dispute resolution relating to the concession agreement is the courts of the country where the investment is located, almost no forensic experience exists in any such jurisdictions relating to these disputes. This absence of experience, along with the complexity of the issues raised, are unfavorable to long-term investments.

Alternative Means for Dispute Resolution

These problems may be mitigated through alternative mechanisms for dispute resolution. One such alternative is to litigate concession agreements in the courts of a foreign jurisdiction with broad knowledge and experience in these matters. This, however, is restricted in some jurisdictions such as Panama and Colombia, while in others it has not been utilized.

Another alternative dispute resolution mechanism is arbitration. Arbitration has the advantage of enabling the parties to appoint arbitrators experienced in the particular area of the dispute and preserving confidentiality. Private investors will generally be interested in knowing whether the laws of a particular jurisdiction allow the government to submit disputes to arbitration and whether disputes relating to concession agreements may be submitted to arbitration. Also, private investors will explore whether arbitral awards are enforceable against the government, and what is the applicable procedure.

Arbitration of disputes relating to concession agreements is expressly permitted in Honduras for concessions awarded for the operation of airports. With respect to other industries, the legislation is silent. The laws of Guatemala, Panama, Colombia and Argentina grant the government authority to submit concession disputes to arbitration. In Colombia and Argentina, arbitral awards against the government are enforceable as court decisions.

Although arbitration is generally the preferred dispute resolution mechanism, there are other alternatives like conciliation and mediation. These may be used either instead of arbitration or as a preliminary mechanism that would lead to arbitration only if the parties were unable thereby to settle their disputes. Under the laws of Guatemala and Argentina, there is no impediment to mediation or conciliation to settle disputes arising from concessions.

Ability to Contract Applicable Procedural and Evidence Rules

Efficient resolution of concession disputes may require that, in addition to submitting the matter to arbitration, the parties have the right to specify procedural rules that set forth time limits and evidence rules. Such rules and timing may differ from the provisions of local laws and may prove instrumental in reaching prompt resolution of disputes. The enforceability of such arrangements is unclear under the laws of Honduras. In Guatemala, Panama and Argentina, procedural arrangements are valid and binding upon the arbitrators, while the laws of Colombia provide that they are not binding.

Conclusions

The laws of the surveyed countries present similarities and differences both in their content and relative degree of development. While none of the legislation is free from certain weaknesses, to some extent those same weaknesses can be mitigated or counterbalanced within the same legal system.

For instance, in Panama, congressional approval of concession agreements is required before they become effective, but the development of a model concession contract may prove conducive to ensuring predictability and facilitating congressional discussion. Another example: in all jurisdictions, post-award challenges are permissible by bidders who have not been selected; however, the laws of Honduras provide fast-track procedures aimed at solving these disputes promptly. Also, although concessionaires may be required to resort to different governmental agencies to obtain the permits and authorizations necessary to operate a concession, in Honduras that burden may on occasion be placed on the government. In all five countries, the government retains the power to impose unilateral amendments to concession contracts, but in Colombia and Argentina such power is limited to a certain percentage of the "value" of the contract or to amendments that do not affect the substance of the contract. In Panama, Colombia and Argentina, concessionaires may seek restoration of the economic and financial equilibrium of the contract following any such actions.

Also in all five countries, the government can terminate a concession contract based upon "public policy" considerations. However, in Colombia, following completion of the construction of a highway the government is precluded from exercising such powers.

Although these examples of mitigation or counterbalancing of weaknesses do not amount to an ideal legal environment for private investment, the coexistence of strengths and weaknesses has so far permitted either the successful implementation or the inception of programs aimed at concessioning infrastructure services.

In more general terms, the laws of the surveyed countries principally follow French doctrine regarding concession awards of infrastructure services. Under this doctrine, concessionaires are an instrument of the government in providing infrastructure services. The government remains the indirect provider of the service and is vested, therefore, with broad powers more consistent with the direct participation of the government in the service rather than with mere private sector investments. This view underlies many of the provisions and regulations described that may have adverse implications for private investments.

Where private investments in infrastructure services through long-term concession agreements are used, doctrines that provide the rationale for intense regulation need to be closely scrutinized. The role of the government ceases to be that of a provider of public services in such cases. This is particularly true when access to the provision of a certain infrastructure service is open to free competition and the authority granted to private investors is not limited in time. However, it may also prove accurate within other mechanisms allowing private participation in infrastructure services. In this new context, the role of the government becomes that of a regulator of a private activity rather than that of a provider of public services. A thorough review of the general doctrines underlying the legal framework for infrastructure services in the surveyed countries could prove helpful for future reforms aimed at creating a more favorable climate for private investment.

Appendix 2.1

Comparative Matrix of Laws on Private Investment in Infrastructure

	HONDURAS	GUATEMALA	PANAMA	COLOMBIA	ARGENTINA
			GENERAL ISSUES		
CONCEPT OF PUBLIC SERVICE	Public service is defined as public ownership of an activity (including its direction and control) with the purpose of satisfying collective needs.	Public services assume the existence of an organization controlled by the government and aimed at satisfying specific needs of general interest.	Public services are not expressly defined but current law identifies certain services (i.e., telecommunications, electricity, water supply and sanitary sewage) deemed to constitute "public services."	Public services are defined as those activities performed by either the government or private parties, aimed at fulfilling needs of permanent importance for the society. Under Colombian law, a special category of public services–the "domiciliary public services"–has been created. These encompass water supply, sewerage, garbage collection, electricity supply, gas transportation and distribution, and certain telecommunications services.	There is no statutory definition of "public service." In general, "public services" encompass activities which are ancillary to those of the administration, with the purpose of fulfilling individual needs which are relevant to the society as a whole, rendered by the government or by entities authorized by, and subject to the control of the government, and subject to a special legal regime.

Appendix 2.1 (cont.)

	HONDURAS	GUATEMALA	PANAMA	COLOMBIA	ARGENTINA
			GENERAL ISSUES		
PARTICIPATION OF PRIVATE INVESTORS IN INFRASTRUCTURE SERVICES	Laws have been passed to allow the granting of concessions to private entities for telecommunication services, electricity supply and operation and maintenance of airports and ports.	In the telecommunications and electricity industry, private parties are granted free access. With respect to other public services, legislation has been passed enabling the granting of concessions or other types of contractual arrangements.	The Constitution and certain laws passed in accordance therewith allow the government to grant concessions for infrastructure services to private parties.	Pursuant to the Constitution, public services may be provided either by the government or by private parties. Concessions are necessary only to the extent the provision of the service by a Colombian private party requires that it uses assets that pertain to the government. In all other cases, private investors may provide the service without need of a concession.	Participation of private investors in infrastructure services generally requires that such private parties be granted a concession, license or other kind of authorization.
			BID PROCESS AND RELATED MATTERS		
PREPARATION OF DOCUMENTATION	Although no experience exists, concession agreements would probably be prepared by the government and the potential investors required to adhere to those terms.	Concessions take the form of "unilateral" documents wherein the government sets forth the terms and conditions of the relevant concession.	The government has developed a model concession contract used as an initial draft for all projects.	The government customarily prepares a draft concession agreement and the interested parties may request that hearings be held for purposes of clarification or discussion.	The government prepares initial drafts of each concession agreement, which are made available to interested parties together with the documents applicable to the bidding process. Generally, within the period granted to submit bids, interested parties may request in writing clarifications or amendments.

SELECTION OF CONCESSIONAIRE	Public bidding.	Public bidding or open public invitations.	Public bidding preceded by a prequalification procedure.	Public bidding.	Concessionaires may be selected through public bidding, contest of integrated projects or public auctions. Generally, infrastructure services have been concessioned through public bidding processes.
POST-AWARD APPROVAL PROCESS	Congressional approval required if the term of the concession agreement exceeds the term for which the president in office at the time of the award was appointed.	Congressional approval required.	Congressional approval required if special benefits or privileges are granted to the concessionaire.	Approval of the executive branch is required.	Approval of the executive branch is required.
CHALLENGES TO THE AWARD	Any party that submitted a bid may contest the award. A fast-track procedure is available.	Award can only be challenged on the grounds that the selected bidder did not submit the best offer.	A challenge against the award may be brought based upon noncompliance with the selection procedure.	Any interested third party and the State Attorney may challenge the award based upon a breach of the rules applicable to its appointment.	The appointment of a concessionaire can be challenged by other bidding parties for violation of the bidding process rules. Parties with an interest in submitting a bid but which have failed to do so for reasons attributable to a breach of the bidding rules may challenge the award. A claim may seek compensation for breach of the applicable regulations or an order nullifying the award.

Appendix 2.1 (cont.)

	HONDURAS	GUATEMALA	PANAMA	COLOMBIA	ARGENTINA
			BID PROCESS AND RELATED MATTERS		
RESTRICTIONS, EXPROPRIATION	Government may expropriate assets of concessionaire, subject to a "fair price" compensation determined within judicial proceedings. Governmental actions relating to expropriation are subject to judicial review.	Government may expropriate assets of the concessionaire and the right to operate the concession. The concessionaire is entitled to a compensation equivalent to the "current value" of the expropriated assets. Governmental actions relating to expropriation are subject to judicial review.	Government may expropriate assets of the concessionaire and the right to operate the concession. The concessionaire is entitled to a "fair" compensation and parties to a concession agreement may agree therein as to the amounts payable by the government to the concessionaire following an expropriation. Governmental actions relating to expropriation are subject to judicial review.	Government may expropriate assets of the concessionaire and the right to operate the concession. The concessionaire is entitled to compensation that must take into account public and private interest. Actions of the government relating to expropriation are subject to judicial review, except for the determination of the "public interest" as a rationale for the expropriation.	Government may expropriate assets of the concessionaire, subject to compensation that must cover the actual value of the assets, direct damages and interest. The determination of "public interest" as a rationale for expropriation is not subject to judicial review.
PERMITS AND AUTHORIZATIONS IN ADDITION TO THE CONCESSION	Granted by governmental agencies other than that granting the concession. The burden of obtaining such permits and authorizations is on occasion placed on the government.	Made available by agencies different from that granting the concession.	The concessionaire must resort to governmental agencies different from that granting the concession.	The concessionaire must resort to governmental agencies different from that granting the concession.	The concessionaire must resort to governmental agencies different from that granting the concession.

RIGHTS OF WAY		Regulations exist for the granting of rights of way in the electricity industry. The concessionaire is required to file an application with the Ministry of Energy and Mines and thereafter enter into negotiations with the owner of the affected estate to determine the compensation. If no agreement is reached, the issue is determined by a court in a fast-track proceeding.			Rights of way are deemed granted upon the granting of the concession and approval of the project in the electricity and fossil fuels industries. The concessionaire must pay compensation that will take into consideration the value and occupation of the affected estate.
	LEGAL STRUCTURES AND RELATED ISSUES				
USE OF PROJECT COMPANIES	Participation of private investors in infrastructure services may be effected either through project companies or direct sponsors' participation.				
LIABILITIES INCURRED BY THE GOVERNMENT PRIOR TO AWARDING THE CONCESSION		The concessionaire is not made responsible for actions or omissions of the government in connection with providing the service prior to the award of the concession.	The concessionaire may be held a successor of the government as provider of the service prior to the granting of the concession, and therefore liable for actions or omissions of the government, except for labor liabilities.		The concessionaire may be held bound by actions or omissions of the government prior to the granting of the concession in relation with certain labor liabilities.
CONTRACTUAL STRUCTURES FOR PROJECT FINANCING	No limitations in any of the five countries.				

Appendix 2.1 (cont.)

	HONDURAS	GUATEMALA	PANAMA	COLOMBIA	ARGENTINA
			LEGAL STRUCTURES AND RELATED ISSUES		
SECURED LENDING: TYPICAL MECHANISMS	Pledge, mortgage and floating charges. Creditors are granted an absolute first priority security interest and must resort to a court of competent jurisdiction to conduct foreclosure proceedings. The bankruptcy of the concessionaire does not affect the continued enforceability of the liens.	Pledge and mortgage. The bankruptcy of the concessionaire does not affect the continued enforceability of the liens.	Pledge and mortgage. Creditors are preferred to all other creditors except for the government and insurance companies. The bankruptcy of the concessionaire does not affect the continued enforceability of the liens.	Pledge and mortgage. Creditors are preferred to all other creditors except for labor and tax obligations. The bankruptcy of the concessionaire does not affect the continued enforceability of the liens.	Pledges and mortgages (including all equipment affixed to real estate). Creditors are preferred to other creditors, subject to certain limited exceptions. Foreclosure of chattels may be conducted through out-of-court auctions, while foreclosure on real estate requires that the creditor resort to a court. Bankruptcy of the concessionaire does not affect the continued enforceability of the liens.

TRUST ARRANGEMENTS	Trust arrangements are permissible and the assets placed in trust constitute an estate separate from that of the trustor and the trustee. Only commercial banks may provide trustee services.	Trust arrangements are permissible and the assets placed in trust constitute an estate separate from that of the trustor and the trustee. Only banks and financial institutions authorized to operate in Guatemala may provide trustee services.	Trust arrangements are permissible and the assets placed in trust constitute an estate separate from that of the trustee and the trustor. The trust property is subject to independent taxation.	Trust arrangements are permissible and the assets placed in trust constitute an estate separate from that of the trustee and the trustor. Only financial and other specially authorized entities may serve as trustees. Trusts are subject to complex tax treatment.	Trust arrangements are permissible and subject to fraudulent conveyance restrictions, which have the effect of isolating the trust property from the estate of the trustor and trustee. In order to offer trustee services to the public or to perform trustee's duties with respect to indebtedness evidenced in the form of publicly offered securities, the trustee must hold a banking license or otherwise be specially authorized.
ASSIGNABILITY OF RIGHTS TO OPERATE CONCESSION OR COLLECT TARIFFS	Probably prohibited.	Doubtful.	Subject to governmental approval.	Subject to governmental approval.	Subject to governmental approval. Approval of an assignment to operate a concession may not be available in all industries.

Appendix 2.1 (cont.)

	HONDURAS	GUATEMALA	PANAMA	COLOMBIA	ARGENTINA
LEGAL STRUCTURES AND RELATED ISSUES					
LENDERS' SPECIAL REMEDIES: CURE DEFAULTS OF CONCESSIONAIRE OR OPERATE THE CONCESSION TO AVOID OR CURE DEFAULTS	Not enforceable.	Subject to governmental approval.	Enforceable.	Enforceable.	Not enforceable.
EXCHANGE CONTROLS	No exchange controls.	No exchange controls for payments abroad.	No exchange controls.	Foreign exchange transactions need to be made through authorized local entities; 30% of the proceeds of loans obtained abroad need be deposited with Central Bank, which makes available funds after 18 months.	No exchange controls. Mandatory conversion rate of pesos into U.S. dollars.
CONCESSION CONTRACT					
ALLOCATION OF RISKS: GENERAL PRINCIPLES			A general principle of concession law exists whereby the concessionaire is required to undertake risks associated with conducting the business and the government undertakes all other risks.		A general principle of concessions law exists whereby the concessionaire is required to undertake risks associated with conducting the business and the government undertakes all other risks.

ENFORCEABILITY OF CONTRACTUAL ARRANGEMENTS RELATING TO RISK ALLOCATION	In general, the enforceability of contractual arrangements relating to risk allocation is doubtful. Parties to a concession agreement, however, may validly agree as to the meaning and scope of certain concepts associated with risk allocation, such as force majeure.	Since the granting of concession generally does not require that an actual agreement be entered into, risk allocation arrangements are not resorted to. To the extent an agreement is entered into, parties may validly agree as to the meaning and scope of certain concepts associated with risk allocation, such as force majeure.	Risk allocation contractual arrangements are enforceable, subject to the general principle of risk allocation embodied in the laws of concessions. Parties to a concession agreement may validly agree as to the meaning and scope of certain concepts associated with risk allocation such as force majeure.	Risk allocation arrangements are enforceable to the extent they are aimed at restoring the economic and financial equilibrium of the concession contract. Parties to a concession agreement may validly agree as to the meaning and scope of certain concepts associated with risk allocation such as force majeure.	Risk allocation contractual arrangements and agreements relating to the determination of the meaning and scope of concepts associated with risk allocation (such as force majeure) are enforceable, subject to the general principle of risk allocation embodied in the laws of concessions and preservation of the concessionaire's right to claim restoration of the economic and financial balance of the concession agreement.
ABILITY OF THE GOVERNMENT TO MAKE UNILATERAL AMENDMENTS TO CONCESSION AGREEMENTS	Government is entitled to make unilateral amendments to a concession agreement.	Government is entitled to make unilateral amendments to a concession agreement.	Government is entitled to make unilateral amendments to a concession agreement to the extent there is a danger that the service will be withheld or seriously affected.	Government is entitled to make unilateral amendments to a concession agreement if a risk exists that the service will be suspended or affected. If the amendments alter in 20% or more the "initial value" of the contract, the concessionaire may seek termination.	Government is entitled to make unilateral amendments to a concession agreement for the benefit of the general interest. Unilateral amendments may not alter the substance of the concession agreement.

Appendix 2.1 (cont.)

	HONDURAS	GUATEMALA	PANAMA	COLOMBIA	ARGENTINA
CONCESSION CONTRACT					
CONSENSUAL AMENDMENTS TO CONCESSION AGREEMENTS	Legislation is silent and there is no past experience on consensual amendments to concession agreements. Nonselected bidders would be entitled to challenge consensual amendments grounded on discriminatory treatment. Substantial amendments are subject to congressional approval.	Legislation is silent and there is no past experience on consensual amendments to concession agreements. Consensual amendments are subject to congressional approval, and congressional a priori approval for future amendments is invalid.	Consensual amendments to concession agreements are permissible but may be challenged by third parties if they result in a substantial change of the terms of the concession.	Consensual amendments to concession agreements are permissible if there is a material change in the circumstances existing at the time the concession was granted. Consensual amendments may be challenged if they entail a change in the circumstances under which the concession was granted. Consensual amendments are subject to the same approval process as the concession agreement.	Consensual amendments are permissible following a change in the circumstances foreseen when the concession was granted, provided such change is not attributable to the parties and is unforeseeable and extraordinary. Consensual amendments may be challenged if they entail a change in the circumstances under which the concession was granted. Consensual amendments are subject to the same approval process as the concession agreement.
RESTORATION OF ECONOMIC AND FINANCIAL BALANCE OF THE CONCESSION CONTRACT			The remedy is available to the concessionaire and may take the form of payments by the government, amendments to the concession agreement (e.g., extension of term) or amendments to the applicable tariffs.	The remedy is available to the concessionaire and may take the form of payments by the government, amendments to the concession agreement (e.g., extension of term) or amendments to the applicable tariffs.	The remedy is available to the concessionaire and may take the form of payments by the government, amendments to the concession agreement (e.g., extension of term) or amendments to the applicable tariffs.

RIGHT OF GOVERNMENT TO TERMINATE A CONCESSION AGREEMENT PRIOR TO THE EXPIRATION OF ITS TERM	Government can terminate a concession agreement at any time, based upon "national security" considerations.	Government can terminate a concession at any time, subject to 90-day prior notice.	Government can terminate a concession agreement at any time based upon public interest considerations.	"Public service" and "public policy" consider-ations entitle the government to terminate concession agreements, except for those relating to the construction and operation of highways, which cannot be terminated prior to their original term, but rather upon completion of the construction.	Government can terminate a concession agreement prior to stated maturity based upon public policy considerations.
TERMINATION RIGHTS OF THE CONCESSIONAIRE FOLLOWING DEFAULT BY THE GOVERNMENT	Legislation does not contemplate the right of a concessionaire to terminate a concession agreement following a default by the government.	General principles of contract law would entitle the concessionaire to terminate a concession agreement following a default by the government.	The laws on concession contracts only address the grounds for the termination by the government, but a concession agreement may include provisions which allow the concessionaire to invoke termination following a default by the government.	The concessionaire must seek a court judgment in order to terminate a concession agreement following a default by the government.	Concession agreements generally entitle the concessionaire to invoke termination following a default by the government.
DETERMINATION OF AMOUNTS PAYABLE TO THE CONCESSIONAIRE FOLLOWING TERMINATION	Matter addressed in each concession agreement. Such arrangements are generally deemed enforceable.				

Appendix 2.1 (cont.)

	HONDURAS	GUATEMALA	PANAMA	COLOMBIA	ARGENTINA
			CONCESSION CONTRACT		
AVAILABILITY OF TERMINATION PAYMENTS	Amounts due by the government need to be included in the next national budget.	Assets of the government are immune from claims of creditors.	Assets of the government are immune from claims of creditors.	Amounts due by the government need to be included in the next national budget. Limitations exist as to the ability of creditors to attach and foreclose on assets of the government.	Amounts due by the government need to be included in the next national budget. Limitations exist as to the ability of creditors to attach and foreclose on assets of the government.

TARIFFS

MECHANISMS FOR DETERMINATION AND TARIFF ADJUSTMENTS	In the electricity industry, tariffs are subject to review upon a change in the price of hydrocarbons or in the official rates of exchange. A tariff increase requires prior regulatory approval. In the telecommunications industry, the regulator may issue regulations regarding applicable tariffs during the period of time the operator is granted exclusivity. Legislation relating the granting of concessions for the operation of airports provides that the relevant concession agreements will contain the applicable tariffs and their adjustments.	The legislation does not contain provisions.	The regulator determines from time to time the maximum tariffs that may be collected by concessionaires. Concessionaires are entitled to apply for revision of such maximums.	The applicable statute provides that the concession contract contemplate adjustment mechanisms that take into account inflation and other similar factors. The statutes vest in the regulator authority to elaborate formulae for the adjustment of tariffs. Such formulae are subject to revision from time to time.	The issue of tariff revision has been customarily addressed in concession contracts and the applicable regulatory frameworks, which entitle concessionaires to apply for new tariffs. In some cases, concessionaires are required to file annual applications for approval of their tariffs. Revision of tariffs is generally based on information provided by the concessionaire about changes in costs beyond its control. Argentine law expressly forbids inflation adjustments and deprives any contractual arrangement to that legal effect. Certain concession agreements contain provisions that entitle tariff adjustments to take into consideration inflation in the United States, and the validity of such provisions has not been contested.

Appendix 2.1 (cont.)

	HONDURAS	GUATEMALA	PANAMA	COLOMBIA	ARGENTINA
		REGULATORY AGENCIES			
NEED FOR TECHNICAL EXPERTISE AT REGULATORY AGENCIES		With respect to certain industries, it is required that certain staff appointed by the government be knowledgeable in the relevant industry.			It is generally required that the individuals appointed by the government to the different regulatory agencies have expertise in the relevant industry.

FACTORS ENCOURAGING OR DISCOURAGING INTERFERENCE	The granting authority and the regulator are the same agency in the telecommunications industry, but in the electricity industry the grantor is the executive and a separate regulator has been created.	Technical requirements for the appointment of officers of regulatory agencies are statutorily provided, and there are limitations on the grounds for their removal. However, there is a general perception that regulators do not perform their duties independently from government and political interference.	The regulator has the power to grant concessions, but the law has been designed to ensure broad independence from the political authorities.	With respect to local public services, the regulator does not grant concessions. However, in the operation of airports, ports and highway systems, the authority granting the concession is also the regulatory authority.	Generally, the granting authority is not the regulator. In gas and electricity, regulatory agencies operate independently from the authority granting the concession. Members are appointed based on knowledge and experience in the industry. Appointments and replacements are subject to rules that purport to make them independent from the government. The executive is required to inform a special committee of the Congress about the proposed appointment or removal, which may be effected only with the committee's consent. This procedure is not applicable in telecommunications, where the executive retains broad powers to appoint and remove regulators. Regulatory agencies for gas, electricity and telecommunications have certain economic independence, while the regulator of postal services does not.

Appendix 2.1 (cont.)

	HONDURAS	GUATEMALA	PANAMA	COLOMBIA	ARGENTINA
			REGULATORY AGENCIES		
TIMING OF REGULATORY IMPLEMENTATION	Generally, regulatory agencies are in operation at the time a concession is granted.	Generally, regulatory agencies are in operation at the time a concession is granted.	Generally, regulatory agencies are in operation at the time a concession is granted.	Generally, regulatory agencies are in operation at the time a concession is granted.	In certain industries, regulatory agencies commenced operating only after the infrastructure services were concessioned.
OVERLAPPING JURISDICTIONS				There is likelihood of overlapping jurisdictions among government agencies.	There is likelihood of overlapping jurisdictions among government agencies.
			ALTERNATIVE DISPUTE RESOLUTION MECHANISMS		
ARBITRATION AS ALTERNATIVE MEANS FOR DISPUTE RESOLUTION	Arbitration is contemplated in connection with the concessioning of the operation of airports. Otherwise, the legislation is silent.	The government may submit disputes resulting from a concession agreement to arbitration. Parties to arbitration may agree as to applicable procedural and evidence rules.	The government may submit disputes resulting from a concession agreement to arbitration. Parties to arbitration may agree as to applicable procedural and evidence rules.	The government may submit disputes resulting from a concession agreement to arbitration.	The government may submit disputes resulting from a concession agreement to arbitration. Parties to arbitration may agree as to applicable procedural and evidence rules.

CHAPTER 3

Effective, Low-Cost Systems to Enforce Infrastructure Contracts

Hugo Palacios Mejia

"The inability of societies to develop effective, low-cost enforcement of contracts is the most important source of both historical stagnation and contemporary underdevelopment in the Third World." —*Douglass C. North, Institutions, Institutional Change and Economic Performance*

Political and economic reasons led many countries during the second half of the 19th century and the first half of the 20th century to believe that provision of public services had to be a government responsibility. As this approach became less pervasive, the idea of granting concession rights to private enterprises to provide such services gained acceptance, provided that the rules and regulations established by the grantor were observed. As a result, following French administrative law—which emphasizes the differences between private and public law with regard to contracts—the *concession agreement* was introduced. It assumes in principle that the private party does not have by itself the right to provide public services because they have been the objects of a government reserve, and that the acquisition of that right is thus subject to a grant from the administrative authorities. Thus, the concession agreement is the typical instrument used by the authorities to allow private agents to overcome entry barriers that are a general rule in the public services sector.

Once it is accepted that public services can be provided through concession agreements—that is, accepting the existence of entry barriers that only government authorities can lift—any number of consequences arise. Authorities monopolize the ability to define the characteristics of the infrastructure project, and may do so according to principles of economic efficiency or any other criteria. Authorities must ensure an equal opportunity to all contractors bidding for an infrastructure project, which implies drafting detailed bidding conditions for the contract. At times, the would-be contractor can only adhere to the bidding documents, and his proposal may be limited to specific items, such as cost and term. This process is likely to prevent authorities from receiving offers boasting advanced technical or administrative features, since the terms and conditions are set forth based on the experience of the user, or his advisors, and not on the experience of those who have to innovate in order to compete in different markets. Though this inconvenience may not be eliminated altogether, its effects can be somewhat mitigated by inviting the potential bidders to comment on the conditions proposed by the authorities, as provided for by Argentine and Colombian law. This allows for incorporating the opinions and concerns of bidders and financing sources.

Later in the concession process, even if circumstances call for an amendment, the authorities may be reluctant to modify the contract because they want to preserve the equality of opportunity among the parties that participated in the bidding process. Otherwise, the authorities may become liable to lawsuits from the losing bidders, who could argue that, had they also been given the opportunity to submit an alternative, the contract would have been awarded to them.

Authorities have the option of including unilateral modification and termination clauses in the contracts, thus increasing the political risk. As shown in Chapter 2, contracts in which the government participates tend to have not only inequitable provisions but also confer on the authorities powers that appear excessive when compared to those of conventional contracts. For instance, some contracts may require a private contractor to continue performing services even when the other party ceases to fulfill its obligations. Governments may have powers such as the ability to unilaterally amend, interpret, allow to expire, or terminate the contract, and to introduce penalty and liquidated damages clauses. In addition to the uncertainties that such powers entail, they may also cause lengthy disputes during the performance of the contract. Such delays are, by themselves, an important element of risk.

Authorities are under pressure to guarantee exclusive rights to the concessionaire in lieu of providing total protection against commercial risks (e.g., poor demand). This and other similar facts may lead to the formation of business monopolies.

Should there be sufficient demand for the services provided by the contractor, the authorities may also be tempted to use the concession as a source of government revenue, which could strengthen monopolies that are harmful to the system, hinder the increase of service coverage, and limit consumer options. By acknowledging or creating a monopoly through a concession agreement, authorities are required to establish controls and regulations, which in turn will exert pressure on the government budget and create new political risks for the concessionaire during the performance of the contract.

Admittedly, there are certain situations that call for the use of concession agreements, such as when the authorities, due to economic, political or legal reasons, cannot do without the ownership of certain assets, yet still want to make additional investments or guarantee more efficient service. For instance, in the case of a public asset such as a road, a public beach or the use of the electromagnetic spectrum, concession agreements are an appropriate instrument.

It is usually argued that in certain instances the entry barriers intrinsic to concession agreements actually benefit consumers by creating natural monopolies with favorable economies of scale. This may be valid from a conceptual point of view; in practice, however, identifying the projects that meet the theoretical economic criteria that justify favoring a natural monopoly may be a complicated task. Projects that in fact are not suited to transfer to the consumer the alleged benefits they should provide are often defended on grounds of being natural monopolies. When in doubt, competition offers the most advantages.

The above leads to the conclusion that the best way to link private capital and management to public infrastructure projects is by ensuring free access to the public services sector. Colombia has done so since 1994 in the areas of energy production, transmission and distribution; local telephone services; water transportation and distribution; and solid waste disposal and sewerage. Though in principle the same rules are in effect for long distance services and gas distribution, certain regulations have made their application less clear.

The principle of free access implies that private entrepreneurs have the ability to define infrastructure projects, identify contractors, establish contract terms, and execute the contracts. The incentives of competition and the principles of economic efficiency and profit maximization guide their actions. They assume the project's inherent risks within the legal framework of civil or commercial contracts and, in particular, those referred to as agreements.

Free access clearly does not mean that the authorities lose their ability to regulate the entrepreneurs' activities. Rather, regulations are advanced with the main purpose of fostering competition, not guaranteeing the viability of a monopoly. When monopolies do appear, regulations may seek to ensure that their rates and operations are similar to those that a free market would have produced. Under this approach neither party to an infrastructure project contract can benefit from unilateral modification and termination clauses during project implementation, although under special circumstances such a clause may be included to guarantee the continuity of the service provision.

Also, free access does not mean the authorities have to waive certain rights in areas such as urban planning or environmental protection. It does assume, however, that the service provider will be subject to general criteria that are relevant to the nature of the activity and not to ad hoc criteria stemming solely from a concession regime.

The principle of free access is compatible with the principles of social solidarity and subsidies, provided that these principles are transparent. While the entrepreneur may charge market prices with the approval of the regulatory agency, the authorities may appropriate budgetary funds to finance a certain percentage of the cost of the service for the poor. Hence, the use of private funds will permit an increase in coverage, something that has significant social value in itself that probably would not be possible under the fiscal restrictions needed to maintain macroeconomic balance. Available government funds can then be used to subsidize service to the poor.

The political risk during the performance of infrastructure contracts is mitigated when the principles of free access to the area of public services are applied. Private sector participation in the construction and operation of public infrastructure projects can be enhanced through explicit legal statements regarding free access to those projects. This would immediately place infrastructure contracts within the realm of civil and commercial laws whose risks are more familiar to private enterprise, and whose application is generally backed by plenty of legal precedents.

The General Counsel of the Eurotunnel project has said that the law of concession agreements is unknown in the United Kingdom. It could also be said that unilateral clauses are relatively foreign to the Anglo-Saxon legal culture. And, as long as the countries that belong to that culture remain an important source of capital, relying on private legal systems is likely to enhance the flow of capital to the Latin American region.

Opportunism in Infrastructure Contracts

Even though free access to the area of public services would mean that infrastructure projects would be subject to fewer political risks—thus making them more attractive to private companies than concession agreements—this does not imply that all major obstacles would be eliminated.

Contracts for the construction and operation of public infrastructure facilities face special problems not only when one of the parties is a government agency, but also when both parties are subject to private sector rules. This chapter examines the difficulties of enforcing such contracts, and considers concession agreements as just one kind of contract that carries more risk than normally found in infrastructure projects.

Disputes between the parties to construction contracts occur more frequently than with any other kind of private legal contract, and such disputes will be more significant if the contractor is also in charge of operating the facility.

The conflictive nature of these contracts stems mainly from two facts. First, compliance does not take place immediately, but rather over a period of time. Second, throughout the life of the contract both parties are subject to conduct and economic provisions that in many cases require them to cooperate so that each can fulfill its duties and exercise its rights.

This opens the door for opportunism by both parties during the different stages of contract implementation. At the time the parties enter into the contract they assess the risks and agree on how to allocate their burden. However, as time passes and some risks materialize and others dissipate, the party that suffers a loss has incentives to avoid the economic consequences, while the party not affected by a loss tends to neglect payments that were agreed to as a means of insuring against losses.

Contractual opportunism will translate into difficulties in enforcing contracts without incurring high costs. The risks of contractual opportunism become more apparent if the legal system lacks effective and low-cost rules and procedures to define with binding force the contents of contracts. Even though a very important source of such rules is the law itself, they only become tangible and meaningful when judges refer to them repeatedly and apply them consistently to specific cases. Although in countries with legal systems rooted in French law the use of precedents is not as prevalent as in countries whose legal system is based on common law, the latter provides information that is key to anticipating the way in which a judge will rule in a current dispute. The use of precedents, and not the law alone, helps determine the exact scope of the rules that settle disputes over infrastructure contracts. It is highly unlikely that enough disputes will arise in a small or medium-sized country to permit the emergence of precedents whose breadth is clearly defined.

Poor regulations or the inadequate use of precedents, the resulting risks of contractual opportunism, and the cost of avoiding those risks (insurance, guarantees, immersion in the country's business and legal culture, legal counsel, etc.) add to the parties' transaction costs and, therefore, interfere with the performance of a public infrastructure contract. These transaction costs will proportionally increase where the knowledge of the regulations and of the risks of a contract can be applied only in a certain country or on limited occasion.

No legal system or contract draft will entirely eliminate legal uncertainties or the possibilities of a dispute, but it is a valid aspiration that the parties to a contract be able to find that such uncertainties and possibilities are similar to, and not significantly greater than, those they know and those to which they are accustomed. A more ambitious goal would be a legal and contractual regime that would actually reduce those uncertainties. In other words, the goal is not to eliminate the risks inherent in drafting laws and contracts; however, it is reasonable to aim for making comparisons between different regimes easier, reducing the differences, and eventually, reducing the uncertainties.

Benefits of Reforming the Legal Framework of Infrastructure Contracts

Raising capital for the development of the infrastructure sector becomes easier as risk allocation in public infrastructure contracts becomes more clear; that is, as more precise and widespread rules and more abundant precedents are made available.

Should the analyses of economists such as Douglass C. North prove to be correct, it could be said that the more a country designs effective, low-cost systems to enforce contracts, the brighter the prospects of overcoming the obstacles of underdevelopment.

On a less distant scenario, an important consequence of having more certain contract regulations would be the possibility of attracting capital from outside the region, particularly from countries whose contract systems are inspired neither by French civil law, such as the United States, England and Japan, nor by an administrative legal system designed by the State Council or French lawmakers.

In fact, the perception of contractual risk is different in the country benefitting from the construction and services of an infrastructure project than elsewhere. Being unfamiliar with a country's legal and business culture, foreigners will naturally tend to consider the enforcement of a contract more risky in those places where they have not done business before. Differences in risk perception will always be a reason why funds available for infrastructure projects in foreign countries are harder to come by and more expensive than domestic capital. If foreign funds are to be obtained in sufficient amounts and at reasonable prices for the construction and operation of public infrastructure projects, an effort should be made to mitigate the risk of contractual opportunism by making regulations and norms as clear as possible.

To a lesser extent, contractual uncertainty also limits the flow of domestic capital. If that uncertainty involves a small or medium-sized economy, circumstances will aggravate the problem even further because, even if appropriate laws are in effect, there might not be enough judicial precedents to easily determine the scope of the laws. The investor's legal counsel will be more willing to give an opinion backed by consistent decisions from judges than an opinion based on a single, isolated legal interpretation.

Contractual uncertainty particularly affects the use of public funds for infrastructure projects. Authorities signing a contract either for public works or for a concession are likely to face problems with contractors more frequently, making the use of governmental savings less efficient. Thus, contracts that can be enforced effectively and at low costs not only would facilitate raising international funds for the region, but also ease the flow of domestic capital and enhance the use of public resources.

Differences in the Legal Frameworks of Infrastructure Contracts

The goal of the comparative analysis in Chapter 2 of the legislation of five different countries[1] was to identify the legal obstacles to private participation in infrastructure projects and to formulate reforms to reduce or eliminate them. Other countries in the region stand to benefit from the lessons yielded from the experiences of the countries studied.

The comparison, of course, should be based on the results of a purely formal analysis. The meaning of the law always goes beyond its text or its context: the judges' rulings, the jurists' opinions, and secondary or regulatory legislation all contribute to the meaning of the law. Making comparisons about the comprehensive meaning of legislation, which is indeed its true meaning, is extremely difficult. Even so, there are some important differences among the legal frameworks that each country uses with regard to public infrastructure contracts. They can be grouped into the five following categories.

Ideological Differences

Some of the differences may have a profound ideological content, particularly those regarding the freedom of the private sector to provide public services.

[1]Argentina, Colombia, Honduras, Guatemala and Panama.

The existence of either freedom or entry barriers immediately determines whether or not the contracts are concession agreements, thus subject to special rules that increase the sovereign risk or locatio operis agreements akin to conventional private legal contracts. The possibility of using expropriations to enforce concession agreements, and particularly the scope of the underlying indemnities, is a sensitive topic that has been debated at length throughout the region.

Differences due to the leverage and level of commitment that certain interest groups have developed in many countries should not be overlooked either. The construction of infrastructure projects may require licenses and government permits, especially related to environmental protection, rights of local communities, and protection of historical heritage. Also very important, when present, are laws that protect workers' entitlements under labor contracts and those that seek to prevent the interruption of public service supply.

Legal reform would hardly redress all these differences in the legal framework because they have an ideological nature. Although reforms regarding the principle of freedom of entry to the sector may be more viable, the political obstacles to their implementation should not be ignored.

Differences That Can Be Overcome with Procedural Rules

As long as an individual has a dominant position in the market by virtue of either owning public service infrastructure or having acquired it through a concession agreement or as the result of the freedom of entry principle, setting the rates to be charged becomes an issue that has immediate social and political ramifications. The application of the underlying regulations will always carry a political risk.

It is possible to pursue legal reforms that, while maintaining the power to prevent abuses in the hands of the authorities, create administrative procedures that guarantee the private company the opportunity to make itself heard. Those procedures would not keep the company from obtaining a reasonable return on its investment, and would enable it to receive from the authorities clear and timely statements about the extent of its rights and duties. A subsequent legal review of those statements with the aid of legal experts would complete a reasonable legal framework.

Economic and Political Differences Addressed in International Treaties

There are differences in the legal approach to certain matters that undoubtedly affect contract risks, but that have already been addressed by international cooperation efforts. These matters are usually related to currency exchange issues. One of the objectives of the International Monetary Fund is to facilitate international payments of goods and services exchanged, and it does not seem right to assume that reducing the differences and uncertainties of infrastructure contracts would lead to legal reforms that are more liberal than those resulting from the Fund's charter.

Something similar can be said about another relevant issue: the treatment and the possibility of government expropriation of foreign investments. This matter usually involves the constitutions of the countries, not only their legal systems. Several international treaties already exist in this area, some bilateral and others backed by the World Bank. Despite the importance of the issue, the infrastructure financing cause would be better served by focusing on other more specific sources of uncertainty.

Specific Differences about Contractual Issues

Chapter 2 points to the existence of some legal discrepancies or instances where the law is silent regarding issues that neither reflect serious ideological conflicts nor have received constant special attention from international agencies. These issues are indeed more likely to be the subject of legal reforms to attract funds to the infrastructure sector. Specific examples are the rules related to issues such as rights-of-way, types of collateral, the scope of fiduciary arrangements, the possibility of lenders taking over the responsibilities of the project builders and operators, lenders' duties, the duty the victim has to mitigate the effects of breach of contract, the discretion the parties have to determine risk-sharing responsibilities within a contract, the amendments to administrative contracts, and the rights and duties of the contractor upon fulfillment of the contract.

A matter not related to political conflicts but surrounded by clearly vested interests and thus deserving of special attention is the issue of the contract's economic and financial equilibrium. This concept covers, in principle, the duty of the contracting government agencies to compensate the private contractor for all the losses caused by burdens or limitations imposed by actions taken by the authorities. However, there are exaggerated versions of this rule that lead to administrative contracts that are free of risk to the private contractor. Therefore, as long as the rules pertaining to contract equilibrium are not precise, possibilities for opportunism will remain, running against the interests of the government agencies. The content of most rules is not clear regarding the reasons for maintaining such equilibrium, when the balance is lost, how it is restored, and who chooses the adjustment mechanisms in each case.

Differences in Conflict Resolution Procedures

Chapter 2 points to the progress made by some countries in incorporating arbitration systems into their laws for the settlement of disputes, even though significant problems remain. There have been substantial recent international efforts in this area to coordinate legal systems.

Prospects for a Standard Infrastructure Contract Format

Insofar as the goal is to provide a common benchmark or to reduce the uncertainty of the rules applicable to infrastructure contracts, one possibility for the region would be to move toward more uniform contract clauses, much in the same way that some engineer trade associations have done it in certain European countries.

Such an effort might not yield useful results at this time. In fact, one common characteristic of several Latin American legal systems is the presence of multiple compulsory public interest regulations that, if in conflict with any contract clause, can render that particular clause or the entire contract null and void. The diversity of legal systems would make the use of a standard contract text in different countries difficult because contracts might then be revoked for violations of public interest regulations.

In many Latin American countries it has been established that, unlike the private sector, authorities may limit their work to those activities expressly provided for in the law. As a result, many contract options available to the private sector are unavailable to government agencies, not because they are prohibited, but because they have not been authorized.

Drafting standard public infrastructure contracts in Latin America would be hampered both by the fact that the provisions would have to defer to many higher order rules, and that in several countries the provisions applicable to the private sector would not be authorized for government agencies.

The reduction of uncertainties and legal differences pertaining to the framework of public infrastructure contracts should be pursued through legal reforms rather than through the development of common contract texts. With time, though, the latter could be the result of the former.

The Aim of Legal Reforms

There is no legal model in any of the countries surveyed to regulate contracts for the construction and operation of public infrastructure projects. Each country's laws reflect unique cultural and economic circumstances that have evolved with time and led to changes in the regulations. Similarly, no international agreement provides for the creation of a common contract framework for public infrastructure projects in countries with significant capital flows, although work to that effect is being carried out by the European Union. Finally, legal reform would be less difficult to implement if the issues involved had not been the subjects of ideological debate.

A starting point would be to determine the possibility of eliminating those features in legal systems that are peculiar to the countries involved and completely foreign to the practices and institutions of countries that export capital. Then, it would be necessary to authorize the private and public sectors to incorporate into their contracts certain business agreements that capital exporting countries frequently use. This does not mean the legal arrangements in those countries are necessarily "better" than those of other countries; rather, it would acknowledge the fact that there is sufficient risk management expertise in using those business agreements, due to the larger volume of operations that capital exporting countries perform. Thus, the work proposed, to a certain extent, requires more information about the legal contractual framework of the countries that handle a significant amount of funds for infrastructure projects.

There are certain specific issues that should be carefully addressed when planning legal reforms to enhance public infrastructure financing. Some refer to the nature of the contract provisions for each party, while others deal with mechanisms used to settle disputes.

Freedom to Allocate Risks

It would be safe to assume that when dealing with companies involved in the construction and operation of infrastructure projects, each of the parties is relatively aware of the variables it controls, the variables controlled by the other party, the risks, and the cost of coping with those risks. Therefore, contractual freedoms in the allocation of risks among the parties involved should not be restricted, especially when most legal systems contain force majeure clauses that waive responsibility.

In this context, the rules for the economic and financial equilibrium of the contract should be used only to compensate the private contractor for losses resulting from legitimate government decisions that affect the contractor's corporate interests; that is, losses that do not affect the community as a whole. The control on the authorities' illegitimate decisions should be carried out according to the rules that protect the contractor against breach of contract, or regular liability rules.

Contract Interpretation Rules

In reviewing the risk allocation provisions of a contract, it is suggested that each party assume those risks it can assess or know more accurately than others, or those that it can mitigate more economically. However, in terms of legal reforms, perhaps it should be established by rule that, in case of doubt, the contract should be interpreted as though the parties had agreed to abide by economic principles like those that ensure the optimal use of resources. This would represent progress, as opposed to the use of conventional rules of interpretation based on formal analyses of the text or on contractual performance that may be subject to several interpretations.

Immediate Conflict Resolution

Few contract provisions are as useful in the implementation of an infrastructure project as those that enable the immediate resolution of conflicts that arise during the performance of the contract.

Studies have identified the following as the most frequent sources of conflict in the performance of infrastructure contracts: new developments requiring projects work unforeseen in or unrelated to the original agreement; unexpected conditions in the construction site, soil or weather; delays, including those due to design errors or revisions; and interference with the contractor's work schedule. Insofar as these problems are not resolved promptly, they can result in work stoppages or delays that may have serious financial consequences for the parties.

It might be more economical to keep certain individuals properly and constantly informed about the performance of the contract so that they are capable of settling conflicts in a timely manner. The alternative is to appoint different arbitrators for each conflict or for a bulk of conflicts once they have accumulated. The presence of these individuals should be prevented from encouraging futile claims and trivial conflicts.

Alternative Methods of Conflict Resolution

A broad consensus has been forming about the usefulness of having several methods of conflict resolution beyond just traditional judicial approaches. Arbitration systems allow for specialized and experienced judges who can gain the trust of the parties and are capable of settling conflicts relatively quickly. Nevertheless, rules in regard to the admissibility of arbitration are usually very strict, and in the case of doubt the rules on settlement of disputes usually favors the jurisdiction of regular judges. In Colombia, there have been many judicial rulings that, based on constitutional interpretation, have denied the possibility of arbitration or have limited the scope of the underlying regulations.

It would be worth considering legal reforms that provide for the automatic use of alternative resolution methods not only for conflicts originating directly from the contract, but also for related issues that could interfere with its performance, even if such issues involve parties that were not part of the original agreement.

It would not be appropriate, however, to submit conflict resolution to international judges, unless there are relevant international aspects in the conflict that could influence the outcome of the dispute. Even though such judges might be experienced in work concession matters and infrastructure contracts, their experience is usually linked to legal frameworks that may be different from those of the country where the conflict should be settled in the first place.

Procedural and Evidentiary Rules

Even if conflicts can be settled through arbitration, it is possible that the rules do not permit the parties to depart from the established legal procedures and evidentiary requirements. Such restrictions can considerably impair the usefulness of arbitration procedures. Particularly in the case of infrastructure contracts, the volume of documents, for instance, can be overwhelming. The application of conventional rules of admission of evidence could consume the arbitrator's time unnecessarily. Therefore, it would be advisable to have the parties agree on the procedural and evidentiary rules to be applied in arbitration or even in conventional procedures. The International Chamber of Commerce accepts such agreements in arbitration.

Defining Administrative Procedures

As long as government authorities are parties to infrastructure contracts, and especially if they can resort to extraordinary clauses during their performance, the law should define the processes and the deadlines for the authorities' decisions. It would be convenient to examine whether the deadlines could be managed through the principle of *estoppel in país* because of the authorities' silence.

Conflicts of Interest When Government Agencies Are Party to a Contract

When government agencies are parties to an infrastructure contract, it is best to avoid situations where the agencies themselves are in charge of regulating the commercial activities of the project after it begins operations. In particular, regulators should not carry out control or oversight or assess penalties related to rule violations. In other words, the authorities should not be parties to and enforcers and regulators of a contract at the same time.

In fact, an agency that is party to a contract may have political commitments that create conflicts of interest at the time of imparting rules about the operation of a project, especially when rates are involved. If the agency that sets the rules has to investigate and punish infractions as well, the problems that would otherwise be blamed on poor or unclear regulations would probably be attributed to misconduct on the part of the private contractor.

Multiple Controls

One potential problem in the performance of infrastructure contracts takes place when different government agencies are in charge of overseeing the fiscal, disciplinary, penal or contractual issues surrounding a contract's performance, or when it is unclear which agency should make a final decision at a given time. Any legal provisions that prevent this kind of duplication will mitigate the political risk involved.

Control of Contract Amendments

Just as at the time of awarding the contract, when the parties agree to introduce amendments to contracts involving a government agency, the desire to preserve equal conditions among the private bidders competes with the need to accommodate the contractor's actual experiences and the changes in circumstances. In many cases, amendments can be seen as a way of sidestepping the terms of the original bid.

Only the supervisory authorities should be able to analyze why amendments are needed and how they are incorporated. However, should the analysis reveal an actual violation of the equal conditions principle, it should not serve as grounds to compensate the losing bidders or rescind the new agreements. Disciplinary penalties may be imposed against the officials involved, or the contractor's undue profits may be reduced. However, the contract should not be rescinded and care should be taken so as not to jeopardize the interests of third parties acting in good faith, e.g., project financing agencies.

Rules Regarding Contract Expiration

Upon fulfillment of a contract for the construction or operation of an infrastructure project, or of one of its stages, questions about the quality of the works may arise, as well as whether the liabilities for breach of contract should be covered by the contractor or the insurance company. The expiration of a contract raises other questions related to payments due to the contractor. In some countries, concession agreements require the contractor to revert to the government the assets linked to the concession, even if they were provided by the contractor. This, however, does not exclude the possibility that the government pay the contractor the remaining value of certain assets. Inasmuch as the circumstances allow, the contract's economic clauses should not provide for payments between parties upon the expiration of the contract, and should allow free separation of project assets contributed by the contractor, whose removal does not interfere with the operation of the project.

Ownership of Assets Linked to the Project

In countries such as Colombia, the law is unclear as to who owns the assets linked to the project during construction, what underlying powers the government agency has with respect to facilities that are part of work in progress when the agency is party to the contract, or what the consequences are of delivery said to be satisfactory, particularly in the case of partial deliveries. These issues may be of special significance in terms of performance bonds and should be incorporated into the corresponding regulations.

Towards a Contract Framework for Infrastructure Investments

The implementation of legal reforms is not an easy task. But it could be made easier if proposals were presented as a part of an international cooperative effort. Multilateral institutions such as the Inter-American Development Bank could provide an additional service to the region by promoting a treaty aimed at reducing the transaction costs associated with infrastructure contracts. This would help attract international private funds to the sector, harness domestic savings, and increase government efficiency whenever it is a party to such contracts.

Although the ratification of treaties usually involves lengthier formal procedures than those required to change laws, the extra work might be offset by the actual prospect of improving the conditions of infrastructure financing for countries of the region. A treaty could favor the development and subsequent use of standard contract terms for infrastructure contracts in different countries, thus further reducing transaction costs due to legal uncertainty. Similarly, a treaty would enhance the regional exchange of engineering, management and legal services.

Conclusions

One of the most attractive reforms aimed at raising capital for public infrastructure projects is to ensure freedom of entry to the sector. Barriers should be exceptions, not the rule. Freedom of entry does not imply, of course, that the authorities waive their power to regulate and monitor, or, when deemed necessary, to use public funds to provide subsidies.

It does not seem possible, however, to draft a standard contract for the region's infrastructure projects. The peculiarities of legal systems may make null and void the most important clauses. On the other hand, there are a number of subjects on contractual law and practice that are not usually associated with particular political views in the region and that could be incorporated into each country's laws in order to increase legal certainty, as well as the confidence of project investors and lenders. The impact of the reforms could also be significantly enhanced by incorporating them into an international treaty.

CHAPTER 4

Regulation by Contract: A Lender's Perspective on Concession Regimes

Jacques Cook

In looking at the political landscape of Latin America and the Caribbean, one is struck by the prevalence of policies for the privatization and structural reform of the region's infrastructure sector. Although these policies share some common themes, each government is in fact developing its own framework for implementing them. It is, therefore, impossible to generalize about the region's experience with privatization and its eventual impact on the economic development. However, most of us assume that when the economic history of the region is written, the privatization of infrastructure will figure as a significant factor in the long-term growth and modernization of Latin America.

While BOT (build-operate-transfer) concessions are part of the first stage of economic liberalization, this mechanism has limitations that prevent it from providing the comprehensive legal and regulatory framework required for sustained privatization of infrastructure.

Although most Latin American countries still have limited experience regulating private sector infrastructure providers, they have a unique opportunity to install new and more effective systems of economic regulation. Forging an effective public-private partnership for infrastructure development in the region vitally depends on creating transparent rules and regulations. This process requires perseverance from the political leadership, competent technical support from key government institutions, and a willingness to experiment with new principles and instruments of legal and economic regulation.

Regulation by Contract: BOT Concessions

One of the most prevalent instruments for economic regulation of privatized services is the private sector concession contract. This form of regulation is widely used for infrastructure because it offers governments a reasonably simple way to oversee the activities of private sector providers. It also offers governments a regulatory instrument that appears to require limited supervision by government agencies. However, economic regulation cannot be effectively carried out on a wide scale only through concession contracts. In fact, this instrument is an awkward and incomplete tool for addressing fundamental issues of economic regulation, which require the creation of comprehensive legal and regulatory regimes based on precise statutory norms, coupled with the legal and procedural safeguards to protect the legitimate interests of the private sector and consumers.

Concession regimes have existed in various guises since antiquity. Broadly speaking, a concession is any arrangement in which a private company obtains from the government the right to provide a particular service under conditions which accord it significant market power.[1] From the standpoint of a project lender, the bankability of the concession agreement normally focuses on the following key features of the contract:

- Provisions concerning required investments, criteria for project completion and the commencement of operations to collect tolls or charge tariffs;
- Provisions affecting the reliability of the revenue stream needed to repay debt and provide a return to equity, including assessment of tariff clauses and other adjustments in the key terms of the concession that affect the economic-financial equilibrium;
- Events of termination and payout provisions;
- Enforceability of lender security interests over the project and its assets.

Experience has shown that failure of the concession contract and concession legal framework to properly address these key issues will result in higher transaction costs to the project sponsors, who may be forced to offer indemnities and guarantees to their project lenders to cover any potential shortfalls. Deficiencies in these areas may also cause delays in securing financing, as the project sponsors often may have to negotiate addenda to the concession or

[1]See Michael Klein, *Concessions—A Guide to the Design and Implementation of Concession Arrangements for Infrastructure Services*. World Bank, 1996.

obtain consents from the conceding authority to fill in the perceived gaps in contractual coverage. Finally, badly designed concession contracts can lead to costly disputes, public dissatisfaction, and the erosion of political support for the privatization of key public services.

The survey presented in Chapter 2 shows that there is no clear consensus in the region on the fundamental principles of concession law. Moreover, for interested lenders and developers, the absence of an agreed concession model means that the task of appraising and assessing the risks involved in infrastructure BOTs is fraught with difficulties and uncertainties. This is obviously not a satisfactory situation either for lenders, developers or Latin American governments.

Unilateral Amendments

The government has the inherent right under most civil jurisdictions to require unilateral amendments to the concession and additional works in the public interest. In Honduras, specific legislation grants the government the right to make unilateral changes in the terms of any concession pursuant to which the service is provided by a private developer. Under the laws of Panama, the government may make unilateral amendments to concession agreements only to the extent that there is danger that the service will otherwise be seriously impaired. Such a determination must be made by a regulator. In Colombia, the government's authority to intervene is triggered by a potential interruption in service. Moreover, if the unilateral changes result in the initial value of the contract being modified by 20 percent or more, the concessionaire is granted the right to claim termination of the concession agreement. Under Argentine law, the authority granting a concession has the right at any time to impose upon the concessionaire an improvement or modification in the service for the benefit of the public.

Although the theoretical basis for the government's right to impose conditions on the concessionaire above those specified in the concession contract is generally accepted in most jurisdictions of the region, the government's discretionary power over the concessionaire creates a level of uncertainty that can adversely affect the economic interests of the private investor. This power introduces an imbalance in the relationship between the private developer and the government that should be redressed through appropriate contractual limitations in the concession agreement, effective dispute resolution provisions, and procedural safeguards in the country's civil procedures and administrative laws that give the concessionaire standing to contest arbitrary and capricious acts by the conceding authority. In the few countries that have such provisions, major statutory changes have been required to protect the rights of the concessionaire.

Project Completion

The typical concession calls for the concessionaire to carry out certain investments in infrastructure and to recover its investment through the collection of fees or tolls. In exchange for these investments, the government provides certain services to the concessionaire that only a government is capable of providing, including expropriation of the necessary land and rights of way. Problems arise when the government fails to comply with some or all of its obligations under the concession, preventing the concessionaire from fulfilling contractual commitments to the conceding authority.

A textbook example of this problem was the Bangkok Expressway Toll road project in Thailand. In 1987, the Thai government granted a concession totaling over $900 million to a Japanese developer for the construction of an expressway. The concession provided that the parties would share the revenues collected on the unified system of toll roads, and that the tolls would be increased from 10 baht to 30 baht when certain specified components of the roads were completed (the Priority Component). However, events occurred that prevented the government from delivering the lands it was committed to expropriate for construction. As a result, the concessionaire was able to deliver only a portion of the Priority Component works within the contractual deadline. This meant that the concessionaire was in technical default of its loan covenants (failure to achieve Project Completion) and, more seriously, would have to cover its debt obligations with contingent equity unless it could share in the toll revenues. Matters got ugly as the government refused to raise the tolls and share revenues until the concessionaire could achieve substantial completion on the Priority Component. Clearly, the government was in a political bind, since it believed that it could not justify raising the tolls on an uncompleted road. Ultimately, the dispute was submitted to arbitration, the Japanese developer was bought out by local investors, and the project was refinanced by local banks.

This project contained a number of useful lessons about concession contracts. First, it showed what can go wrong when the contracting parties leave key provisions unclear. For instance, although the contract contained several clauses dealing with the rights and obligations of the parties in case the lands were not delivered in timely fashion by the government, it failed to provide any clear monetary remedy for the concessionaire. Under the concession agreement, the concessionaire was allowed to request an extension of the concession period, an increase in the tolls, or an adjustment in the sharing formula. However, the agreement did not *require* the government to raise tolls or to share the toll revenues. This placed the risk of untimely delivery of the rights of way on the concessionaire and the lenders rather than on the government, which was the party best able to deal with this project risk. Thus, the concession contract misallocated one of the key project risks and failed to provide a mechanism for making timely midstream corrections in the project documents. This doomed the project and eventually produced a breakdown in relations between the government and the concessionaire.

One can ask why the parties agreed to such ambiguous terms. Why place so much money at risk when the contractual terms are by definition imprecise and the likely results so patently unfair to one party? The answer is that it is probably impossible to allocate risks in many of these projects through contracts alone. Although lawyers may not willingly acknowledge this fact, it is not always possible to design the perfect contract that anticipates every conceivable problem that may arise in the course of a long-term concession. Also, as is so often the case, the parties may have thought they could work out any problems through amendments or adjustments later on. Experience has taught us that this perception of the contractual relationship in infrastructure concessions is unrealistic. Unless mandated by law, governments cannot always be trusted to protect the interests of the concessionaire and to ensure that contractual fairness is maintained throughout the life of a concession. And it should not be forgotten that political and social realities change over time, making it unlikely that common sense and good faith will be maintained throughout the life of a lengthy concession. Regulation by contract thus may become a trap for the unwary who become prisoners of their own imperfect legal instruments.

Early Termination

For most concession regimes in Latin America, the government is empowered to terminate the concession prior to its stated maturity due to a material default by the concessionaire if the concessionaire becomes insolvent or by mutual agreement of the parties. In addition, most systems recognize the right of the government to terminate the concession in the public interest even where neither party is in default. Ironically, the right of the concessionaire to trigger an early termination because of a default by the conceding authority is not uniformly recognized. For instance, Honduras does not provide for the right of the concessionaire to terminate a concession upon a default by the government of its obligations. In Ecuador, although the concessionaire may terminate a concession because of a default by the government, it must first obtain an arbitral decision or an administrative decision of a court before it can initiate the termination; yet no such procedural restriction is placed on the government's right to early terminate. In Panama, concessionaires do not have the right to early terminate the concession even if the government defaults on its obligations under the concession agreement. To an outsider interested in investing in projects in these countries, this situation does not appear reasonable. If the concessionaire must continue to provide services and cannot early terminate the concession because of a default by the conceding authority, there is a serious risk that the concessionaire may have no effective way of mitigating damages through suspension of its performance. This contractual imbalance is not consistent with the need to create an environment favorable to private investment in infrastructure. For this reason, governments should offer the concessionaires the same contractual rights that governments enjoy, with appropriate procedural safeguards to protect the interests of both the public and the private developers. This would be consistent with prudent standards of public administration and would provide a more balanced basis for a true public-private partnership.

Buyouts and Termination Amounts

Although the legal procedures for early termination are often a source of confusion in concession contracts, the more troublesome issue relates to compensation to the concessionaire in the event of an early termination. Here, too, there is inconsistency in the various regimes. In some countries, concessionaires have been provided with clear formula to compute the compensation amount based on the net asset value of the concession. In others, the BOT contract will have only the vaguest reference to the amount of compensation, with the amount often left to be determined by some third party or through arbitration. In Chile, the amount is determined through an auction supervised by the secured lenders. Finally, some concessions provide for no payout amount in case the concession is terminated because of a default of the concessionaire. Clearly, from a lender's standpoint, this is the harshest and least acceptable arrangement, since it does not provide fair compensation for the investments made by the concessionaire and opens the possibility that the government could be unjustly enriched by a default by the concessionaire.

The significance of the termination buyout cannot be overlooked in any financial and legal appraisal of a private sector BOT project. Ambiguities on the computation of this amount or potential difficulties in securing payment from the local government can be major political and commercial risks that can imperil the project's ability to secure long-term financing. This is because in a nonrecourse or limited recourse financing, lenders' security interest is usually restricted to the cash flow generated by the project. In BOTs, lenders will often be unable to foreclose on the property of the project company because the land and fixtures remain property of the state. In such circumstances, the termination buyout provisions of the concession are the only way to provide fair compensation to the lenders and the developer. It should therefore not be surprising that the Inter-American Development Bank's first political risk guarantee was used to secure financing for a water treatment plant in Colombia, and that the guarantee covered the risk of nonpayment of the termination amount by the municipality.[2]

Force Majeure Risks in Concession Contracts

Although concession contracts purport to establish a framework for regulation of privatized infrastructure, force majeure risks in such projects should be apportioned fairly between the contracting parties. Political force majeure risk should clearly be assumed by the conceding authority, while insurable commercial force majeure risks should be borne by the concessionaire. However, allocation of these risks is often impossible to evaluate on the basis of the contractual provisions of the concession agreements because of the absence of clear definitions of force majeure events. References are often made to the civil code of the respective country, but the scope of the force majeure provisions are unclear.

Finally, lenders are not always clear on how the existence of a force majeure event is to be procedurally defined in the underlying concession contract. If force majeure must be invoked, there has to be a reasonable procedure for

---

[2]See Appendix 4.1 for a more complete discussion of the Rio Bogotá Water Treatment Project and the IDB's first partial risk guarantee.

determining the existence of a force majeure event. But in many concessions, only the government agency is allowed to determine the existence of such an event. This opens up the possibility that the concessionaire may be unable to invoke force majeure relief if the government agency acts unreasonably. There have been some recent attempts to be more precise in the treatment of force majeure risks in concession contracts. Still, more work needs to be done to provide clearer standards and procedures for dealing with force majeure in concessions now being awarded by national and municipal governments throughout the region.

Lender Security Interests in BOT Contracts

BOT concessions must also provide legally enforceable mechanisms to protect the interests of secured lenders to the concessionaire. Although most of the concession laws in the region acknowledge the rights of secured lenders, many do not provide clear procedural safeguards to protect those interests in the event the project company defaults on its obligations under the concession, is adjudged bankrupt, or defaults on its financing agreements. For instance, most of the property controlled by the concessionaire cannot be mortgaged or pledged to third party lenders (e.g., toll roads). Also, most jurisdictions in the region do not allow the concession contract to be pledged to lenders, although many concession regimes allow the pledge of the rights emerging from the concession, such as toll revenues and other economic entitlements of the concessionaire. Finally, many of the concession contracts require that the property of the concessionaire be returned to the conceding authority upon termination of the concession, free of all encumbrances.

In light of the precarious nature of their interests in the concession, lenders might look to the following to strengthen their legal position in the concession:

- It should be stipulated that the government will not take any action to amend, rescind or terminate the concession without first providing timely notice to the secured lenders.
- Secured lenders should be given a contractual right to cure any default by the concessionaire and to exercise step-in rights to protect their economic interests.
- Secured lenders should be afforded a security interest in any proceeds that stem from the sale or transfer of the concession to another third party. In the absence of a buyout by the conceding authority, this would provide lenders

with a means of covering their loss in the event of a premature termination of the concession.

• Secured lenders should be given standing to intervene in any proceeding involving a dispute under the concession, including any administrative proceeding to adjust the concession terms.

Finally, the law on secured transactions in many jurisdictions does not always provide a convenient way of recording the interests of lenders to a concessionaire. This may become very important in a bankruptcy workout situation. It may be useful to establish special mortgage instruments to deal with the particular characteristics of project finance lending to concessionaires.[3]

Tariff Regulation

Perhaps no issue in concession contracts is as important as provisions affecting the tariffs or fees collected by the concessionaire. Obviously, the concessionaire will have little incentive to fulfill its obligations under the concession if the applicable tariffs do not provide a reasonable rate of return on the investment. And for the government authorities, political support for the privatization initiative will depend vitally on its ability to deliver quality services to the public at reasonable costs.

Experience shows that the public's willingness to pay tariffs is heavily influenced by its clear perception of the real costs of the services, regardless of whether they are provided by public or private entities. For instance, in many countries, governments have provided water and sewerage services to the public at heavily subsidized rates. In most instances, the availability of cheap water is an illusion, since the state-run enterprises typically underinvest in the sector and therefore are unable to provide a safe and reliable water supply to the general public. In such instances, a BOT concession with a reputable private supplier may offer the opportunity to improve the quality and reliability of the services. But this would require appropriate incentives for the private company and a fair and reasonable tariff regime. Governments should therefore educate consumers about the benefits and costs of privatization so that the public reac-

[3]For instance, in Chile, a *prenda especial de la concesión de obra pública* was created allowing lenders to record their interests in private sector concession contracts. (Public Works Law No. 164 of 1991 as amended by Law 19,460 of 1996).

tion to higher prices in the short run does not jeopardize long-term gains attainable through the BOT.

In a BOT concession, the tariff provision must allow the concessionaire to make periodic tariff adjustments to reflect changes in the CPI or foreign exchange rates. Also, the tariff structure may need to be adjusted to reflect changes in the concessionaire's rate base or shifts in consumption patterns, especially if the concessionaire is guaranteed a rate of return on its investments.[4] In countries that are introducing price cap regulation,[5] the regulators also have to ensure that tariff levels provide incentives for improvements in productivity. In most countries of the region, experience with rate making and economic regulation is still evolving. However, the important point is that BOT concession contracting cannot be carried out in an institutional vacuum. An effective legal and regulatory framework for dealing with rates is a necessary complement to the tariff provisions included in the concession agreement. Without it, the concessionaire will be exposed to considerable political, economic and financial uncertainty, which cannot always be addressed through improvised negotiations and adjustments during the life of the concession.

Governments should be urged to develop procedural mechanisms for reviewing rates for vital services in order to ensure orderly and sustainable privatization of infrastructure. These deliberations should not take place behind closed doors and must provide fora for public discussion and debate of key issues. If telephone, water or electricity rates must be increased, users should have an opportunity to comment on the requests and, if appropriate, present contrasting views. The investment programs of the concessionaire also must be exposed to public scrutiny, especially where these programs are providing the basis for rate increases. These open fora will provide consumers and the private developer with avenues to engage in an orderly dialogue on public policy issues and, if properly managed, should strengthen public acceptance of privatized infrastruc-

---

[4]A rate of return tariff system ensures that the service provider will receive a tariff that covers the costs of operation and maintenance, depreciation and taxes, and a return on its investment. Determining an appropriate rate of return is also contentious, with arguments focusing on the amount of the investment and proper costing thereof. Consumers in many countries have been dissatisfied with rate of return guarantees because of the technical and legal difficulties that are involved in enforcing and supervising the private concessionaires.

[5]Price caps of RPI-X methods for setting tariffs effectively provide the private operator with a guaranteed return subject to performance incentives, which discourages wasteful overinvestment to inflate the rate of return. This method also requires careful monitoring of tariffs and periodic reviews by the regulator based on a full disclosure of information on the operations of the regulated entity.

ture. The alternative could be street protests punctuated by distorted reports in the press, all of which could undermine the privatization initiative.

International experience has confirmed that rate setting is perhaps the most difficult aspect of privatization. In the United States, rate setting has been one of the most complicated aspects of public utility regulation. In transport, electricity, water and sanitation, the state and federal regulatory agencies have struggled for many years to achieve a proper balance between public and private interests. The results have not been entirely satisfactory, as evidenced by recent initiatives to deregulate and introduce more market incentives.[6] In the United Kingdom, the privatization of railroads and electricity sectors has further highlighted the difficulties of creating a new regulatory regime. It should therefore not be surprising that the countries of Latin America are facing a daunting challenge in establishing new regulatory frameworks for privatized infrastructure.

Aguas Argentinas, S.A. provides an example of what can happen when the tariff provisions of the concession contract are not properly coordinated with an effective regulatory framework. Press reports have indicated that one of the key problems in that concession has been the tariff provisions.[7] The original concession granted in 1993 provided that new customers of the system were to be assessed an infrastructure charge. However, the concessionaire apparently concluded that this charge ($800) would be too low and therefore requested that a connection charge of $200 be added to this amount to allow the company to recover its investment. It soon became clear that many new customers would be unable to pay this charge. The concessionaire also requested an increase in water fees. Accordingly, the Argentine government and the concessionaire renegotiated terms of the concession clauses dealing with tariffs, and last year the government issued a decree that authorized an amendment to the concession. Once implemented, the amendment would allow imposition of a Universal Service and Environmental Improvement charge (SUMA) (equal to $4 bimonthly) payable by all customers in lieu of the infrastructure charge payable by new users, a 14 percent increase in water fees, and the imposition of a $120 connection fee for new customers. This amendment was reportedly challenged in court by consumer groups that, among other things, claimed that the regulatory agency created to supervise the concession, the *Ente Tripartito de*

---

[6]See *Infrastructure for Development: World Development Report 1994,* Chapter 3, Regulatory Cycles in the United States, p. 57. (New York and London, 1994).
[7]See *Oxford Analytica,* Argentina: Water Politics, 3/19/98.

Obras y Servicios Sanitarios (ETOSS), had not adequately protected consumer interests.

Basically, what appears to have taken place in this case is that the government and the concessionaire sought to address a major rate adjustment through direct negotiations between the conceding authority and the concessionaire, rather than through an administrative proceeding of the regulatory authority established to supervise the concession. In light of the political and legal issues that have arisen in connection with that proposed adjustment, one can question whether it is reasonable to handle these anticipated rate adjustments throughout the life of the concession through direct negotiations. Will the general public and organized consumer groups remain satisfied with this process? Will they launch legal challenges to negotiated rate increases? Is there a more transparent legal process in Argentina that would provide for an orderly resolution of controversies over these key policy and tariff issues? What will be the eventual role of the regulatory agency, ETOSS, if the national government undertakes a formal amendment of the concession for future rate adjustments? These are as yet unresolved issues that the Argentine authorities will certainly have to address if they want to install a stable and effective regulatory framework for this important concession.

It would be naive to assume that implanting new regulatory frameworks will be quick and easy and that the governments of the region will be able within a very short time to do what has taken decades to achieve in countries more experienced in privatizing infrastructure. But it will be important for the countries of the region to start with some basic principles:

• Rates cannot be designed based solely on political considerations. Keeping tolls low may be politically acceptable, but it may not provide enough revenues for private sector investment. Some form of public subsidy may be required if tolls cannot be raised to cover investments. In any event, governments need to establish clear and transparent rules for setting rates for all concessions. On the other hand, relying only on market incentives may not be politically viable, especially where the market may produce natural monopolies that adversely affect consumer welfare.

• Regulatory agencies must be created as soon as possible and given the financial and human resources needed to competently monitor and gather data on the affected sector. This process is not easy. Critical issues such as the respective roles of local versus national institutions must be resolved. In large federal systems, state and municipal regulatory functions will have to be defined in a manner consistent with a national norm. The degree of autonomy of the agencies must be determined together with mechanisms to ensure their political accountability.

• Procedures must be set in place that ensure that all interested parties have access to the basic information on the performance of the private sector concessionaires. Performance standards should be publicly known and disseminated to the public at large.

• Rate-setting principles and guidelines should be publicly enunciated so that consumers are fully educated about the process and policies that are to be applied in establishing rates.

It should be clear from this chapter that a simple concession contract, no matter how artfully drafted, cannot fully address all of the complex issues involved in rate setting and economic regulation of private concessionaires. Agency regulation, statutory norms and procedural safeguards are needed to complement the concession and thus ensure that a viable relationship between the parties is maintained throughout the life of the contract.

Conclusions

Contracts have been widely used to attract specific investments in BOT concessions. These contracts have not only served a regulatory function, but have also been instruments for allocating project risks between the public and private sector. Concession contracts are also therefore important factors in securing financing for infrastructure projects in the region. As an instrument of risk allocation, the concession contract is not always well designed, and often leaves gaps and troublesome ambiguities. Experience has also shown that regulation by contract is fraught with difficulties, not the least of which is drafting an instrument that is clear to all the parties while providing sufficient flexibility to deal with many issues likely to arise during the life of the concession. It is not always easy or possible to reconcile these conflicting objectives in the context of a single contract expected to operate over an extended period of time.

Public policy requires consistency and predictability. However, individualized concession contracts open up the possibility of inconsistent and incompatible results, which may not be viable in the long run. For instance, a concession contract for a toll road negotiated in 1998 may contain provisions inconsistent with contracts awarded three or four years later. The public and the investor community will be confused by these inconsistencies, which will be difficult to justify and maintain.

What is needed in the long run is a statutory framework for regulation that defines the rules of the game and fairly enforces them. Although the possibility for abuse and overreaching cannot be avoided in all instances, improprieties can be minimized through the introduction of statutory checks and balances that force both the public and private sectors to competently execute these projects in the public interest.

Successful public-private partnerships ultimately depend on the implementation of a regulatory scheme that is transparent, predictable and reasonably free of corruption. Historical precedent should be of some assistance to the leaders of the region in developing these new systems of economic regulation.

The countries of Latin America are at a critical crossroad in their path to sustained development based on private sector-led growth, and they have a unique opportunity to introduce modern principles of economic regulation to strengthen and sustain the privatization of infrastructure services.

Appendix 4.1

In 1997, the Inter-American Development Bank approved its first political risk guarantee for a water treatment plant in Bogotá, Colombia. The guarantee covered the risk of nonpayment of the termination amount. Briefly, its main features were the following. The project was a 30-year concession granted by the Santa Fe de Bogotá capital district to a project company formed by Lyonnaise des Eaux and its Degremont subsidiary, of France. The project cost for the first phase of the construction was $135 million, consisting of $35 million in equity and $100 million in long-term notes. The sponsors approached the IDB for a guarantee for the termination payment and currency convertibility coverage for both the termination payment and the debt service.

Under the concession, a termination event could occur in four instances: (i) default by the project company, (ii) unilateral termination by the District of Bogotá, (iii) default by the district under the concession, or (iv) force majeure that extends beyond six months. Following a termination event and the appropriate determination by a third party arbitrator, the district's obligation to make a termination payment would arise and would vary depending on the cause of termination; in any event, the payment amount would be sufficient to cover outstanding debt. The IDB guarantee would be triggered only after the termination amount had been set and the government had failed to honor its contractual obligation to pay those amounts. The maximum amount of IDB coverage would only apply to the minimum amount needed to cover outstanding debt on the Series A notes and would not provide coverage for equity payout. The IDB guarantee applies to Series A notes totaling $30 million, while Series B notes totaling $70 million were unguaranteed. The Series A guaranteed notes were priced at 87.5 basis points over U.S. treasuries, while the Series B notes carried a 237.5 basis point premium over U.S. treasuries. The notes were successfully sold in the U.S. private placement market and carried a 13-year maturity. In other words, the rating agencies viewed the IDB guarantee covering both the termination payment and the currency convertibility risks as providing substantial credit enhancement to the financing. This transaction provided the IDB with a clear demonstration of the importance of termination provisions in concession agreements and the need in some instances to mitigate the political risks attached to these provisions.

CHAPTER 5

Renegotiation of Concessions in the Latin American Context

Fred Aarons

A government generally transfers activities to the private sector because of major investment needs, the need to improve the "value for money" in government procurement, limited tax revenues, and deterioration of services. Governments must consider the most efficient and rational approach to achieve the twofold goal of attracting private sector investment while ensuring the fulfillment of straightforward policy goals.

Prior to transferring activities to the private sector, governments have to take the necessary steps to understand what is needed to win the private sector's confidence and attract investment. The three principles that should be considered are continuity of the service, nondiscrimination between users of the service, and adaptability of the service to the needs of the public.

Since 1990, Latin American governments have pursued more active privatization programs. Many have resorted to concessions as opposed to direct sales of previously state-owned companies in order to facilitate private sector involvement in the construction, operation and maintenance of such public services (generation, transmission and distribution of electric power, ports, toll roads, airports, railroads, water and wastewater systems, and in some instances, mail service).

Consideration should be given to public bidding as part of the initial step by governments interested in transferring these public services through concessions. Concession contracts should be awarded through competitive bidding rather than directly and should be negotiated with a single entity. Direct awarding and negotiation may jeopardize the inherent benefits of the project due mainly to the government's relative inexperience in providing services on a commercial basis. Direct awards also preempt the possibility of attracting several potential project developers, which lowers costs and ensures a better transfer of know-how. A competitive process offers transparency, ensures maximum efficiency and builds much needed public confidence. Governments may even consider private entities operating infrastructure services as "contracting authorities." In this way, the private companies would be obliged to follow public procurement procedures in awarding their own contracts. In addition, governments should avoid rushing bids and bid evaluation processes that can result in an inaccurate basis for establishing tariff structures and revenue forecasts.

Because governments in developing countries are increasingly using concession programs, it has become important to ensure the sound and efficient transfer of services and to facilitate a long-term partnership between the public and private sectors. The process by which these concessions are granted and carried out must ensure that investment costs can be taken off a government's books, result in efficient and competitive projects, and encourage the public to accept paying real prices for services.

Whenever a project involves a government concession, the concession agreement becomes the primary document of the transaction. While provisions of concession agreements vary depending on the sector and the characteristics of the service, the bottom line is that the project must be bankable. From the investor's point of view, a concession must offer protection against the possibility of a government defaulting on its contractual obligations. This requires realistic, clear and comprehensive provisions that ensure the project's revenues will be forthcoming. Only projects with such features have a chance of attracting financing from international bank syndicates or investors through public or private placements in capital markets.

Testing the Bankability of Concessions

The concession codifies the credit-financial structure, and in certain instances does the same for the regulatory structure. These legal documents are executed by the local, provincial or central entity (known as the granting authority) and the project developer or concessionaire to create what should be an airtight set of provisions acceptable to all parties to the transaction. Several key provisions must be included in the concession agreement to meet the litmus tests of bankability.

The operation period must be for a fixed term sufficient to pay back the project debt and provide a return to equity. For this reason, the agreement should contain provisions for extension of the operation period. If a project's financial return is jeopardized by a government's default on its contractual obligations, then the period of the concession should be extended, or adequate guarantees provided to the concessionaire in order to avoid inappropriate development of the project or negative effects on the parties to the concession agreement. Adequate termination provisions must also be included, along with proper compensation (e.g., establishing liquidated damages) to those affected. These termination provisions must ensure that compensation terms are clearly stated in terms of amount and its determination method, the period within which payment should be assessed and paid, and the method for payment. This should make it possible for both concessionaire and lenders to assess the project risks in the event of early termination of the concession, and consequently of any loan given to the concessionaire.

Due to the risk that the contracting parties may default on a concession agreement, safeguards are necessary to provide adequate security to the project's lenders. Standard techniques to at least partially mitigate the effects of such an event also include offshore escrow accounts, and the assignment of the benefits of various contracts to the lenders, as well as the lender's right to "step in" and take over the rights of the project company. In the case of the assignment of rights, lenders should seek and obtain the prior consent of the government to ensure project continuity and loan repayment. Governments, however, are usually reluctant to assign concession rights. If they do, their preference is for assigning these rights just before the actual transfer is required so that the granting authority can maintain direct control over selecting the new concessionaire. A sound assignment provision is necessary to provide comfort to the lenders that their loans will be repaid, and to allow for verification by the government that the recipient of the concession ("assignee") will be capable of satisfying the terms of the contract.

Regulatory issues of particular importance that must be addressed in all concession agreements include (i) whether the public is willing to pay for services previously subsidized; (ii) whether regulations will restrict the freedom of the operator to set and review appropriate tariff levels; (iii) whether and when the concession will revert back to the granting authority; (iv) what the policy will be on competing infrastructure providers; and (v) whether the legal framework for awarding concessions, permits and land acquisition is well defined.

Operational risks arise from an operator's technical inability to fulfill its obligations, the failure of equipment to meet specifications during commissioning, or a host of other factors. A concession agreement must address these factors, while providing comfort to each party without encouraging the abandonment of the project. To mitigate some operational risks and ensure that the service is provided to the entire target population, the contract can require implementation of an operation and maintenance manual or the use of performance bonds as mechanisms to monitor and control proper project operation.

Concession agreements are normally governed by laws of the country where the project is developed. Consequently, governments are not always forthcoming in accepting alternative dispute resolution mechanisms (such as mediation and arbitration) to resolve controversies arising from a concession. These mechanisms are internationally recognized and provide a viable means to resolve disputes between the contracting parties in an expeditious and transparent manner. Their inclusion in the concession agreement can provide comfort and reliability to the parties involved and therefore should always be considered. There is particular reluctance to adopt alternative dispute resolutions in countries with a civil law system, where the state prefers to submit these controversies to judicial courts, even though those courts often have serious case backlogs.

In the context of interpretation of contracts, and particularly in civil law countries, any specific provision not expressly incorporated in the concession agreement is usually regulated by the applicable local law. For example, while force majeure may not be defined in the concession contract, its definition is usually based on the country's existing civil law code. As part of its due diligence, a project sponsor should spend substantial time and resources making sure that key definitions are not missing from the concession agreement, and that other issues that could undermine the bankability of a concession are addressed in a timely fashion.

Changing the Rules of the Concession

In the world of concessions, theory and practice are not necessarily the same. Numerous concession agreements executed in different sectors throughout Latin America are affected by a constant changing of rules. As the fundamental documents that establish performance parameters expected from the contracting parties during the life of the concession, the agreements are often adjusted to correct deficiencies related to the lack of an appropriate regulatory framework. In Latin America, there has been a tendency to overlook specific circumstances having a material impact on the success of the concession and, ultimately, to mitigate their impact with amendments to the concession agreement. The lack of appropriate planning prior to the bid process has increased the need to tackle certain deficiencies that prevent maintenance of the adequate financial and economic equilibrium of the concession.[1] Increasingly in Latin America, concessions are used as a tool to regulate the relationship between the concessionaire and the granting authority. After several years of granting concessions for public services on a consistent basis, renegotiation of the concession agreements has again become the main mechanism to mitigate failures. Some may argue about the convenience of renegotiating concession agreements as a method to cover for deficiencies in the regulatory framework. The reality, however, is that most Latin American governments have relied heavily on concession agreements to address intricate regulatory issues that have an impact on the appropriate rendering of the public service and ultimately on consumer satisfaction.

Concession agreements integrate several usually complex structures, which reflect the compromises undertaken by the different parties to ensure productive efficiency, while ensuring investors that desirable and viable projects are developed. Although the technical provisions vary by sector, most concessions contain similar structures, and more importantly, address a set of core issues that must be dealt with in the vast majority of contracts of this type. As a result, experience has shown that the purpose behind renegotiating concessions revolves around those common core issues. This circumstance may facilitate a review of the variables that usually prompt renegotiation of concession agreements.

Renegotiation of concession contracts is usually related to three fundamental needs that appear in different forms: to ensure the financial viability of the concession, to reduce uncertainty for lenders on the terms agreed upon, or to adjust circumstances created by political interference. The renegotiation of these or other elements of a concession should be undertaken while considering the purpose and extent of the concession as a fundamental premise.

Financial Viability

One of the main causes of renegotiation of a concession agreement is the need to put in place proper mechanisms to ensure adequate compensation for developing the project. Lack of financial viability results in part from the inappropriate allocation of risks between the parties to a concession. This is par-

[1]Financial and economic equilibrium of a concession relates to the allocation of risks to those parties most apt to bear them, with the expectation that those parties will be compensated accordingly during the life of the concession for bearing such risks.

ticularly relevant when considering that risks are not regularly borne by the party able to assess, control and manage them, nor by the party with the best tools to mitigate them at a lower cost for the transaction. Since concessions are structured based on the price that services can be sold to users, it is critical to establish from the outset clear rules related to tariff levels, structure and adjustment mechanisms. One typical financial viability problem, which may provoke the renegotiation of the terms of a concession after its award, occurs when the eventual winner offers the highest annualized payment to the granting authority to be covered by revenues obtained through implementation of a tariff structure. Let us assume that the annualized payment offered in exchange for the concession was considered as the key variable for the granting authority to award the concession. Once the concession is implemented, its financial viability may be jeopardized because it overlooked the ability and willingness of the public to pay the tariff needed to cover the annualized payment. There are several ways to address the problem, but there is an immediate tendency to renegotiate the tariff structure to obtain a more viable income stream. Renegotiation may prove even more cumbersome when lenders are facing the prospects of a different concession structure than the one considered when they committed their financial support to the transaction. The renegotiation usually involves scaling back the financial inflows and outflows with a reassessment of the assumptions used to raise financial funding. In some cases, there may even be an extension of the terms of the loan granted to the concessionaire or an adjustment of the original structure of the financing in order to mitigate the underlying risks through alternative instruments. But the successful development of the concession may be undermined if the granting authority does not try to restore a sustainable regulatory framework to support the concession agreements already in place.

Nonbankability for Lenders

Another typical factor that may provoke the renegotiation of a concession agreement is the vagueness and uncertainty of the stipulated terms and conditions. This is usually related to the lack of clarity on such key aspects as reasons for termination and the rights derived from such events, assignment of the concession and its revenue streams, tariff adjustment mechanisms, cost overruns, force majeure, and dispute resolution mechanisms.

In other words, irrespective of the interpretation that may apply to the terms and conditions of a concession agreement, lenders try to ensure that all the risks are appropriately mitigated in a binding agreement that will serve as the cornerstone of their financial structure. This reflects most clearly the apparent differences between the common law approach of Anglo-Saxon countries and the civil law approach of Latin American countries. Lenders tend to rely on the common law approach and as a result show preference for "airtight" and self-contained contractual terms and conditions, without relying on extra-contractual interpretations of the law, legal doctrine or jurisprudence. For their part, granting authorities initially unexposed to the standard international requirements to finance projects implemented under their privatization programs fail to recognize the need for an unequivocal set of objective rules less prone to political detours.

Political Elements

A third factor that induces renegotiation of concession agreements is generated in part by the lack of a well thought-out and implemented regulatory framework, along with the ambiguity of the terms and conditions of the concession agreement. Although the level of commitment on the part of governments to any privatization scheme should be demonstrated by establishing clear, viable and sustainable regulatory frameworks for the underlying sector, granting authorities in Latin America have resorted to the renegotiation process as a tool to reassess the merits of privatization. Governments must create a reliable political environment open to private sector participation in order to mitigate the uncertainties created by the constant and unwarranted changes of law that may undermine any effort to privatize public services.

Leaving the Fundamental Terms and Conditions of Renegotiation Frameworks Unaltered

When confronted with the need to renegotiate a concession, it is imperative to consider the privatization scheme used at the time the concession was originally awarded. The renegotiation process may be limited by the need to preserve the fundamental variables or postulates of the bid. In other words, the renegotiation process must not be used to alter variables that ultimately determined the winner of a concession. For example, if the fundamental economic factor in awarding a concession was the price of the tariff, then the tariff structure should not be altered in a manner inconsistent with the parameters established when considering the bid proposals. Otherwise, a case of moral hazard would be created, since the winning bidder has an unfair advantage: he was awarded a concession based on a "low, successful but unviable bid," with the expectation that this would be improved after awarding the concession. In public infrastructure projects, it is common to encounter concession agreements awarded on the basis of an annualized payment by the concessionaire to the granting authority (or the lowest traffic guarantee requested, for example, in a toll road project). In such cases, it would damage the credibility of any privatization program to allow a winning bidder who had offered the highest annualized payment or requested the lowest traffic guarantee to request a revision of the concession based on the lack of viability of the premises considered at the time of the bid. Hence, it is essential to establish a clear and transparent framework for the renegotiation process so that moral hazard is averted, while improving the structure of the underlying concession to ensure appropriate long-term viability.

Several elements to consider before renegotiating a concession agreement are fundamentally tied not only to the terms of the bid (the economic and political conditions and regulatory environment), but also to the net worth and experience of the concessionaire, sources of interpretation of the concession, external influences, and mechanisms to resolve disputes. Each of these elements plays a key role in the overall renegotiation process, and their impact should thus be carefully assessed in order to obtain a renegotiated concession agreement that is legally binding and enforceable.

The scope of the renegotiation of concession agreements varies as much as its implications. In general terms, renegotiation may be presented as a clarification or interpretation process, a full amendment, or even as an amended and reinstated version. In the event of a clarification or interpretation process, both the granting authority and the concessionaire limit the scope of the renegotiation to terms and conditions that would increase the unequivocal character of the underlying agreement. A typical case that requires clarification relates to the definition of force majeure, which is generally understood as a superior or irresistible force that causes problems beyond the reasonable control of the contracting parties, and will excuse their performance. The definition is aimed at protecting the parties in the event that at least one provision in a contract cannot be performed due to causes outside the control of the parties, and which could not be avoided by exercise of due care. Many concession agreements granted by governments in Latin American countries do not stipulate in an unequivocal fashion the concept of force majeure and its implications for the concession, such as the compensation owed by the government in the event of termination of the concession, and in particular, the compensation owed for investments executed and not recovered by the concessionaire. Such lack of clarity may have a negative impact not only on the concessionaire or the granting authority, but also on lenders who rely on termination rights to collect the outstanding loan amount in case of early termination of the concession. In such cases, an interpretation or clarification of the terms of the concession agreement may be warranted to ensure the bankability of the underlying contract and ultimately the financing of the public service given in concession.

A full amendment may be warranted, without affecting the fundamental principles upon which the concession was granted, when the parties to a concession agreement do not include terms related to the rights of the concessionaire and the granting authority in the event of termination of the concession. Most concession agreements granted by Latin American governments over the last five years have overlooked the causes of concession termination and, more importantly, the compensatory rights owed to the contracting parties. Such failures cause difficulties in assessing the financing viability of a project and can provoke the inadequate allocation of risks among the granting authority, the concessionaire and its sponsors, and the lenders. In certain instances, an amendment to the concession may require simultaneous adjustments to several provisions of the agreement. Once again, the prevailing principle must be not to alter the fundamental elements of the original concession. An amendment related to the concessionaire's compensation mechanism may also be required due to the lack of definition of the parameters for adjusting tariffs (periodicity, alternative mechanisms, and procedures to implement such tariff adjustments). From a formal viewpoint, concession amendments should be approved by the corresponding official authorities to ensure their legal validity and enforceability. It is also important that a public entity independent of the granting authority issue an opinion about the scope of the renegotiation and the legal adequacy of any amendment. This helps to avoid legal challenges by losing bidders or other parties with a substantial interest in the terms and conditions of the concession or the service rendered. Verification of such requirements varies by country, but it is a critical element that must not be underestimated given the potential detrimental effects on public service delivery and financial consequences for the parties involved in the transaction.

To illustrate in a more comprehensive manner the aspects discussed above, the sections that follow look specifically at concession agreements related to water and sewerage and toll roads in Latin America. These sections highlight some of the pitfalls that governments may encounter when privatizing public services, as well as bidders' problems, particularly when they are over-eager to win concessions for public services without realistically considering the business fundamentals. The degree of privatization of a public service is inversely related to the uncertainty surrounding the project. Transportation and water and wastewater are not the object of full privatization, but rather characterize activities in which the state relinquishes service provision to the private concessionaire while maintaining a fundamental regulatory role. Therefore, the level of uncertainty surrounding such projects is relatively high by nature. Indeed, these two sectors are often affected by complex and imperfect regulatory structures and public service restrictions that require an adequate balance in order to achieve a viable and sustainable public-private partnership. As a result, any attempt to ensure viable concession proposals must include a careful assessment of risk as well as of economic and financial circumstances.

Water and Wastewater Concessions

Even the most successful experiences in water and wastewater concessions have thus far demonstrated that there is a constant struggle between the viability of the concession and the social costs relating to the public service rendered by the concessionaire. Generally, the transfer of the provision of water and wastewater services to a private concessionaire has been received well by customers. Nonetheless, the terms of the concession are often based on attaining certain targets instead of completing specific works. While this provides flexibility and discretion to the concessionaire on technical matters during the life of the concession, it also gives enormous discretion to the regulatory entity to interpret the flexible structure of the concession. Thus, political variables—even at the regulatory agency level, which should be a technical body—play a fundamental role during development of the concession whenever there is a progress assessment of the concessionaire's performance. Political variables are even more at play when a tariff adjustment depends on such a progress assessment. There are cases in which the apparent success of an underlying concession has been verified by the fact that the concessionaire's capital expenditures are higher than required for a specific period of the concession, and by the customers' general approval of the services provided. Yet, the broad terms of the goals to be achieved by the concessionaire under a particular investment plan has prompted a fairly restrictive interpretation by the regulatory agency of the capital investment requirements under the underlying concession, triggering, as a result, nonapproval of a tariff increase. Another difficulty in water and wastewater concessions relates to the allocation of cost coverage for the expansion of potable water and sewerage services in a concession area. Experience shows that a partial cross-subsidy mechanism covered by current customers in favor of potential customers is much more sound than covering the cost of expansion of services with connection and infrastructure charges collected from new customers usually located in lower-income areas. Nonetheless, contracting parties to several concessions in the region have not been able to address this issue appropriately, and when a cross-subsidy is adopted, its implementation has been derailed by multiple exogenous variables. The limitations imposed on the expansion of water and wastewater services have been a deterrent for maximizing the social benefits expected from concessions in the sector. The inability to structure a balancing scheme from the outset has created bottlenecks that have prompted the renegotiation of concessions in order to restructure tariff adjustment mechanisms and cost coverage methods for service expansion. These renegotiations undermine the credibility of the privatization process, and have a negative impact on the service to customers and on the institutional framework under which the service is provided.

Toll Road Concessions

Bankability of toll road concessions is a constant concern of lenders. Several cases in Mexico, Ecuador, Brazil, Panama, Colombia and Venezuela demonstrate the difficulties encountered when granting toll road concessions. Traffic reliability is the fundamental factor in the success of a toll road project. In one case, the government granted two different road concessions, one with a reliable traffic flow and the other without any track record other than the developmental benefits to be generated in the zone surrounding the road with reliable traffic. In other words, the government established a concession under a cross-subsidized toll road system in order to attain the development policies established from the outset. The bankability of the concession, however, was at issue due to the lack of definition of terms relating to termination rights and compensation, cost overruns, force majeure, and the effect of delays in construction of road segments. The different interests of the government, the concessionaire, and the lenders were in conflict due to the poor allocation of risks under the concession agreement. This led to renegotiation of the agreement, resulting in separation of the different toll road segments so that each one would be part of the concession on a stand-alone basis, reducing the level of cross-subsidy. In addition, the tariff adjustment mechanism was clarified to provide certainty and incentives to complete the project. A general characteristic of toll roads across the region is the lack of appropriate planning and structuring, even in cases where the traffic flow may be more certain.

In another toll road case, the government had to interpret the concession agreement in order to ensure its legal certainty and provide adequate comfort to prospective lenders. Political considerations played a special role and ultimately limited the scope of the renegotiation. Once again, lack of definition regarding termination rights was a key factor in determining the need to renegotiate the concession agreement. Renegotiation of the concession consumed more than a year, causing higher transaction costs than originally budgeted. In the case of the toll road concession with two distinctive segments, the government balanced its legitimate interest to promote the development of an important economic sector with the prospects of losing the aggregate benefits of the concession roads. In this second case, the government adopted a more cautious position to changes requested by lenders to conform with the so-called bankability of concession agreements.

Conclusions

Concession agreements vary depending on the sector, the goals of the government, the nature of the public service to be provided, the size of the concession area, the level of development of the regulatory framework, and the exposure of the underlying granting authority and bidders to the requirements of the international financial markets.

Whereas concession agreements must have a clear and flexible structure that allows for appropriate implementation throughout the life of the concession, renegotiation of concession agreements has been utilized as a tool to readdress essential elements relating to the viability of the privatization process. Experience with the first generation of concessions has provided a reference point to ensure appropriate attention from the outset of the privatization process to the fundamental elements that facilitate a more successful partnership between the public and private sectors.

Governments, bidders, lenders and regulatory entities must pay special attention to the underlying principles that ensure the viability of concessions and the standard implementation of the diverse set of goals represented by each party. The experience accumulated not only with the granting of concessions but also with their renegotiation is instrumental to avoid pitfalls and as a guide for upcoming concessions in Latin America.

CHAPTER 6

Obstacles and Incentives to Private Infrastructure Investment and Financing

Gustavo Ramírez and María Angela Parra

This chapter analyzes two issues essential to achieving success in the second stage of instituting private participation in Latin American infrastructure. The first is the need for local financial sectors to further evolve and adapt to the needs of emerging infrastructure projects. The second is the importance of continuing and successfully concluding institutional and regulatory reforms.

The absence in the region of a national private infrastructure industry has meant that most large projects have had to be financed with foreign capital by strategic investors. Local and regional projects with smaller investment requirements experience difficulties in obtaining this type of financing, as they are perceived to be riskier and unable to take advantage of economies of scale. Domestic investors' knowledge of the local environment implies a reduced perception of risk, and allows them to finance these projects more efficiently. In order to take full advantage of this capability, traditional indicator-based credit analysis must be modified and made suitable for use with projects financed without recourse, or with only partial recourse, and with no guarantee other than the cash flow generated by the project. The other source of funds for this type of project is the capital market, which in many countries of the region is not yet fully established. However, the development of capital markets can be promoted by means of the privatization process, as long as the aim of privatization is not to maximize fiscal revenues from the sale of public assets.

In many countries of the region, private participation processes have been delayed and, in some cases, have failed because of the lack of continuity in implementing institutional and regulatory reforms. The most successful processes have come about as a result of in-depth reforms, either in countries with strong governments and the capacity to implement change despite the efforts of opposition forces, or in countries experiencing such acute economic crises that reforms were inevitable. In terms of institutional economies, the actual potential for carrying out reform depends on cost ratios. Consumers may generate change through the electoral process, but the costs of generating such votes may be so high as to prevent an electoral process from bringing about any change at all. Change can only occur when the cost to the consumer that is implicit in the inefficiencies of service provision exceeds the cost of generating change. Otherwise, reforms will be only partial and may turn out to be more costly than inaction.

More than a decade ago, the countries of Latin America initiated a process for linking private capital to infrastructure development. The objectives have been many and varied, depending on the particular country and situation. Among them have been to improve and expand service provision as part of the strategy for addressing the challenges of the global economy; to improve the quality of life; to encourage competition; to attract foreign investment; to develop financial and capital markets; and to solve fiscal problems. Although results vary by country, investment has not only been boosted by the privatization of existing enterprises, but also by the development of new projects. According to International Finance Corporation figures, between 1990 and 1995 enterprises valued at more than $32 billion were privatized, while investments in new projects reached $30 billion.[1]

This process has required institutional reforms aimed at redefining the functions of the state as regulator as opposed to service provider, and particularly at strengthening sectoral regulatory schemes in such a way as to maximize the economic benefits resulting from private participation in infrastructure service provision.

Broadly speaking, private participation to date has focused on larger enterprises and projects that are either national or urban in scope, have some type of strategic importance, and have a low level of relative risk.

Each country now faces the challenge of adapting its private participation scheme to smaller local and regional projects and enterprises in such a way that the benefits associated with more numerous and better highways, telecommunications and energy and water services can be extended to the 120 million people residing in rural areas.[2]

---

[1]International Finance Corporation, *Financing Private Infrastructure, Lessons of Experience 4*, World Bank and IFC, 1996.

[2]Inter-American Development Bank, 1996 Report on *Economic and Social Progress in Latin America.*

But are the region's financial and capital markets prepared for this type of business? Does the current stage of institutional and regulatory development allow this step to be taken? This chapter offers some reflections based on the Colombian experience that might contribute to the current debate.

Local Project Financing

Some 40 percent of private investment in the region during the first half of the 1990s originated abroad and was destined to sectors characterized by their high technological content, large resource requirements and competitiveness, such as the telecommunications and electric energy generation sectors.[3] Reflecting this situation, legal norms, regulatory schemes and process structuring have all contributed to the creation of this particular investor and investment profile, which is appropriate for the large projects implemented to date.

However, in cases involving projects requiring smaller investments and located in local and regional markets, a more advantageous approach is to encourage the participation of national investors and sources of financing. It is more difficult to attract foreign investor interest to projects perceived to be riskier and in which economies of scale are not as great or are simply nonexistent. This becomes critical if we bear in mind that the competition for external resources has become particularly high with such places as China, India and Eastern Europe, which because of their size and current state of development demand significant amounts of capital for projects with enormous growth potential, given the considerable level of unsatisfied demand.[4]

This situation makes it necessary to encourage the participation of national investors in new local and regional projects. These investors have a lower risk perception because they are familiar with local conditions. They are also able to finance such projects more efficiently.

However, it is here that the credit restrictions and the depth of the capital markets in these countries begin to be felt. In the case of Colombia, for example, in order for the local financial sector to take maximum advantage of

---

[3]International Finance Corporation, *Financing Private Infrastructure, Lessons of Experience 4*, World Bank and IFC, 1996.

[4]Indeed, annual growth in flows of foreign capital to China in recent years has averaged 36 percent, with rates of 30 and 31 percent, respectively, recorded for India and Eastern Europe, while growth in the rates of flow into Latin America and the Caribbean has been only 25 percent. *Global Development Finance*, 1996.

such opportunities, increased sophistication in credit analysis and a complete shift in the policy governing credit guarantees are required.

A defining characteristic of infrastructure loans is that they are nonrecourse loans; the only guarantee is the cash flow generated by the project. This is anathema to the institutions operating in the traditional Colombian credit culture (including regulatory agencies), which base the quality of credit on real guarantees, even though they may have little or no value as loan security when actually executed.

To encourage the mobilization of a greater volume of nonrecourse or partial recourse credit, the credit analysis process must become more sophisticated so that banks will come to fully understand project characteristics, including legal and regulatory aspects. In this regard, there is much work to be done. Financial entities still prefer to require guarantees, focusing on details deemed essential for ensuring the maximum creditworthiness of a project, such as supporting contracts or the soundness of sectoral regulatory systems.

On the other hand, although capital markets are the funding source most suited to the conditions of infrastructure financing (both in terms of longer maturities and increased flexibility for accommodating different maturity structures), they are not sufficiently developed to be a significant source of resources. The Colombian market for bonds with maturities greater than one year is particularly small. For 1997, total demand will be close to $3.8 billion,[5] of which only $460 million is available to the private sector, including infrastructure projects. This accounts for only 12 percent of the country's total infrastructure requirements for 1997.

The greatest hope for growth in capital markets lies in pension funds and, to a lesser extent, severance and layoff funds. However, the volume of these funds continues to be small, totaling approximately $2 billion.[6]

Regulation in the area of options and coverage, which would be one way to efficiently adapt to the conservative requirements of valuation, is still in an incipient stage, thus limiting their participation in infrastructure projects.

This contrasts with the case of Chile, where not only is the volume of assets administered by pension funds 15 times greater than in Colombia but, to mention a single case, such funds hold 30 percent of the shares of the principal enterprises operating in the Chilean electrical sector.[7]

---

[5]Assuming an average life for securities of two and a half years. *Estimación del mercado disponible para colocación de nuevos títulos de largo plazo en 1997.* Document for Discussion No. 1, Nicolás Botero and María Angela Parra, Corporación Financiera del Valle, 1997.
[6]Asofondos, 1997.
[7]Merrill Lynch, *Latin American Electric Utilities*, Quarterly Valuation Guide, 30 June 1997.

The situation characterizing Colombian funds will tend to perpetuate itself if the effective involvement of such funds in similar processes is not encouraged. In Chile, Bolivia, Argentina and Peru, the democratization of ownership has been a fundamental objective of private participation. This is based on the understanding that democratization will encourage private savings, redistribute wealth and strengthen the capital shares market. Naturally, this requires a reconsideration of short-term objectives, including maximizing fiscal revenues from the sale of public assets.

In Colombia, for example, the norms governing the privatization of state enterprises provide for two rounds: an initial round when the total amount of shareholder participation must be offered for sale at a fixed price to workers, worker associations and pension funds; and a second round when the remaining participation is offered to the general public. However, since the objective has been to maximize the amount of the sale, generally successful efforts have been to ensure that only a small percentage of shares is sold in the first round in order to negotiate a sale to the highest bidder during the second round. The second round sale is based on a process of prequalification, which restricts the bidding to strategic investors.

Such a scheme favors short-term fiscal objectives and wastes a unique opportunity to increase the depth of local capital markets and effectively improve the distribution of wealth. In short, the establishment of close ties between the financial and infrastructure sectors of the countries of Latin America would contribute to the sustained development of both sectors over the long term.

Evolution of Institutions and Regulatory Systems

In reviewing private participation processes in the various countries of the region, a number of questions have emerged. Why have certain countries or sectors successfully achieved such a profound level of development that has enabled them to become regional leaders in the fields of telecommunications or electric energy, while others have failed to privatize even their largest and most promising enterprises? Why have most countries had to face strong opposition from both organized labor and public opinion in the process of establishing links to private capital?

In Colombia, the processes of privatization and private participation in telecommunications have been stifled by labor union opposition. As a result of pressures applied by regional groups and the failure to implement efficient tariff and subsidization schemes, it has been equally impossible to successfully launch private participation processes in the electricity and potable water distribution sectors.

Countries with more successful reform processes have included Chile and Argentina. Reform in Chile was carried out under an authoritarian government that had been in power for almost two decades. Although a dictatorship is perhaps the easiest context for instituting far-reaching reforms, it is difficult to conceive of such an approach as being the most recommendable one for other countries on the region.

Argentina, which has already begun developing sewerage and water distribution systems for cities with fewer than 300,000 inhabitants,[8] launched its reform process in the late 1980s following years of economic stagnation, high inflation and a profound fiscal crisis. The chaos in public services was more than evident. In 1988, the waiting time for telephone service was 22 years, while the average delay in responding to requests for water and sewerage repair in Buenos Aires was 180 hours.[9] This crisis, coupled with frequent water shortages, created the appropriate scenario for the wave of reforms over the past decade. As the cases of Argentina, Bolivia and Peru illustrate, chaos has a sweeping effect in terms of generating solutions.

With regard to institutional economics, the effective potential for instituting reforms is dependent on a simple cost ratio. As long as the political cost of reform is greater than the costs implicit in the inefficiency of service, reforms will be exceedingly difficult to implement.

Simply stated, there are three types of agents in the area of infrastructure service provision: producers, consumers and the government, which acts as intermediary between the other two. The relationships between these agents are mediated by the costs they create. The government, through either direct intervention or regulatory action, generates costs for producers for the common good. The producers, in turn, generate costs for consumers as a result of the inefficiencies in service provision. Consumers, who can generate costs for the government only through the electoral process, find themselves without any effective means to change the situation.

In a country such as Colombia, which in economic terms is located at the mid-point on the scale, with no enormous crises but likewise no great achieve-

---

[8]*Managing Government Exposure to Private Infrastructure Projects*, Latin America and the Caribbean Region, Economic Development Institute, World Bank, 1997.

[9]International Finance Corporation, *Financing Private Infrastructure, Lessons of Experience 4*, World Bank and IFC, 1996.

ments, it is difficult to develop a consensus with regard to the need to take efficient advantage of the public patrimony by establishing links to private capital. In some cases, the government, ceding to the interests of pressure groups or fiscal considerations, has opted to undertake partial reforms, thus minimizing short-term transaction costs.

Described below are two examples of how the evolution of reform can determine the success or failure of privatization, since reform processes can go so far as to become obstacles effectively preventing or permanently limiting private investment.

In 1992, one year after the implementation in Colombia of electric energy rationing that brought service outages lasting up to 10 hours, a decision was made to open electricity generation to competition and private participation. As in other countries of the region, the first mechanism for encouraging private participation in power generation was the Power Purchase Agreement (or PPA) with government guarantee, by means of which a public enterprise purchases the entire generating capacity of a private plant, regardless of actual government or system requirements.

This represented a fundamental step forward by eliminating the construction risk and a significant portion of the financing risk. However, all of the price and distribution risk was transferred to the state enterprise, which not only generated a severe fiscal contingency but also, over the long term, distorted the development of market prices. Competition was inhibited by limiting the subsequent emergence of private generators with the ability to compete without guarantees.

At the start of the process of selling the generating plants, PPAs were perceived as obstacles to the establishment of private sector links and were on the verge of thwarting the process. But in reality it was the incomplete reforms rather than the PPAs that had the potential to generate a crisis—one even more serious than the blackouts that had led to reforms. Fortunately, a regulatory process evolved and the crisis was avoided through the establishment of a charge for installed capacity. In very general terms, this involves payment of the fixed costs of the generating plants required during periods of critical water shortage. In this way, it is possible to provide a rational and efficient solution to the risk of nonrecovery of investment due to lack of distribution, allowing full private sector entry into the field of electricity generation with no need for government guarantees. Something as simple as establishing the long-term marginal cost eliminated fiscal risk from the outset and made possible the consolidation of private participation in Colombia's electricity generation industry. (Private participation now exceeds 40 percent of installed capacity.)

Telecommunications in Colombia is another clear example of the importance of regulatory and institutional reform, but without such a happy ending. Private participation has not occurred in this sector, perhaps because the economic costs associated with the inefficiency of government-operated telephone services are still lower than the transaction costs with which the government finds itself faced in implementing reforms against the efforts of organized labor and political pressure groups.

Reforms in this sector have attempted to promote competition and private participation in the provision of local and long distance telephone service. However, increased openness to competition has been successful only with regard to local telephone service. Long distance service is provided by TELECOM, a government-owned state enterprise whose labor union succeeded in pressuring the government to reject privatization and delay the decision to allow competition. In addition, regional politicians and labor unions have successfully opposed the privatization of the large municipal-owned local telephone enterprises.

Half-hearted reform efforts, pressure from vested interest groups and a weak regulatory system lacking well-defined objectives have led to singular mishaps. The Bogotá Telephone Enterprise, a city-owned enterprise with the largest captive market in the country, has an unmet demand of 500,000 lines, equivalent to 30 percent of its installed capacity. Both the city council and the telephone company labor union have refused to allow the establishment of links to private capital to secure the technical, financial and administrative resources needed to improve service. At the same time, the regulatory scheme, which is applied at the national level, has divested the telephone enterprise of its monopolistic privileges, reducing with the stroke of a pen the value of the company by almost $800 million and opening the market to competition. Yet rules remain confusing and fail to prevent abuses resulting from monopolistic predominance, cross-subsidies and tariff distortions.

The vacuum left behind by the inefficiency of the municipal enterprise has not been filled by private investors. TELECOM, the monopolistic government-owned long distance operator, decided to enter this market. However, since the required resources exceeded its economic potential, the firm sought to mobilize private capital through the use of joint venture contracts, the amount of which is currently approaching $1 billion. Such contracts protect partners from existing regulatory risks by means of guarantees that generate contingent liabilities but that, in addition, are secured by their long distance revenues, which will be affected by competitive changes.

The result has been competition between two public enterprises, one national and the other municipal, a reduction in the value of both firms, fiscal contingencies and considerable doubt as to whether the public, in exchange for absorbing these costs, will receive sufficient, timely and high-quality service—the opposite of the results expected in any process for developing private sector ties and market deregulation. Moreover, all of this has taken place in a sector rightly considered to be the most attractive for private investment because of its dynamic nature and potential for expansion.

The above examples demonstrate that the particular dynamic of these two sectors requires that both institutions and the regulatory system itself be adapted to the current state of sectoral evolution, as opposed to attempting to adapt the sectors to a restrictive and incomplete institutional and regulatory environment. Further attempts to do so not only may cause the nation to miss out on the benefits of private participation, but also subject it to situations worse than those in which it is now immersed.

Conclusions

Many countries find themselves at a critical juncture in the process of promoting private participation in infrastructure. Past success is no guarantee of future success. Project and market characteristics change as the private participation process moves forward. Accordingly, it is necessary to further entrench both the reform process and the regulatory and institutional changes being introduced.

This new stage of privatization will be characterized by smaller regional projects, the financing of which will be more efficient if procured locally. Toward this end, local financial sectors need to adapt to the conditions under which infrastructure projects operate, which in turn will contribute to the sound development of the financial and infrastructure sectors of the countries of the region.

Moreover, if economically and socially successful private participation processes are to be continued, both the regulatory process and institutions themselves need reforming. Far more than any short-term cost, incomplete reforms can end up being so expensive as to undermine the fundamental objective for which they were undertaken.

CHAPTER 7

Commitment and Governance in Infrastructure

Pablo T. Spiller and William Savedoff

Governments are unique social institutions. Like other political institutions they act as agents of their constituents. Unlike other institutions, though, they have a monopoly on the coercive power to establish, change and enforce laws (Weingast, 1995). Thus, a major task of public policy is to establish commitment. Without commitment, the expectation of future policy reversals may become self-fulfilling prophecies, defeating the original policy goals.

Nowhere is the problem of commitment more important than in the worldwide movement toward private sector participation in infrastructure, particularly in the developing world. Private sector investors are already involved in projects ranging from the by now familiar electricity and telecommunications sectors to water and sanitation, roads, ports and airports. Even the postal service is not immune to privatization.[1]

The movement toward private sector participation, however, is hampered by a basic governance problem inherent to infrastructure sectors: the overarching political temptation to behave opportunistically vis-à-vis infrastructure operators. In order to promote private investment, governments may offer contracts or establish regulatory environments that are attractive to the private sector and reserve certain discretionary powers to protect the interests of constituents. Once investments are made, however, the polity has an increased interest in using its unique powers to shift the balance in what it may perceive as the interests of its constituents. Knowing this in advance, private investors hesitate to enter a game that appears rigged against them. The government's unique strength becomes a hidden Achilles' heel. As much as the government wishes to serve the long-term interests of its constituents, which includes attracting investors, it may not be able to establish an institutional framework that provides

[1]Argentina recently privatized its postal service.

policy credibility—that is, a framework that provides sufficient assurances that the current government or its successors will not behave opportunistically.

The temptation to behave opportunistically also implies that the organization of infrastructure sectors is exceedingly fragile. A major point of this chapter is that although multiple equilibria are possible in infrastructure sectors, low-level equilibria are the only stable ones. These low-level, stable equilibria are characterized by low investments, low quality, low prices, poor service and poor customer appreciation and support for the operator. Low-level equilibria are frequently characterized by public ownership but not because the private sector is immune to low-level traps. Rather, when a low-level equilibrium develops under private ownership, the political reaction will usually lead to a government takeover of the sector or the operator, thereby moving the low-level equilibrium inside the public sphere.[2]

The key advantage of private sector participation in infrastructure has less to do with inherent efficiencies than it does with the possibility of creating a credible policy environment. When the government contracts with its own agencies to undertake investments or improvements, the budget constraints and potential penalties are not credible, since the public sector would essentially need to sanction itself. Sanctions become a credible threat when infrastructure is in private hands (see Perotti, 1995).

Thus, the challenge for those political entrepreneurs who rightly perceive that private participation provides a better chance of moving out of a "low-level equilibrium" is to design a governance structure that fosters policy credibility and commitment—limiting the ability of governments to behave opportunistically. The purpose of this chapter is twofold: first, to explain the inherent stability of low-level equilibria; and second, to demonstrate how various governance structures fare in moving the sector away from them.

Opportunism in Infrastructure Sectors[3]

The regulatory issues arising from private sector participation in the infrastructure sector are not different from those in the utilities sector. Elsewhere it has been shown that these issues relate to three basic characteristics: large sunk costs,

---

[2]Examples of transfers to public ownership of utilities include the Montevideo Gas Company and the Jamaica Telecommunications Company. See Spiller (1992).

[3]This section draws heavily from Spiller (1992).

economies of scale, and massive or large-scale consumption (see Spiller, 1992; Levy and Spiller, 1994). The combination of these three characteristics implies that the pricing of infrastructure sectors is going to be politically sensitive.

The reason for the politicalization of infrastructure pricing is threefold. First, the fact that a large component of infrastructure investments is sunk implies that once the investment is undertaken the operator will be willing to continue operating as long as revenues exceed costs. Since operating costs do not include a return on sunk investments (but only on the alternative value of these assets), the company will be willing to operate even if prices are below total average costs.[4] Second, economies of scale imply that in most infrastructure services, there will be few suppliers in each locality. Thus, the whiff of monopoly will always surround infrastructure operations. Finally, the fact that infrastructure services tend to be massively consumed implies that politicians and interest groups will care about the level of infrastructure pricing.

Thus, massive consumption, economies of scale and sunk investments provide governments (either national or local) the opportunity to behave opportunistically vis-à-vis the investing company.[5] For example, after the investment is sunk, the government may try to restrict the operating company's pricing flexibility, require the company to undertake special investments, purchasing or employment patterns, or restrict the movement of capital. All these are attempts to expropriate the company's sunk costs by administrative measures. Thus, expropriation may be indirect and undertaken by subtle means. While the government may uphold and protect traditionally conceived property rights, it may still attempt to expropriate through regulatory procedures, that is, disallowing costs, lowering prices, or requiring special investment patterns or purchases.

The implications of these three structural features to the development of regulatory structures have been analyzed elsewhere. In particular, it has been shown that it is important to link regulatory reform to a country's institutional environment in a discriminating fashion (Guasch and Spiller, 1995; Levy and Spiller, 1994 and 1996; Spiller, 1992 and 1996). Regulatory structures cannot be directly copied from one country to another, and similarly, regulatory reforms that attempt to improve upon current regulatory structures have to pass

[4]The source of financing does not change this computation. For example, if the company is completely leveraged, a price below average cost will bring it to bankruptcy, eliminating the part of the debt associated with the sunk investments. Only the part of the debt associated with the value of the nonsunk investments would be able to be subsequently serviced.

[5]This incentive exists vis-à-vis public and private companies.

the acid test of implementability. In other words, first best is seldom achievable, and an inexorable tradeoff between flexibility and credibility exists everywhere, although to varying degrees. Unfortunately, infrastructure sectors are such that for private participation to take place in a way that improves the public welfare, regulatory credibility is a necessary ingredient. Thus, regulatory proposals that attempt to grant regulators substantial discretion to reform and correct perceived market imperfections may, in turn, eliminate investment incentives. This paradox is at the essence of the tradeoff between credibility and flexibility developed in Levy and Spiller (1994). Indeed, this tradeoff reflects a more general problem inherent to commitment in governments. As Weingast (1995) states in his opening paragraph: "A government strong enough to protect property rights and enforce contracts is also strong enough to confiscate the wealth of its citizens."

The Political Profitability of Governmental Opportunism

Expropriating sunk assets may be advantageous for a government if the direct costs are small compared to the (short-term) benefits of such action, and if the indirect institutional costs are not too large. The direct costs are related to the government's potential loss of reputation among other operators of infrastructure projects, which will reduce investments in the infrastructure and utilities sectors. The institutional costs are related to the implications of disregarding judicial findings or evading proper, or traditional, administrative procedures. The short-term benefits are frequently related to expected electoral gains from reducing operators' prices or attacking monopoly suppliers.

Thus, incentives for expropriating sunk assets will be largest in countries where direct costs are small, indirect institutional costs are low, and the government's horizon is relatively short. Direct costs will be smaller when there are fewer private operators in the infrastructure sector; when the sectors do not, in general, require massive investment programs; and when technological change is not an important factor in the sector. Institutional costs will be low in countries where formal or informal governmental regulatory procedures (checks and balances) are weak or absent; where regulatory policy is centralized in the administration; and where the judiciary has little tradition, or authority, to review administrative decisions. Perhaps most important, the government's time horizon is strongly affected by the periodicity of elections, and whether or not the government faces highly contested elections and a need to satisfy key constituencies. Private operators will recognize and evaluate these factors, often choosing not to undertake investments in the first place. Thus, direct government provision of infrastructure may become the default mode of operation.

Implications of Government Opportunism

If, in the presence of such incentives, a government wants to motivate private investment, then it will have to design institutional arrangements that limit its own ability to behave opportunistically once the private utility invests. Such institutional arrangements are nothing more or less than the design of a regulatory framework. They will have to stipulate pricesetting procedures, conflict resolution procedures (arbitration or judicial) between the parties, investment policies, etc. In other words, regulation, if credible, solves a key contracting problem between the government and the utilities by restraining the government from opportunistically expropriating the utilities' sunk investments (Goldberg, 1976; Williamson, 1975). This does not mean that the utility has to receive assurances of a certain rate of return, or that it has to receive exclusive licenses,[6] although in some countries such assurances may be the only way to limit the government's discretionary powers.

Unless such a regulatory framework is credible, investments will not be made, or if undertaken will not be efficient. Investment inefficiencies may arise on several fronts. A first order effect is investment that never takes place. In countries where the government's commitments not to expropriate investments explicitly or implicitly are very weak, private investors will not invest. Under such conditions, even public entities with any degree of decisionmaking autonomy will underinvest.

A second effect of noncredible frameworks is that when operators do invest, they may do so exclusively in areas where the market return is very high and where the payback period is relatively short. This has been the experience in a variety of sectors, from mining to water, where very high initial profits are used by investors to essentially offset the risk of their sunk assets. In some cases, the risk of expropriating fixed assets is reduced by charging customers for the fixed costs of expansion. For example, in several Latin American countries (and also in Japan) the installation charge for a telephone line may range from $400

[6]Indeed, Colombia's initial deregulation of telecommunications involved deregulation of value-added networks. It specifically stipulated that the government could not set their prices and that there could not be exclusivity provisions. Thus, regulation meant total lack of governmental discretion.

to $600. Given that the fixed investment cost for a new line ranges from $600 to $1,200 in less developed countries, that initial charge substantially reduces the payback period for the investor, partially protecting the utility from the expropriation of its sunk investments. This may be one reason why investment in telecommunications, whether public or private, has proceeded much more quickly than in the water sector. In most Latin American water systems, the combination of low prices and low hookup charges has made it difficult to attract operators who might otherwise be willing to face the regulatory risk by exploiting particularly profitable service segments.

A third effect of noncredible government policies is that operators may keep maintenance expenditures to a minimum, thus degrading quality. This has been an important cause of the intermittent supplies in the utility sector across Latin America.

Fourth, investment may be undertaken with technologies that have a lower degree of specificity, even at the expense of reducing the quality of services. In this regard, it is not surprising that private telecommunications operators have rushed to develop cellular rather than fixed link networks in Eastern Europe.[7] In the solid waste sector, too, private haulers will use general purpose trucks or handcarts rather than invest in specialized compacting equipment, even though the latter may be more profitable and environmentally sound, simply because it is more difficult to resell or convert them to other uses (Cointreau-Levine, 1994).

Fifth, operators may insist upon high up-front rents achieved through very high prices. Although these may provide incentives for some investment, they may also be politically unsustainable. To privatize Argentina's telecommunications sector, prices were raised well above international levels. Subsequent to privatization, however, the government reneged on many aspects of the license.[8] Aguas Argentinas, on the other hand, obtained generous pricing terms after being granted the concession for Buenos Aires, which allowed it to reduce its exposure to regulatory risk (Artana et al., 1997).

---

[7]While cellular has a higher long-run cost than fixed link, and on some quality dimensions is also an inferior product, the magnitude of investment in specific assets is much smaller than in fixed link networks. Furthermore, a large portion of the specific investments in cellular telephones is undertaken by the customers themselves (who purchase the handsets).

[8]License provisions, such as indexation, were initially not implemented—allegedly because of the passage of the Convertibility Act that prohibited indexation—and later modified by the government. The initial high prices, though, allowed the companies to remain profitable, even following the government's deviation from the license provisions (see Spiller, 1992).

By strongly encouraging inefficiency and poor performance, a noncredible regulatory framework will eventually create the conditions for a direct government takeover. Thus, government ownership has become the default mode of operation. Government ownership, then, represents neither the best way to promote the public interest nor the most efficient way to provide services, but simply the failure to develop institutions that limit the temptation for opportunistic governmental behavior.

Governmental Opportunism and the Performance of Public Enterprises

Government opportunism, in its basic form, implies low prices—so low, in fact, that they fail to provide either the public or private operator with the ability to finance its business expansion, whether current or past.[9] Lowering prices, however, is not simply a one-time reversible action. Rather, once the short-term political interest in lower prices is seized upon, the low prices trigger a downward spiral in which mutually reinforcing factors make low prices and low quality an equilibrium. This downward spiral is depicted in Figure 7.1.

Politicians, in their clamor for lower prices, delayed billing or unprofitable activities, can purport to support the public interest while blaming the operator for inefficient performance. But low prices imply that the public operator will depend on government transfers for expansion and investment. The need for government transfers, in turn, limits the operator's ability to expand, since the investments are not evaluated relative to their own profitable returns but against the competing uses of funds in the national budget. In Chile, for example, one of the key constraints on investment in expanding water supply and treatment is the fact that the water companies remain public entities whose expenditures form part of the national budget. Although these investments might be easily recovered through tariffs, and therefore incur little or no claims against future tax revenues, the investment budgets are limited by competition with other sectors, such as education, for which little or no cost recovery can be anticipated (Morandé and Doña, 1997).

A cash-poor company that needs direct government transfers to finance its investment program will also be subject to substantial scrutiny and intervention, thus limiting its autonomy in matters of personnel, allocations and expansion. Once it becomes politically convenient for the polity to set oppor-

[9]That is, servicing the debt.

Figure 7.1. The Downward Spiral

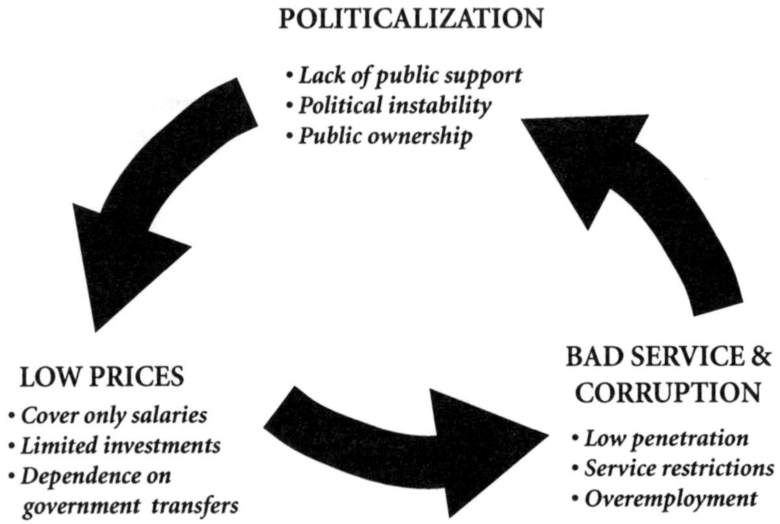

tunistic prices, the budget for maintenance and investment may disappear, leaving only the minimum required to cover salaries (which are themselves protected by a strong lobby). Under such scrutiny, a cash-poor company also loses much of its ability to protect its autonomy through strategic manipulation of its information. As a consequence, the company's asset base will depreciate, its maintenance program will suffer, and its service quality will deteriorate. These factors will further tighten its investment capabilities, making expansion programs sporadic and generating low coverage levels and probably shortages and rationing as well.[10]

Although investment programs by public enterprises usually require approval by the Ministry of Finance, some cash-rich companies may protect their autonomy by using their information advantage to forestall close government scrutiny. This is where the reinforcing dynamic forces start to make this a low-level equilibrium. As the company is stripped of cash, management and the union have a clear incentive to engage in "cash hiding." That is, since extra cash cannot be used for investments without government authorization, it will be

[10]Shortages will naturally arise in a low price environment, where prices do not cover expansion costs.

used to increase employment, whether permanent (if the company has the ability to do so), or temporary.[11] Corruption can then become endemic, resulting in bad service and low quality and making the company a public eyesore. This in turn reinforces the public perception of bad management, and discourages public support for continuing fiscal transfers. Thus, there is successively less political incentive for elected officials or the Finance Minister to support government transfers.

A stable, low-level equilibrium has then been reached: prices are kept low, government transfers are limited, service quality and coverage are low, and no one—neither the service operator, the government, consumers nor constituents—has an interest in changing their position. Although attempts at reform may occur, they commonly fail.

To understand this point, consider how the low-level equilibrium responds to the most common reforms: increasing prices and changing management. When prices are raised to cover operating costs and finance investment, they are rarely raised enough, because the low efficiency of the system means that actual costs are much higher than long-run marginal costs. Consumers resist the hike in prices unless service is first improved. As a result, the cash generated by a price increase is easily dissipated by the existing management structure and eventually repealed or eroded by inflation. Thus, reforms that introduce price changes without making an institutional change in the way prices are set are not sustainable.

Introducing new management is also generally insufficient to make sustainable changes because the new management faces exactly the same incentives as the old guard. Although not necessarily corrupt, the new management will find that it is better to keep any excess cash in the company rather than transfer it (directly or indirectly) to the government.[12] Since there are no effective incentives to expand or improve service, the cash is used in ways that are not perceived by consumers. Thus, a basic implication is that public companies subject to governmental opportunism will have managerial rotation without substantive operational improvements.

A further implication is that high-level equilibria are inherently unstable unless there are institutional restraints to governmental opportunism. In their absence, a political shock may call for a price freeze, a change in the company's

[11]It is indeed not surprising that most public enterprises in the developing world have a large number of long-term nonpermanent workers.

[12]An indirect transfer back to the government means that excess cash crowds out government transfers, probably on a one-to-one basis.

investment pattern, or any other operational change that has the effect of expropriating the sunk investments of the public company. Indeed, the movement down from a high-level equilibrium could be stochastic—precipitated by random political and economic shocks, like high inflation and political and social unrest.

This analysis, then, shows that low-level equilibria are stable because there is no public support for increasing government transfers or higher prices for the service. The government will have very little incentive to spend scarce investment funds on a mismanaged organization. And attempts to improve management will fail unless there is a basic institutional change.

Breaking Low-level Equilibria

It should be obvious that low-level equilibria have high social costs.[13] While well-developed infrastructure reduces the costs of business transactions and improves the health of the nation, poorly developed infrastructure reduces the country's competitiveness and the extent of its domestic integration. Expensive, congested or unreliable communications, for example, constrain sectors that need rapid access to information. In modern economies, even such "low-tech" industries as exports of flowers or garments require access to sophisticated communications (see Box 7.1). Unreliable or unavailable power and water prompts firms to invest in generating their own supplies, increasing their costs and reducing their international competitiveness. Similarly, poor transport infrastructure (and badly designed access charges to infrastructure) increases direct and indirect (congestion) transport and insurance costs, affecting direct labor and input costs, limiting the extent of domestic integration, increasing export costs, and reducing the set of potential export industries.

Poor infrastructure also has environmental and health implications. Lack of proper water infrastructure, for example, has a negative impact on health conditions. It also degrades the environment by diverting too much water from aquifers and streams due to excessive losses. Inefficient and expensive electricity and gas force families in poorer conditions to burn fuels such as wood that deplete scarce resources and cause soil erosion.

Thus, moving out of low-level equilibria *should* be an important governmental priority. But as the previous discussion suggests, simple fixes will not

---

[13]The following draws from Spiller (1992). For an example from the Honduran water sector, see Walker et al. (1997).

Box 7.1

The Costs of Poor Telecommunications Services: Flower Growers in Colombia and Garment Companies in the Philippines

Colombia's flower growers are located in the savannas surrounding the cities of Bogotá and Medellín. Their location is based not just on weather but also on proximity to airports. Since flower exporters require day-to-day communication with markets, and since access to international lines is difficult from the flower farms, growers have found it necessary to keep offices with minimal staff in Bogotá. The Association of Colombian Flower Growers, taking advantage of the current telecommunications liberalization policy, has obtained bids to build a private satellite network to connect all members to the central office and to the association's offices overseas, providing them direct access to international communications. The association estimates that such a network will cost $1,500 per grower, approximately the cost of a telephone line in Bogotá at black market rates (Spiller, 1992).

A similar situation exists in the Philippines. A World Bank study cited by Ferreira and Khatami (1996) reports that "although the larger garment companies have access to telephones, waiting time for additional lines averages three to five years. In order to communicate with their subcontractors, the larger garment companies have resorted to alternative modes of communication, such as investing in radio equipment, motorcycles, and courier services...The smaller companies typically have their production facilities outside of Metro Manila and need to maintain a separate office in the capital (at an average cost of P35,000 [$1,400] per month) to have access to communications services for import/export transactions. Companies in Mindanao do not maintain a separate office in Manila because the quality of telecommunications services between Manila and Mindanao is unreliable."

do the job. Efforts that have failed in the past include the standard set of international agency recommendations, like price increases, performance contracts or other types of temporary performance improvements, and even hiring private firms under build-operate-transfer (BOT) contracts.

A standard international agency recommendation is that prices should cover operating and investment costs. In negotiations on a particular sector development loan, a government may agree to a price increase. Once that price increase is introduced, the political forces that triggered opportunistic pricesetting will kick in again sooner or later, depending on the extent to which inflation erodes the imposed price increase. In the longer run, the increase will be nothing more than a blip in the chart.[14]

A second approach has been to introduce performance contracts between management and government, under which management receives some part of the expected increase in profits. The evidence provided by Shirley and Xu (1996) suggests that, in general, such contracts have failed to improve public sector performance because they change neither the basic discretionary power of the government nor the asymmetry of information between management and government. Since managers know that surplus and profits will eventually be taken away, they operate the firms to redistribute cash to themselves and their workers, rather than to increase efficiency. These contracts fail because the government lacks credibility—it can neither establish hard budget constraints nor effectively monitor management's actions. Hence, the use of management contracts as a solution to a credibility problem is ultimately self-defeating.

Finally, there is the use of BOTs to expand systems. BOTs are an attractive way to expand the system because they require neither any basic change in the way the company operates or is managed nor any direct transfer from the government. BOTs simply add capacity without changing the corrupt and inefficient nature of the corporation. Such arrangements require substantial governmental guarantees, very high initial prices, and relatively inflexible contract terms. Since the overall credibility problem is not resolved, BOTs are appropriately perceived as costly, further reinforcing the public impression of corruption and favoritism that circles the company.

The basic question, then, is what set of changes could move an infrastructure sector away from a low-level equilibrium. The previous discussion suggests that the key is to develop a process that limits government discretion in pricesetting. Once such limits are in place, attempts to improve management and to set prices at reasonable levels may actually work.

For a process to be effective in limiting government discretion, three complementary mechanisms must be in place. First, substantive restraints on regulatory discretion must be embedded in the regulatory framework; second, formal or informal constraints must limit the ability of the polity to change the regulatory framework itself; and, finally, institutions must be in place that en-

[14]Between 1979 and 1989, average tariffs fell by an average of 1.5 percent following loans by the Inter-American Development Bank to national electricity sectors in 12 Latin American countries, compared to an average increase of 7.2 percent before, despite contractual clauses requiring that tariff levels be maintained.

force those substantive or procedural constraints (Levy and Spiller, 1994). These three mechanisms are easier to implement in countries where decisionmaking is naturally decentralized. In countries where decisionmaking is heavily centralized, regulatory credibility requires more rigid institutions and restraints.

Regulatory commitment can be introduced in different forms. It can be achieved, for example, by writing very specific legislation and delegating its implementation to a regulatory agency whose decisions on both substance and process can be reviewed by the judiciary. Alternatively, regulatory credibility can be achieved "à la McNollgast," that is, by hard-wiring the decisionmaking process so that the interests of the regulated companies are safeguarded against administrative expropriation (see McCubbins, Noll and Weingast, 1987; on hard-wiring; see also Hamilton and Schroeder, 1994, and Macey, 1992). Here again, the courts may review agencies' decisions both on substance and procedural considerations. Finally, regulatory credibility can be achieved by granting the operator a license that specifies the regulatory process through which its prices will be determined. Deviations from the license could be challenged relatively easily through the courts.

These three regulatory instruments have different implications for both regulatory credibility and flexibility, and perform differently depending upon the context (Spiller, 1996). The difficulties in building commitment can be seen even in the United States, a relatively propitious system with decentralized decisionmaking. The United States has a government structure that fragments power between a directly elected president, a legislature composed of two chambers elected under different rules and at different times, and electoral rules designed to tie legislators to their local constituencies, which limits (but does not eliminate) the power of political parties. The U.S. judiciary is reasonably well respected by the population, and its decisions are widely accepted and even implemented. However, in such a situation, specific legislation may be difficult to introduce because the political fragmentation inherent to the political system increases legislative costs. Thus, the saliency of a policy problem must be very high before legislators will spend time in negotiating and drafting specific legislation (Schwartz, Spiller and Urbiztondo, 1993).

Hard-wired decisions, on the other hand, are easier to draft and adopt, but are, as everything, potentially imperfect. In particular, they run the risk of being diverted by future judicial interpretation. Finally, although licenses as regulatory schemes are feasible in the United States, they may be too rigid given the nature of the political system. Thus, the commitment potential of American regulatory structures is quite strong, and allows most of these mechanisms to function much better than in less propitious environments. It is not surprising, then, that hard-wiring solutions are the regulatory norm in the United States (McCubbins, Noll and Weingast, 1987). Hard-wiring solutions provide politicians with the necessary political flexibility, while at the same time the credibility of the judiciary and its traditional protection of property and contract rights provides investors with some assurances against opportunistic behavior.[15]

In nations with centralized decisionmaking processes, the first two approaches do not provide much regulatory credibility. Nations with centralized political decisionmaking can change laws relatively easily, hence very specific laws (in substance or in process) will not effectively constrain governmental decisionmaking. Indeed, it is quite interesting to observe that while in the United States the evolution of the electricity sector was undertaken almost without federal legislation, in the United Kingdom (a highly centralized system), major regulatory changes were mostly undertaken via legislative changes (Spiller and Vogelsang, 1996). Similarly, in these type of political environments, courts will tend not to challenge administrative decisions (see Spiller, 1996, for a theory of the evolution of independent courts).

Various countries have attempted different approaches to limit governmental discretion when privatizing infrastructure sectors. Chile, a country with substantial checks and balances, introduced specific legislation regulating pricesetting in electricity, telecommunications and water. Similarly, Chile's antitrust legislation limits political interference through a very complex decisionmaking process (Corbo, Luders and Spiller, 1997). On the other hand, Argentina, a country with substantial credibility problems, privatized its water and electricity distribution utilities with a specific regulatory framework embedded in operating licenses. These licenses substantially limit the ability of the regulatory agency to deviate from the prescribed pricesetting process. Bolivia, almost alone, has maintained private ownership of electricity since the turn of the century through the use of specific concessions.[16] Given the limited

---

[15]This does not mean, though, that American utilities haven't had their share of regulatory difficulties. The inflationary process, the increase in the real price of oil, and the environmental concerns that started in the 1970s required substantial changes in the regulatory process (Joskow, 1974), costing the electric utilities substantial market value. One of the lasting effects of this period is the increase in the perceived change in the regulatory risk. Capacity additions (mostly nuclear) undertaken during the oil shock period were challenged in courts by environmental groups and eventually required to be withdrawn from the rate base.

[16]The other long-lasting private electricity firm in Latin America is the Caracas Electricity Company, which has had no regulatory structure but has had widely diffused local ownership.

tradition of administrative law in the developing world, it is not surprising that few countries have experimented with administrative procedures as ways to provide regulatory credibility. But regulatory structures by themselves may not be enough. Ancillary structures may have to be developed.

Maintaining High-level Equilibria

Once high-quality equilibrium is achieved, the design emphasis shifts toward how to sustain it, which means providing the political support to maintain a process that limits governmental opportunism. Such support will come from interested parties. Thus, a polity interested in preserving high-level equilibrium will need to design an industry structure that increases the number of interest groups involved in supporting it.

A basic strategy to increase political support is to fragment the industry, which has the advantage of creating multiple sources of political support for proper governmental behavior. Similarly, fragmenting the industry and creating at least potential competition limits the informational advantage enjoyed by each company and reduces the potential for regulatory capture. At the same time, it reduces the appearance of monopoly and makes it less attractive as a target of politicians seeking to garner political support against the operator.

Fragmentation has been extensively utilized by the Argentine reformers. A clear example is the privatization of the electricity sector: today the wholesale electricity market has more than 600 players (see Spiller and Torres, 1996, for a discussion of the Argentine electricity reforms). Although not as extensively as the Argentine case, Chile has also fragmented many of its utility sectors, including the water sector.

A second basic strategy is to privatize the sector. Privatization creates an interest group interested in limiting opportunistic behavior and willing to spend substantial resources to do so. It also provides the opportunity to grant large segments of the population direct interest in the profitability of the operator. Popular capitalism—whether through investments by private pension plans, as in Chile or Bolivia, or via selling large chunks of the company to citizens, as in the United Kingdom or in the Czech Republic—is in a certain sense superior to selling the company to a foreign investor. Foreign investors from large and politically strong powers may utilize their countries' influence to achieve some political support; on the other hand, a lack of direct political support of foreign investors will increase the risk of governmental opportunism.

Finally, each of these strategies will be limited in effect if the mechanisms for establishing prices are not insulated from governmental opportunism. The more fragmented and competitive the market, the less justification for government involvement in price determination. But when fragmentation is limited and operators are private, the temptations for governmental opportunism in pricesetting are very large. It is precisely such conditions that prompt the need for independent pricesetting boards with spelled-out procedures and formulaic pricesetting, or for contractual licenses. This will help achieve the goal of institutionalizing a credible government policy toward pricing in the sector.

Conclusions

Although usually built in concrete, infrastructure pertains to sectors that have the most fragile of structures. Because of their basic features, these sectors are prone to governmental opportunism, triggering a downward spiral of low prices, investment, quality and coverage, as well as high levels of corruption. To avoid this, and to maintain high-quality levels, three basic design features should be introduced: first, development of a price determination process that drastically limits governmental discretion; second, a policy of industry fragmentation, coupled with the elimination of exclusivity so as to promote potential competition; and finally, privatization of the sector, with emphasis on domestic participation.

REFERENCES

Artana, D., F. Navajas, and S. Urbiztondo. 1997. Argentina: La regulación económica en las concesiones de agua potable y desagües cloacales en Buenos Aires y Corrientes. Inter-American Development Bank, Washington, D.C. Mimeo.

Corbo, V., R. Luders, and P.T. Spiller. 1997. The Foundations of Successful Economic Reforms: The Case of Chile. Universidad Católica de Chile. Mimeo.

Cointreau-Levine, Sandra. 1994. *Private Sector Participation in Municipal Solid Waste Services in Developing Countries, Volume 1: The Formal Sector*. Urban Management Programme Series Paper 13, World Bank, Washington, D.C.

Ferreira, David, and Kamran Khatami. 1996. *Financing Private Infrastructure in Developing Countries.* World Bank Discussion Paper No. 343, Washington, D.C.

Goldberg, Victor. 1976. Regulation and Administered Contracts. *Bell Journal of Economics* 7(2) Autumn: 426–452.

Guasch, J.L., and P.T. Spiller. 1995. *The Path Towards Rational Regulation in Latin America and the Caribbean: Issues, Concepts and Experience.* World Bank Directions in Development Series. Washington, D.C.: World Bank.

Hamilton, J.T., and C.H. Schroeder. 1994. Strategic Regulators and the Choice of Rulemaking Procedures—The Selection of Formal vs. Informal Rules in Regulating Hazardous Waste. *Law and Contemporary Problems* 57(1–2): A111–160.

Inter-American Development Bank. 1993. Evaluation Report on Electric Power Sector, Tariff Policy and Lending. ORE, RE-187, IDB, Washington, D.C. March.

Joskow, P.L. 1974. Inflation and Environmental Concern: Structural Change in the Process of Public Utility Price Regulation. *Journal of Law and Economics* 17: 291–327.

Levy, B., and P.T. Spiller. 1994. The Institutional Foundations of Regulatory Commitment: A Comparative Analysis of Five Country Studies of Telecommunications Regulation. *Journal of Law, Economics and Organization* 10(2) October: 201–46.

———, eds. 1996. *The Institutional Foundations of Regulatory Commitment: A Comparative Analysis of Telecommunications Regulation.* Cambridge: Cambridge University Press.

Macey, Jon. 1992. Organizational Design and Political Control of Administrative Agencies. *Journal of Law, Economics and Organization* 8(1): 93–110.

McCubbins, M.D., R.G. Noll, and B.R. Weingast. 1987. Administrative Procedures as Instruments of Political Control. *Journal of Law, Economics and Organization* 3: 243–77.

Morandé, F., and L. Doña. 1997. *Los servicios de agua potable en Chile: Condicionantes, institucionalidad y aspectos de economía política.* Serie de Documentos de Trabajo R-308, OCE, Inter-American Development Bank, Washington, D.C.

Perotti, E.C. 1995. Credible Privatization. *American Economic Review* 85(4) September: 847–59.

Schwartz, E.P., P.T. Spiller, and S. Urbiztondo. 1993. A Positive Theory of Legislative Intent. *Law and Contemporary Problems* (1-2): 51–74.

Shirley, M. And L. Colin Xu. 1996. *Information, Incentives and Commitment: An Empircal Analysis of Contracts between Government and State Enterprises.* World Bank Working Paper 1769, Washington, D.C.

Spiller, P.T. 1992. Institutions and Regulatory Commitment in Utilities' Privatization. IPR51, Institute for Social Policy Reform, Washington, D.C. September.

Spiller, P.T. 1996. A Positive Political Theory of Regulatory Instruments: Contracts, Administrative Law or Regulatory Specificity? *Southern California Law Review* 69(2): 477.

Spiller, P.T., and C. Torres. 1996. Argentina's Electricity Regulation: Its Performance, Credibility and Options for the Future. World Bank. Mimeo.

Spiller, P.T., and I. Vogelsang. 1996. Regulations, Institutions and Commitment: The Case of British Telecom. In B. Levy and P. Spiller, eds, *The Institutional Foundations of Regulatory Commitment.* Cambridge: Cambridge University Press.

Walker, I., M. Velásquez, F. Ordoñez, and F. Rodríguez. 1997. *Regulation, Organization and Incentives: The Political Economy of Potable Water Services. Case Study: Honduras.* Working Paper Series R-314, Inter-American Development Bank.

Weingast, Barry, R. 1995. The Economic Role of Institutions: Market Preserving Federalism and Economic Development. *Journal of Law, Economics and Organization* 11(1): 1–31.

Williamson, O.E. 1975. *Franchise Bidding for Natural Monopolies: In General and With Respect to CATV.* Philadelphia: Fels Centers of Government, University of Pennsylvania.

CHAPTER 8

Economic Principles to Guide Post-Privatization Governance

Robert Willig

Achieving the public interest goals of the privatization process requires a commitment to planning the structure of post-privatization governance ahead of time. While it is commonplace to hear loud mandates for ex ante planning from project analysts who are active at the keyboard rather than at the negotiating table, in practice the process usually proceeds pragmatically, with little more planning than the flow of implementation steps needed to avoid total confusion. Due to the very nature of privatization, however, its implementation requires that ex post governance be thought through and, in essence, designed in advance.

Economic analysis offers much in the way of principles to help plan the post-privatization market and governance structures, whose organization and architecture are critical to the ongoing success of the privatization process. Both logic and experience show that successful privatization requires that the government prepare to limit its power to intervene in the operations and finances of privatized enterprises. As a consequence, the ex ante planning must include the mechanism of post-privatization governance, as well as the guideposts for the substantive content of that governance.

The kind of post-privatization governance necessary to meet the public interest depends on the ability of the markets to sustain effective competition. This ability is a creature of the institutional and market settings that surround the privatized entity's activities, and it may be crucially dependent on deliberate policy choices made at the time of privatization or subsequently. Restructuring state-owned enterprises, and structuring new concessions, may seek to organize competitive markets if the technology permits. However, public utility style regulation may be needed if the technology of production is one of natural monopoly. In this domain, economics offers a relatively clear analytic framework for deciding where and how competition should be pushed, by means of the policy decisions that attend the structuring of the privatized entities.

Effective competition cannot always be expected to arise with sufficient power and speed following privatization. To discipline enterprise decisions and make them consistent with the public interest, there is a need for ongoing regulation of privatized enterprises, particularly in key areas of infrastructure. Economic theory has much to say about the issues that regulation must be ready to address and resolve. These issues are important to the directly affected firm and its customers, rivals and suppliers, as well as to the economy as a whole. How these interests can influence regulatory decisions and provide vital information to regulators will determine the success of the entire reform effort. Thus, the architecture of regulation is crucial, particularly the way the regulatory body is organized, how it is to function, and how it is to relate to the interested parties, the political arm and the rest of the government.

For privatization to unleash the forces of private enterprise, regulation cannot be just another form of state control like the one that preceded the reform. Thus, both regulation and the privatized enterprises they regulate must be insulated from political control. This requires an appropriate regulatory structure and, most importantly, some credible commitment to limit the discretionary powers of the regulatory apparatus. However, these limitations must be designed to avoid becoming excessively rigid and unresponsive to market changes, which require adapting behaviors and strategies.

This chapter advances a hypothesis about a socially desirable way to limit government regulatory powers over privatized enterprises. In essence, the regulatory body should be committed to reaching decisions and resolving disputes on the basis of transparent application of economic principles that are publicly articulated before the commercial investment is ever made by the private operator.

This solution would provide appropriate limits on the discretionary exercise of regulatory power, while avoiding the paralysis and unnecessary rigidities that attend post-privatization governance based on adherence to detailed micromanaging terms of a privatization agreement or concession. The controlling economic principles would set the framework under which negotiations and arbitration would yield dynamic adaptations to changing circumstances and resolutions of disputes, serving the needs of both the parties involved and the public interest.

The controlling principles could be articulated within a concession or privatization agreement, thus becoming part of the contractual agreement between the enterprise and the government. Alternatively, the principles might be contained within an overarching statute. The feasibility and credibility of each of these approaches may well depend on the structure of the surrounding legal system, since existing commercial laws may be inconsistent with particular principles articulated in a privatization agreement or in a special statute.

This chapter ends by articulating economic principles that might be included in a statute or a concession agreement as the foundation for transparent decisionmaking and dispute resolution. These principles cover issues including the primacy of financial returns expected from the privatization agreement, the processes by which tariffs are set and coordinated with quality and reliability of services, and the efficient adaptations that impending competition may warrant.

A Policy Plan for Industry Structure, Regulation and Political Insulation

The widely articulated rationale for the move toward privatization focuses on perceptions of inefficiency, waste, poor quality output, underinvestment, and unresponsiveness regarding operations of public enterprises, as contrasted with expectations of dynamism, cost effectiveness, ample capital availability, responsive output quality, and creative productivity in the operations of private enterprises. But there is widespread reluctance to relinquish public control over infrastructure activities, linked to genuine concerns about the incentives of private owners to avoid serving the public interest, as well as to the attractiveness of the status quo with its accustomed flows of benefits to the politically favored and powerful. It is important to uncover just what it is about privatization that actually invigorates infrastructure and other sectoral activities emerging from state-owned enterprises. This would address the natural reluctance to undertake reform and aid in formulating plans to maximize the gains while avoiding the pitfalls of privatization.

Conventional wisdom holds that privatization is effective because market responsiveness, cost efficiency, productivity and economical applications of capital are key to the pursuit of profit, and profit is the overriding goal of private enterprise. It further assumes that, on the basis of periodic financial disclosures and audits, investors and managers of enterprises can effectively assure that they are well monitored. In contrast, state-owned enterprises are managed without the profit incentive, but rather under the control of political agendas that may foster market unresponsiveness, low productivity and inefficiency. Political agendas are difficult to reconcile with long-run commitment, since they are endemically discretionary and subject to change and reinterpretation. They are also difficult to monitor since their goals are generally not compatible with quantification and audit.

This conventional wisdom about private and public enterprises still does not explain all of the differences in performance, since one must consider the possibilities for strong political interference with the profit-maximization goals of private enterprises, as well as the possibilities of using profit incentives to guide the management of a state-owned enterprise. Political interference is particularly likely through the regulation of private infrastructure enterprises. And private-public infrastructure partnerships might be particularly attractive candidates for profit-oriented incentive mechanisms.

The deeper explanation of differences between public and private enterprise performance focuses on the inevitability of political influence over the operations of public enterprises, and the haphazard relationship that must be expected between political agendas and economically efficient performance. There can be no credible commitment that walls off public enterprise from political management. For activities that belong in the public domain, like those related to security and public safety, that is perfectly appropriate. However, genuine privatization is inevitably accompanied by some form of committed assurance of insulation from political interference.

After all, owners of private liquid capital will be unwilling to invest in the sunk assets needed to supply infrastructure services unless there is a convincing commitment that the government will not explicitly or implicitly expropriate the resulting private value, including by means of political interference with management. The danger of such expropriation will be perceived by investors as threatening, particularly for politically sensitive infrastructure activities recently undertaken by state-owned enterprises. The prospect of partial expropriation that decreases rather than eliminates investor value may not completely deter private investment, but will inhibit it and raise investor risks and the resulting costs of capital that must ultimately be borne by consumers.

Thus, in order for genuine privatization to occur, there must be a credible commitment to investors that the value of their investments will not be subjected to political expropriation. Such commitments might flow from features of the legal system that protect private property from government, from tight contracts implementing the privatization, from reputation effects that would sorely punish the government's ability to borrow or to further privatize in the event political expropriation were attempted, or from threatened sanctions from international banks or development agencies.

Two intertwined lines of thought follow. First, policy must pay attention to the need for a mechanism that can provide the requisite credible commitment against expropriation of private capital upon privatization. The policy plan underlying a privatization program must be sensitive to this need, particularly in the case of infrastructure privatization. A regulatory body for post-privatization governance may need to be put in place, and the policy plan must cover how this body's powers will be circumscribed to maintain the necessary credible commitment against expropriation, while acting to control monopoly power to protect the public interest.

Second, the commitment to investors is the source of the efficiency gains from privatization. The commitment mechanism means that if the government wants the privatized enterprise to act against its profit interests for the sake of its political agenda, it will have to compensate the firm. With its superior information concerning the costs of acquiescence, and its superior bargaining position, the privatized firm would be in the position to extract a profitable payment from the government. Consequently, the government would find it more costly to induce the privately-held (albeit possibly regulated) enterprise to act than would have been the case for an otherwise identical public enterprise. The higher costs of political interference with management of a privatized enterprise are likely to mean that less interference is sought, resulting in an enterprise more insulated from political forces due to its privatization. This independence enables the enterprise to experience the full force of market incentives, develop its entrepreneurial capacity, and operate efficiently.

To summarize, privatization requires a credible prior commitment to a policy plan that includes protection against political expropriation. This is also crucial in order to insulate the privatized enterprise from political interference and to realize the hoped-for gains in efficiency and entrepreneurship. A privatized enterprise that is subject to effective competition in its markets does not require targeted intervention. A generally market-friendly policy stance by the government will protect a newly privatized enterprise from expropriation in the same way that other investments are protected in the economy. However, infrastructure services sold by privatized enterprises are likely candidates for specially targeted public utility style regulation. This raises a far more daunting challenge both in terms of protection against expropriation and political insulation.

Public utility style regulation is necessary to control market power if, and only if, the fundamental economic characteristics of the relevant market are inconsistent with the workings of competition and contestability. Because infrastructure services and other areas of privatized activities may or may not fit into this category or require restructuring to promote competition, it is important to consider how market structure analysis should be conducted for privatization planning.

Testing Whether Public Utility Style Regulation Is Needed

In general, economic analysis of market structures makes use of information about the scopes and sizes of firms active in the marketplace; about firms that would become active if opportunities arose; and about firms that might come into existence with the right stimulation. Analysts also focus on the underlying characteristics of production and distribution technologies and market demands to ascertain what might be the prospects for competition or for monopoly. Where the market structure has been strongly influenced by state-owned enterprises or by other means of direct governmental influence, the number and scope of extant firms are probably not reliable indicators of what the technology and demands would yield as an efficient configuration of supply. Here, more reliance may be warranted on inferences drawn from the fundamentals of the properties of supply costs and demands.

As an initial point of focus, the test for whether public utility style regulation is needed to shape market outcomes as a replacement for competition is based on there being a natural monopoly in the relevant market, high barriers to entry into the relevant market, and sufficient demand for significant monopoly profit in the relevant market.

In this case, natural monopoly means that the technology is such that production of the quantities demanded by the market is most efficiently accomplished by a single enterprise, rather than splintered among two or more enterprises. This would be the case, for example, if the economies of scale were so great that a single plant could produce the entire market demand more cheaply than several plants due to the replication of fixed facilities. This would also be the case for a network industry, like electric power distribution, where building two parallel sets of distribution facilities would be wasteful.

It is crucial to recognize that the natural monopoly condition, along with the other two conditions, must be assessed "in the relevant market." Relevant markets have the dimensions of both geographic and product markets. The relevant product market contains all the varieties of substitute products that provide significant competition to the product that was originally at issue. The relevant geographic market contains all the areas from which supply of products in the relevant product market could originate in order to compete for business. The relevant geographic market may be international in its scope if trade barriers do not interfere, and if the necessary transport costs do not disable imports from contention.

For example, the relevant geographic market for the generation of electricity bought by the residents of the capital city of country ABC might include a neighboring country if power generated there could serve the target population economically and prices were just some 5 or 10 percent higher than normal. In this example, even though the production of electricity in the environs of the capital of ABC might be a natural monopoly, this is not the relevant market. In addition, if the broader geographic market holds sufficient alternative sources of generated power, then the residents of the capital are served at least somewhat competitively.

As another example, the residents of ABC have access to at most a single supplier of wireline telephone service in their houses, and it would be highly inefficient for a second wireline network to be built. However, as its costs fall, cellular telephone service becomes a substitute for wireline services, and cellular service joins the product market. Thus, the conditions of natural monopoly change and become duopoly as geographic competition among alternative telephone providers becomes heated.

As a final example, distribution of electricity to homes in the capital is a relevant product and geographic market, since nothing is a close substitute for electricity in the home, and since alternatives elsewhere are irrelevant. Similar considerations apply to distribution of water and sewerage services, and all three may well be natural monopolies in their relevant markets.

The second condition of the test for public utility style regulation is high entry barriers into the relevant market. This means that any firm not presently serving the relevant target market with a product would not be induced to immediately start doing so by a 5 or 10 percent rise in the prices currently paid. Firms may be unable to enter the relevant market because of right-of-way issues, or a lack of key inputs or requisite technology. The combination of substantial economies of scale and high sunk costs creates a significant economic barrier to entry, since economies of scale imply that the firm must plan on entering with a production volume set by a significant share of market sales in order to attain a competitive level of unit costs. When this level of production is added to that of the incumbents, market price will likely be driven significantly lower, thereby making the sales unattractive. No suppliers would feel compelled to exit, however, since they would not thereby be saving on sunk costs, which are irreversible by definition. Thus, the consequence of entry in this scenario would be long-lived losses, and a well-managed firm would not enter in response to moderately higher prices.

For example, as a result of economies of scale in technology, a firm considering entry into the local generation of electricity might face the need to build sizable capacity compared to local demand. Since the costs of the generators of the incumbent and the entrant would be largely sunk, the entry would predictably lead to losses, and would not occur in the first place.

By contrast, even though a single trucking firm is efficiently handling all the freight between cities X and Y today, it would induce competitive entry by a rival firm or even by a startup if it were to raise its prices significantly above costs. The entrant could come in with just one truck carrying a few loads, or it could bid on all the business. If it won the bid, it would displace the incumbent, which could then move its trucks elsewhere since trucks do not constitute sunk costs in any one region. Or, if it lost the bid, it too could redeploy its trucks elsewhere. Thus, even if trucking were a natural monopoly in some relevant market, potential competition from possible entrants would provide customers with competitive alternatives, in the absence of high barriers to entry, and thereby make public utility style regulation unnecessary.

The third condition that completes the test for public utility style regulation is that there be sufficient demand for significant monopoly profit in the relevant market. Thus, even when the natural monopoly is protected by high entry barriers, if there is not enough demand in the relevant market to cover the costs of the monopoly supplier and yield a substantial excess, then public utility style regulation may well be superfluous since, if it were there, it would hardly constrain the monopolist anyway. Here, demand is measured both in terms of its level and in terms of how inelastic it is; i.e., how much of it would persist in the face of price rises.

If the three conditions all hold, then it is highly likely that consumers will have no realistic alternative source of supply to protect them from exploitation of market power. Two or more firms would be unlikely to be active in view of the natural monopoly conditions. No new firm is likely to enter due to the entry barriers. And the incumbent monopolist would be able profitably to hold prices well above costs, to the harm of the economy. It is this economic harm that public utility style regulation could prevent, if carried out effectively.

If these three conditions do not all hold, then there is a strong economic case for foreswearing public utility style regulation, and as a matter of policy, relying instead on open market competitive forces. There is no doubt that where competition can work, the market solution to allocation and supply issues is the best vehicle for meeting the public interest. It is critical to recognize, at this phase of the strategic policy analysis, that competition has its own prerequisites for a market-friendly legal, economic and cultural environment.

Prerequisites for Competition

Even when structural market conditions are propitious, competition needs an appropriate framework set by government and the commercial culture in order to work effectively. The framework includes laws that establish rights to tangible and intellectual property and create the ability to undertake transactions at reasonable costs; contract law and contract dispute resolution that facilitate striking up flexible and reliable commercial agreements without undue costs and delays; and laws to credibly protect consumers and employees from torts and fraud, not for the purpose of promoting litigation, but to inspire due care and truthful dealings. And it falls to the government to maintain central banking services and orderly structures for capital markets that foster the efficient provision of currency transactions and credit.

Other prerequisites for the propitious functioning of markets based on private ownership and entrepreneurship involve the business culture and code of conduct, as they are shaped by competition law, enforcement mechanisms, and the social ethics of the business community. It is of critical importance that competing suppliers not conspire against customers by rigging bids, dividing markets, or engaging in boycott tactics. Successful suppliers must be restrained from coercion that forecloses entry or expansion of other suppliers. Access to needed business infrastructure services and facilities must not be foreclosed either through business agreements or informal cultural restraints.

Government itself must show the utmost respect for property and commercial freedom, and must be subject to accessible procedures that can contain and deter arbitrary and discriminatory interventions. The government must exhibit a genuine commitment to limit its actions and powers to those explicitly enabled by law. Also, the government can help create competing alternatives for consumers and sources of inputs for suppliers by encouraging free international trade.

Post-Privatization Competition

Where the appropriate framework and fundamental structural conditions are in place to make post-privatization competition reasonably feasible, it would harm the public interest to privatize a monopoly and then foreclose competition via some form of exclusivity arrangements or legal entry barriers. Experience teaches that bidders for enterprises to be privatized often request forms of legal protection from competition based on oft-heard arguments that such protection can better enable them to support investments advantageous to consumers, and to support much higher bids of great value to the nation's fiscal health. Such bidders will seek terms of protection as long or as short, and as narrow or as broad, as they think will seem attractive to the government agencies involved.

As a matter of economics, all of these varieties of offers are a bad deal for the public. The added fiscal benefit that might be forthcoming to the treasury from privatizing a protected monopoly is not worth the added costs to consumers from having to deal with a monopoly, to say nothing of the subsequent losses to the economy from foregone industry vitality and progressivity. If the bidder and the governmental agency find it mutually advantageous to commission some elements of investment that the bidder would not voluntarily undertake, then linking such an investment agreement to the creation of an artificial monopoly is typically bad policy. The economy would predictably create more total real income, and consumers would be better off on net, if such an investment agreement were linked to a straight cash incentive funded through taxes.

At the other end of the spectrum, it would be another serious policy error to force competition by supporting, for example, overlapping concessions where natural monopoly technological conditions might prevail, along with heavy sunk costs. Here, the economies of scale and scope mean that social resources would be wasted as a result of needless duplication, and the naturally ensuing price war would predictably undermine the ability of the competitors to sustain their services.

On the other hand, it might be a socially beneficial policy to seed competition—to deliberately bring a newcomer into a proximate market from which it could more readily enter the market that would otherwise be monopolized. Here, the social benefit from the enhanced potential competition need not be offset by inefficient duplication, since the newcomer need not be any less efficient than the incumbent in serving the proximate market.

Any policy planning for privatization must include consideration of procompetitive restructuring. The enterprise as it was defined under state ownership might not have been set up for efficiency in operations, transactions or management. The enterprise might become more efficient if treated with karate economics—a series of judicious horizontal and vertical karate chops that create a more competitive industry structure. Horizontal chops create separate independent entities that own assets and facilities that can produce supplies in competition with each other. Where horizontal chops avoid the loss of scale economies and other possible efficiencies of the organization, they per force create more independent alternative sources of supply that increase competition.

Vertical chops separate portions of the enterprise that deal with one another as suppliers of goods or services for productive activities. In mature markets, there is generally little reason to restructure along vertical lines. However, where markets are less well developed, vertical separations can create independent sources of supply of critical business inputs that might otherwise be unavailable to entrepreneurs and new entrants. As such, where they do not interfere with economies of scope and with important transactional efficiencies, and where they have the effect of creating new market interfaces, vertical chops can play a valuable role in fostering competition in immature market economies.

Most important for the infrastructure sectors is adoption of a policy of actively enabling competition. This entails dropping all legal barriers to entry, aggressively pushing to open bottlenecks with standardized interconnection protocols, and insisting on procompetitive fair access prices. As a result, competition for the stages of service that make use of the bottlenecks may arise, be robust, and bring serious social benefits from service innovation and cost savings. This competition may lead to entry into competitive provision of the bottleneck services themselves, since success in the adjacent markets can serve as a springboard to overcome the economic entry barriers into the bottleneck stages of production.

Public utility style regulation is unnecessary and probably counterproductive if the relevant market is not a natural monopoly; if it is a contestable market unprotected by legal or economic entry barriers; if a monopoly could only cover its ordinary costs of doing business; if procompetitive restructuring or seeding competition is expected to eliminate market power; or if opening up the bottlenecks is expected to lead to effective full-service competition. Such regulation is costly to operate, and more important, it inevitably causes its own distortions and impediments to the efficient workings of competitive markets. Thus, reasonably effective active or potential competition should be left free of public utility style regulation. Fundamental post-privatization governance is needed to sustain the market-friendly environment and extract a credible commitment from the government to desist from unnecessary, arbitrary, discriminatory or overly stiff regulation. While these issues are far from trivial, and complete success may seem daunting, the challenges are small compared to those posed by post-privatization governance where public utility style regulation is needed.

Tasks, Organization and Culture of Successful Regulation

In the context of a traditional infrastructure industry, privatized enterprise may very well be expected to have characteristics that impart strong monopoly power—natural monopoly market conditions, high economic entry barriers, and large profit potential from ample and inelastic demand. Under these circumstances, public utility style regulation is likely to be needed to perform a full range of challenging tasks so that the economy can reap all the benefits from privatization.

The economic tasks of public utility regulation are many, complex and fraught with internal tensions. For example, while the principal task may be to restrain monopoly power by keeping prices down and quality up, equally important is to respect investor value in order to maintain incentives for supply, entrepreneurship, efficiency and new investment for growth. Yet more subtle is the goal of meeting consumer needs flexibly through the balance, structure and responsiveness of rates. Regulation must accept responsibility for fostering competition in markets adjacent to the natural monopoly by encouraging unbundling, developing interfaces, and appropriately overseeing access prices. All of these tasks become intertwined not only with one another, but also with the challenges of allocating public resources and meeting allied social goals in ways that avoid distortions and embrace competitive neutrality.

A closely related but fundamentally different task of infrastructure planning that corresponds to a broad partnership—including experts of the regulatory body, the political side of the government, and the involved suppliers, competitors and customers—is for the politicized arms of the government to participate in long-range planning for regulated infrastructure sectors, set long-term goals, establish nonmarket goals and determine sources of funding for achieving them, and consider sectoral investment goals and participate in decisions matching up enterprise market participants with projects partially financed with public funds.

In contrast, the distinct functions of public utility style regulation must be performed with organizational and financial independence from the politicized arms of the government, and the decisionmaking processes of regulation must be insulated from political pressures by means of the culture of the administrative bodies. Public utility style regulation should play the role of substituting its influence for the missing disciplinary forces of competition—missing due to conditions of natural monopoly and high entry barriers. The forces of competition generally are ruthlessly effective in driving markets to efficiency in ways that soon enough show their benefits to consumers and to the economy as a whole, despite temporary discomfort. It is these forces that privatization is intended to unleash, and which can only survive under regulation if the regulatory functions are carried out with independence and insulation from political influence.

The regulatory body itself must foreswear any political style of discretionary decisionmaking. Otherwise, it will create regulatory risks for the owners of capital, and its discretionary power will increase costs for commercial enterprises. Thus, regulation must have a culture that renders decisionmaking as transparent as possible, for the sake of predictability as well as responsibility.

There is a valid role for the regulatory body to listen to the voices of industry suppliers, both to collect information and to hear concerns. However, conflicts among competing suppliers are inevitable and healthy, and it is important for the regulatory body to resist the institutional temptation to act as a source of compromise or a platform for negotiations among competitors. The regulatory body must avoid becoming a venue for chilling competition among actual and potential rivals, because in general the outcomes of such negotiations and deal-making are not consistent with the interests of the public, but rather with the interests of an industry cartel that inappropriate regulation may unintentionally foster.

In contrast, the public interest is likely to be well served by the outcomes of informed negotiations between suppliers and consumers. It is a valid and constructive function of a regulatory body to facilitate such deal-making, and it may be useful for an office of consumer representation to be formed to participate in regulatory processes on behalf of the diffuse interests of small consumers. This style of negotiation is unbalanced where there is natural monopoly, but it can become appropriately balanced when negotiations are conducted as reactions to or in parallel with regulation as a source of fall-back positions that would control the exercise of market power.

Commitment vs. Flexibility in Regulatory Architecture

Regulation can proceed by means of deliberately constructed mechanisms that control the exercise of market power and, at the same time, provide enterprises with efficient incentives while allowing market incentives to operate. While no such mechanisms are perfectly free of distortion and costly disputes, they are the best solutions to known regulatory problems. The artful and experienced regulator will choose from such instruments as contracts, privatization agreements, concessions, inflation-indexed price caps, stand-alone cost ceilings, quality floors, performance carrots and sticks, open entry, unbundled-bottleneck interfaces, and the efficient component pricing rule for access to regulated bottlenecks.

Thus, the structure of public utility style regulatory organizations must navigate between two contrasting goals and twin dangers. Well-functioning regulation must be creative and responsive to the nature of the market power that makes it necessary, ready to adapt to shifts in demand and supply, and alert to new opportunities to harness the workings of competition in the directly regulated or adjacent markets. These goals all argue for discretion placed in the hands of skilled and well-intentioned regulatory bodies. Yet, that same discretion may be seen as a mortal threat by the owners of sunk assets under regulatory control, whose value can be destroyed by excessively aggressive regulation that, in essence, forbids revenues beyond those that recover variable costs. The mere fear that otherwise socially valuable regulatory discretion can expropriate asset value can have predictable, rational and unfortunately destructive consequences for the incentives to invest privately in the market.

The most direct solution to the problem of actual or perceived regulatory risk is for the privatization or concession agreement to stipulate the regulations and associated penalties and rewards in great detail. Unfortunately, it is clear that this solution itself generates new risks to the public interest; that is, the inflexibility and inability to deal with new problems as they inevitably arise.

While the strength of the commitment value of the privatization agreement is in rigid adherence to systems of narrowly detailed micromanagement stipulations, this approach will make it difficult and costly to adapt regulation to changing needs and circumstances, or to benefit from the experiences of other regulated sectors. Thus, there is a need to find a different solution that reconciles the seemingly inconsistent challenges of regulatory discretion and predictability.

A Transparent, Flexible and Rational Regulatory Process

This section advances a hypothesis for limiting government's discretionary powers over privatized enterprises in a socially desirable way. In essence, the hypothesis is that the body that performs the regulatory function should be committed to reaching decisions and resolving disputes through the transparent application of economic principles that are publicly articulated before the initial commercial investment is made by the private operator. These principles may be articulated within a concession or privatization agreement, so that they become part of the contract between the enterprise and the government, or they might be contained within an overarching statute, if feasible and credibly stable.

According to this hypothesis, these economic principles should be the continuing guidepost for ongoing post-privatization governance. On the one hand, this solution would provide appropriate limits on the discretionary exercise of regulatory power. On the other, it would avoid the paralysis and rigidities that attend post-privatization governance that adheres to detailed micromanaging terms of a privatization agreement or concession. The controlling economic principles would set the framework under which negotiations and arbitration could yield dynamic adaptations to ever-changing circumstances and resolve disputes.

While there is no uniquely correct articulation of economic principles that might be included in a statute or a concession agreement, the principles must cover issues ranging from the primacy of the financial returns expected from the privatization agreement, to the processes by which tariffs are set and coordinated with quality and reliable services, and to the efficient adaptations that impending competition may warrant.

Guiding Principles for Public Utility Regulation

The following are some of the guiding regulatory principles that would generate efficient solutions to a wide range of disputes and issues that might arise in a regulated infrastructure sector:

- Preserve promised investor value;
- Allow competition to function where it can without distortion;
- Weigh the costs of rules against the benefits;
- Assure service quality and price levels that offer consumers no less than the competitive standard of comparison;
- Assure that prices provide signals and incentives for efficient actions by consumers, suppliers of complementary and substitute services, suppliers of inputs, and investors;
- Allow open access to bottlenecks on terms that reflect competitive parity;
- Pay efficient and competitively neutral attention to social goals pertinent to the sector.

Preserve Promised Investor Value

This principle must be a priority because without it, investors will not permit their liquid capital to become sunk assets vulnerable to effective expropriation through regulation. As discussed in the opening sections of this chapter, regulators of natural monopoly services delivered by sunk assets are inevitably tempted by the possibility of forcing prices down to variable costs. At this level, further production is still motivated, since its forward-looking incremental costs are to be recovered, at least in the short run. Consumers receive optimum benefit in the short run, since these are the lowest prices consistent with continuing production. Of course, this is a myopic policy for the regulator, inasmuch as investors, even if fooled once, will be less likely to be fooled again. They will not voluntarily finance other investments under this sort of regulation, including renewal of the assets that will eventually be necessary for the sector at issue. Nevertheless, private sources of capital are apt to be justifiably concerned that regulators will succumb to the expropriation temptation, and thus will either balk entirely or require an outsized risk premium on any investment unprotected by a credible commitment to the principle of preserving promised investor value.

This principle is susceptible to many different interpretations, with correspondingly different implications for regulation, incentives and economic efficiency. For example, the principle might be inadvertently interpreted to mean that the regulator should shield the investor from market-driven risks of loss of investment value. This is not the intention, since removal of investor risk would inefficiently dull incentives to choose investment projects effectively and employ assets productively.

Instead, the efficient interpretation is that the regulator desist from unilaterally imposing changes in policy or other regulatory directives that would diminish investor value (recognizing that that value is properly and inevitably subject to a wide variety of uninsured risks). The baseline for the mandated preservation of value is the original privatization "deal," or the most recently renegotiated evolution of the deal. Regulator and investor are certainly empowered to negotiate further alterations in the deal. It is an open policy question whether the regulator should be permitted, under the principle, to unilaterally impose alterations in policy that can be shown to preserve investor value, or whether, instead, investor concurrence should always be required.

Allow Competition to Function Without Distortion

This principle mandates that the regulator desist from intervening in activities of the regulated firm that relate to competitive markets, or at least to markets that fail to be identified as protected natural monopolies. The principle thus requires that direct regulatory interference be confined to monopoly markets. It also can be interpreted more aggressively to require that the regulator take steps to enable competition to take place without distortion by requiring, for example, open access at compensatory prices to bottleneck assets and positions.

Weigh Costs of Rules against Benefits

This principle constrains the regulator from expanding its domain of intervention without showing that the benefits would outweigh the costs. As such, it expands upon the admonition to leave competitive markets free of regulation by further requiring that even restraints on monopolists be justified by demonstrating significant benefits to consumers.

Assure Competitive Service Quality and Price Levels

This establishes the entitlement of consumers to combinations of prices and levels of service quality consistent with the competitive standard. Under this principle, the regulator cannot sustain a privatization deal with an infrastructure monopolist that results in prices higher than financially necessary to support the level of service quality. Applied carefully, this principle would allow consumers to challenge arrangements that charged them more in return for flows of cash to the treasury, or in return for investment projects that do not benefit the consumers. The principle is inconsistent with cross-subsidization, and it invites the use of stand-alone cost estimations as ceilings on rates charged for monopoly services. It also invites the use of price cap mechanisms to control the levels of regulated monopoly prices over time, on the theory that average competitive prices would not rise faster than inflation adjusted for productivity gains. And it directly links the regulation of prices and the quality of service, so that one cannot be constrained without consideration of the other. Thus, the principle establishes the right of consumers to seek rate reductions if the quality of service provided falls significantly short of that promised.

Assure that Prices Provide Signals and Incentives for Efficiency by Consumers, Suppliers and Investors

This principle establishes the general connection between the structure of regulated prices and the economic efficiency of the behavior of all parties who might be influenced by those prices. Most directly, it is the gateway for applying the basic idea that prices should be related to economic costs—both marginal and incremental costs over the pertinent time frame on a forward-looking basis. It also is the vehicle for applying the framework of Ramsey pricing, which maximizes consumer benefits subject to the stipulation that prices yield sufficient revenues to cover total costs. Such optimal Ramsey prices are responsive to the relative values of service on the part of consumers, as well as to marginal costs. The expressed idea that prices should encourage efficient reactions by suppliers suggests, for example, that prices should not fall below incremental costs and thereby discourage the supply of efficient substitutes; that prices should not rise above stand-alone costs and thereby artificially encourage the supply of inefficient alternatives; and that prices should not be held down below costs and thereby discourage supply by input providers and even by the regulated monopolist itself.

Allow Access to Bottlenecks on Terms that Reflect Competitive Parity

This principle aggressively asserts that infrastructure monopolists should be impelled by regulation to give open access to their bottleneck facilities to rivals. It directs that prices charged for such access reflect competitive parity, i.e., the access prices should carry the same markups as do the competing end-user services sold by the holder of the bottleneck. Under this principle, then, the incumbent and its rivals can compete on a level playing field for end-users' business with services that make use of the bottleneck. Predictably, the firm with the more efficient offerings will prevail in the market. Meanwhile, the terms of competitive parity for access mean that the bottleneck holder is not denied its net revenues from the use of the bottleneck by its rivals, so that investment in facilities is not discouraged, even for facilities that might become bottlenecks themselves and fall under the sway of this regulatory principle. The principle leaves open whether regulators would require bottleneck holders to proactively establish organized access offerings at tariffed rates, or whether, instead, the principle would be used more sparingly to resolve disputes that may arise from flexible negotiations over access issues.

Pay Efficient and Neutral Attention to the Sector's Social Goals

This principle holds that where social goals are to be attended to by firms in the regulated sector, those goals should be pursued efficiently and without distorting competition. Thus, if revenues are to be collected to support social goals, the surcharges or taxes should affect the prices charged by competing suppliers equally, so as to leave the relationship between the competitors' prices undistorted. If subsidies are to be conferred on particular services earmarked for particular consumers, then the subsidy payments should be offered to any supplier who is able to commit to performing the requisite services. These elements of competitive neutrality are designed to permit achievement of social goals without standing in the way of the forces of competition to select and reward efficiency. Moreover, the subsidies should be granted in as targeted a fashion as is possible, consistent with their goal, to avoid distorting decisions made by those outside of the intended ambit of the program, and to hold down the size of the subsidy only to what is necessary.

Conclusions

This chapter has proposed a specific approach for how a government can foster effective infrastructure privatization by committing itself credibly to post-privatization governance that serves the public interest. The approach entails commitment to transparent economic principles that serve as a basis to resolve disputes and solve problems that arise from needed regulation of privatized monopoly suppliers of infrastructure services. These principles are sufficiently flexible, wide-ranging and adaptable to cover most circumstances, yet sufficiently concrete to yield definitive conclusions where necessary.

Many open questions remain. Would the economic principles be credible and effective if they were written into privatization or concession agreements, or even into special legislation? It could be that the existing legal framework would undermine application of the principles, or that the disputes could not be kept out of courts that would not be bound to follow them. This chapter has not attempted to assess the extent to which adherence to the principles would have improved actual outcomes of post-privatization regulatory problems that arose in Latin America and the Caribbean. Nevertheless, the ideas and open questions are offered here with considerable promise, because it appears that this transparently principled approach to post-privatization governance has the potential to make privatization better fulfill its promise for the region.

PART II

Infrastructure for Latin America: Experiences in Water and Sewerage and Energy

CHAPTER 9

Water and Sewerage Privatization and Reform

Sylvia Wenyon and Charles Jenne

Private sector participation in water and sewerage systems is a relatively recent phenomenon in Latin America. The movement towards privatization started in the early 1990s, but some of the programs were introduced as recently as 1995. Although there are some lessons to be learned about the different contracting approaches, institutional frameworks and the competitiveness of the contracting process, there is less experience to draw on in relation to how contracts have worked in practice in terms of service performance and achievement. This chapter looks at nine cases of private sector participation involving several countries and different contractual forms. The countries are Colombia, Argentina, Trinidad and Tobago, Mexico and Venezuela, and the contract approaches range from service contracts to management contracts, BOTs and concessions.

The approach chosen is not uniform for each case (see Table 9.1). Mexico, for example, has chosen service and management contracts in the Federal District and BOTs in several municipalities. Colombia has chosen a mixed company-based management contract in Cartagena but a management/concession contract in Tunja. Argentina is one of the few countries that adopted a uniform approach by developing concession contracts in all the provinces involved.

The diversity of approaches within countries, together with the different circumstances surrounding each specific case, means that it is only possible to explain why some countries have performed better than others in relation to a few specific parameters. This chapter therefore concentrates on drawing strengths and weaknesses from each specific case in order to glean the lessons that could be applied generally to several types of contract.

Table 9.1. Case Studies

	Type of contract	Starting operations
Argentina		
Buenos Aires	30-year concession	1993
Santa Fe	30-year concession	1995
Tucuman	30-year concession	1995
Colombia		
Cartagena	30-year management contract mixed company	1995
Tunja	30-year management concession contract	1996
Mexico		
Mexico, DF	10-year service/management contract	1994
Puerto Vallarta	BOT	1994
Trinidad and Tobago	3 to 5 year management contract to end in concession	1995
Venezuela	25-year concession	No

Approach

Assessing the case studies has involved examining the actual approaches adopted and the circumstances that form their context, and applying the economic and organizational principles that pertain to the water sector in order to interpret the evidence. The overall objective has been to develop a systematic understanding of events grounded both in theory and experience.

A key theme running through the chapter is the need for effective limitation and proper allocation of risk. Risk management is particularly important where the aim is to involve the private sector in water service provision. All the evidence suggests that there are certain risks the private sector will not accept at any price. Unless uncontrolled risk can be eliminated or significantly reduced—through good regulatory design and thorough preparatory studies, or by allocating risk to the public sector through contract terms—private sector participation in the water sector may achieve disappointing results. On the other hand, if appropriate controlled risk is allocated to the private sector, this can create powerful incentives for improving performance.

In carrying out the study, particular attention has been given to risks that arise in each case and to the effectiveness of the chosen reforms in allocating or mitigating these risks.

Industry Structure and Regulation

The water industry has several important characteristics that differentiate it from other utilities. It has a particularly important impact on health and the environment and also a vital social dimension, both because it is essential to life and because it is considered a good to which everybody has a right. At the same time, the economies of scale involved in the transmission and distribution network, and the difficulties involved in sharing networks, mean that water provision is a local natural monopoly.

The *natural monopoly characteristics* of the water sector mean that for reasons of economic efficiency, only one entity should provide the main service in any geographical area. If the entity is privately owned,[1] adequate economic regulation is needed to prevent it from charging consumers excessive prices and delivering low quality outputs.[2] When reforms introduced affect the structure of the industry, the geographical scope of service provision should not be reduced by, for example, subdividing existing service areas into small units where economies of scale cannot be realized.

Because the role of economic regulation is to reduce the pressures for cost efficiency and customer service that would exist if the water sector was an economic activity subject to normal market forces, a central function of such regulation is to ensure that resulting benefits flow through to service users. Another key role of economic regulation, also linked to its basic function of simulating market pressures, is to ensure that efficient enterprises supplying services for which there is a genuine market demand are allowed to charge tariffs that maintain their financial viability.

Health and environmental externalities in water service provision mean that there is also a need for environmental and drinking water quality regulation.

Environmental regulation must ensure that water resource pollution is controlled through wastewater discharge licenses, abstraction licenses, and minimum quality standards for such discharges. Drinking water quality regulation is necessary to ensure that the health of the population is protected through appropriate water quality standards. Separate regulatory authorities

---

[1]In this context, it is the beneficial ownership by the private sector of all or a significant part of the profits from water service provision that creates the need for effective economic regulation. Ownership of the assets of the business is unimportant in this respect.

[2]Competition should be encouraged when it is efficient, such as for potable water and wastewater treatment, where minimum efficient plant size is lower and the service may be awarded to several firms within large enough towns or cities, or where the population of the city is so large that economies of scale in the provision of the whole service are realized even when dividing the city into several sections.

for each are desirable to ensure that there is full accountability for issuing licenses and for setting and enforcing standards.[3]

The environmental externalities of water service provision also mean that when restructuring the industry, consideration should be given to the possible economic advantages of establishing service boundaries that embrace whole river basins. Provision covering the entire river basin has the advantage of making it possible for the company concerned to internalize possible pollution externalities from wastewater discharges and also to realize the benefits of better wastewater treatment.[4]

The health and environmental dimensions of water are closely interrelated with its *social dimension.* The fact that water services have positive effects on health means that extending the service to all groups, including the poor, is an important public policy goal. Potable water has a positive sanitary effect, thereby reducing disease. Connection to sewerage service is fundamental to reducing disease and mortality due to water contamination from untreated sewage disposal, which pollutes water courses and aquifers.

Expending the effort and resources to establish appropriate water and sewerage services is therefore an effective form of investment in health. Policies that provide incentives to reduce water operators' costs, together with an approach to economic regulation that ensures that a significant proportion of efficiency savings is passed on to customers in the form of lower tariffs, are particularly important in ensuring access to service for low-income groups. When user-cost reductions achieved by these means are not enough in themselves, direct payments[5] or other forms of subsidy to low-income groups may be necessary to ensure that those otherwise unable to pay can gain access to services.

---

[3]However, mechanisms have to be in place to ensure communication between the environmental and water quality regulator and the economic regulator regarding the costs of enforcing higher environmental standards.

[4]The importance of covering whole river basins was recognized in England and Wales, prior to privatization. In 1973, multiple local companies were integrated into single units covering a whole river basin. These companies were subsequently privatized in 1989, preserving the same structure. A similar approach to environmental regulation is used in France, but water service provision is not structured along the same lines.

[5]The externalities arising from provision of water services mean that customers will buy less than optimally if services are priced at economic cost. This is the economic rationale for subsidizing lower-income groups.

Conditions for Successful Private Provision

Successful introduction of private sector participation in the water sector is only likely if the following conditions have been established:

- Reforms affecting the structure of the industry that take into account the possible loss of economies of scale when splitting the area of provision into small units;
- Where practicable, service provision covering whole river basins, because of the potential it gives companies to internalize environmental externalities;
- Adequate and effective economic regulation to ensure that private operators are appropriately rewarded and that there are incentives for the private operator to reduce costs, together with mechanisms to ensure that some of the benefits of efficiency improvement are passed on to customers;
- Adequate and enforceable drinking water and environmental regulation to ensure that drinking water quality standards are enforced, that contamination of water sources is prevented, and that water resources are managed efficiently;[6]
- Necessary provision of direct payments to low-income groups to ensure they can gain access to services.

Case Studies: Industry Structure and Responsibility for Water Provision

Table 9.2 presents a summary of the strengths and weaknesses of the industry structure and institutional arrangements adopted in each of the cases studied.

In Colombia and Mexico, as in many Latin American countries, recent constitutional reforms have granted powers to municipalities to provide water and sewerage services. While this ensures greater local accountability for the services, there are also several potential disadvantages. These include fragmentation of the industry beyond what is justifiable for economic and geographical reasons, and the establishment of inefficient structures, unless municipalities are amalgamated. Although this reform permits the presence of companies with large-scale operations in the bigger cities, there are many municipalities where companies are restricted to an inefficiently small size.

---

[6]And avoiding excessively demanding environmental standards by establishing mechanisms that take account of the cost involved in setting and enforcing them.

Table 9.2. Industry Structure

	Size (too many small units: uneconomic=★)	Municipality/ province in charge of service (political priorities=★)	Municipality as regulator and regulated (conflict of interest)	Municipality as provider of investment finance (potentially=★)
Argentina				
Buenos Aires	✓✓	✓		
Santa Fe	✓✓	★		
Tucuman	✓	★★		
Colombia				
Cartagena	✓	★	★★	★★
Tunja	★✓	★		★★
Mexico				
Mexico, DF	✓	★		★
Puerto Vallarta	✓	★		★
Trinidad and Tobago	✓			

Key: ✓ = Positive
★ = Weakness
★✓ = Good in theory but not in practice

The problem of municipal responsibility has not in itself negatively affected Mexico City in terms of the size of the operation, given the city's population (eight million people). The division of the city into four zones, each allocated to a separate company for eventual management, may, however, involve the loss of some potential economies that could have been obtained from the operation of an integrated network. This said, the arrangement has the potential advantage of introducing scope for some form of comparative competition in the future. It is not possible at this stage to reach a conclusion on which way the balance of advantage lies.

A second problem arising from municipal responsibility for water services is the strong political element it introduces, which may impede development of long-term contracts with the private sector. More specifically, municipalities may insist on reducing tariffs for political reasons without adequate regard for the need for cost recovery. The resulting higher risk for the private sector provider and its financiers means that forms of contract with intrinsically greater potential for improving efficiency (such as long-term operational, maintenance and investment contracts) are less attractive to them. Private sector participation is therefore restricted to arrangements that are more limited in scope, such as service and management contracts rather than long-term concessions or even BOT contracts.

Political interference by municipal and, to a lesser degree, provincial governments that disallow necessary tariff increases has been a major problem in Tucuman, Argentina, and to a lesser extent in Puerto Vallarta, Mexico. In both cases, an incoming government resisted tariff increases. This led to financial difficulties for the municipality in the case of Puerto Vallarta, and rescission of the concession contract by General des Eaux in the case of Tucuman. There are signs that this issue is also likely to become problematic in Mexico City, where the recently elected mayor has previously campaigned for low water tariffs.

One possible solution to the problem of political interference by municipalities and, in particular, their tendency to press for lower tariffs regardless of cost recovery, is to ensure equity participation by the municipality, thereby aligning interests more closely with those of the private sector participant. This has been the path chosen in Cartagena, Colombia. This type of arrangement has the important disadvantage, however, of making the municipality both a regulator and a participant in the regulated entity, with potentially serious conflicts of interest resulting.

A third issue arising from municipal responsibility is that municipalities are themselves often in financial difficulties and may therefore be unable to maintain their contract commitments. This is a problem in contracts where payment comes directly from the municipalities (service contracts, some management contracts, and BOTs), as well as in management-concession contracts such as those adopted in Cartagena and Tunja in Colombia, where the success of the contract depends on the municipality being able to finance the investment necessary to achieve expansion plans.

Financial difficulties of this kind have arisen in Mexico City and Puerto Vallarta. However, since municipal revenues necessary for payment have come from payments by customers, the problem here has had more to do with inability to raise tariffs than with the overall financial position of the municipality. Poor financial management of municipal revenues has been reported to be serious enough to potentially put at risk the success of expansion plans in Cartagena and Tunja.

Environmental Regulation

Environmental regulation is an area to which reforms undertaken to date in the region have given less emphasis. Most countries are just beginning to allocate responsibilities for environmental aspects of water to specific institutions and to define and enforce wastewater quality discharge standards. In Argentina, for example, where great efforts have been made to set up adequate economic regulation, there are no abstraction charges payable when drawing water from the River Plate, nor are there any discharge charges payable by the private operator.

Economic Regulation

All forms of private sector participation require some form of economic regulation in order to protect the interests of customers. Economic regulation may be carried out either by establishing a regulatory body with specific responsibility for this activity or through the specific terms of the contract itself. The advantages and disadvantages of each approach are summarized in Boxes 9.1 and 9.2.

In practice, the choice depends to a significant extent on the degree of uncertainty attached to the private sector operation over its lifetime and to the nature of the customer base that the regulation is designed to protect. The greater the degree of uncertainty over the future evolution of the private sector service targets, investment needs and operating environment, the greater the need to create a regulatory regime to adapt to changes that cannot adequately be anticipated at the outset. In addition, the more dispersed the customer base that private sector participation serves, the greater the need for a regulatory institution to act on the customers' behalf in monitoring the operation and charging of the private firm. These points are illustrated by the contrast in circumstances between a concession and a conventional BOT project, as characterized in Figure 9.1.

A concession typically involves the provision and expansion of service across a system-wide network with a large customer base. New investment will usually be an ongoing requirement that cannot be predicted with full certainty in advance. Concessions often involve the transfer (or lease) of existing assets, the condition and performance of which cannot be guaranteed, giving rise to another source of uncertainty over replacement investment needs and service levels. Under these circumstances, it would be difficult to write a contract that would anticipate all of the contingencies that might arise. It would be more appropriate to create a regulatory authority that could respond to new circumstances as they come up, and do so with a clearly articulated set of principles as to how, after an initial period, price adjustments should be related to service levels and investment needs.

Box 9.1. Regulation by a Specific Regulatory Body

Advantages:
• Flexibility of the approach, which, using prespecified principles, allows tariff controls and standards of service regulation to be modified in light of changing circumstances unforeseen when the private sector contract was put in place. In principle, this flexibility should operate to the benefit of both the operator and service users.
• Regulation can be undertaken by an expert body with full understanding of water sector economics and operations.
• Regulation is clearly separated from responsibilities for service provision, avoiding conflict of interest and making the regulator clearly accountable for its actions.

Disadvantages:
• In order for the arrangement to be effective, the contract must leave scope for the exercise of discretion by the regulatory body. Where there is not a strong tradition of effective independent regulation, this may be perceived as a source of regulatory risk by potential bidders and lead to a reduction of interest in the scheme.
• It may be more costly to establish and administer than is regulation by contract.

A BOT, by contrast, usually relates to a single new investment with limited uncertainty over the service obligation over the contract life (and, such uncertainty as there is can be handled by contract variations within a well-understood framework). Moreover, the BOT service is typically provided to a single customer (e.g., a municipality or industrial customer) or a small group of customers capable of negotiating with the service provider directly without the need for a separate regulator to act on their behalf. Accordingly, BOT schemes are usually regulated via the contract itself, with specific pricing formulas designed to survive throughout the contract life.

The attraction of private sector capital to meet investment needs is a feature of both concessions and BOTs. This is not so for service contracts and management contracts, where no capital from the private sector is involved and where the risks to the private sector participant and the users (from the

Box 9.2. Regulation by Contract

Advantages:

- It should, in principle, provide a clear framework for tariffs and standards of service regulation, thus minimizing uncertainty for operators.
- Relies on existing contract law and the courts for enforcement and does not require institutional change.

Disadvantages:

- Relatively rigid, requiring contract renegotiation if unforeseen circumstances or requirements arise.
- Although there can be provision to appoint an expert to assist in dispute resolution, the ultimate recourse is to the courts under contract law. These courts may be ill-equipped to deal with technical and economic matters.
- Considerable effort is required in initial contract design to ensure that the regulatory requirements are fully and correctly stipulated.

exercise of monopoly power by the provider) are lower. This makes the need for a separate independent regulator less pressing.

Economic regulation and the cases studies. Among the countries studied, separate regulators have been established in Argentina and Colombia, which have followed the concession route to private sector participation. Trinidad and Tobago has followed a phased approach, whereby regulation is being developed at the same time that contractual arrangements evolve from a basic service contract to a more complex concession. With the exception of Venezuela, whose case is discussed below, the other cases involve BOTs or management contracts with less pressure for independent regulation. In these cases, regulation is incorporated within the contract and administered by the municipality as the client.

In theory, creation of separate regulatory institutions should involve a degree of independence from political interference so as to increase transparency and lend some stability and predictability to the regulatory regime. In practice, it is hard to achieve complete independence. The regulators in all of the Argentine and Colombian cases have some degree of political dependency, since members of their board are either representatives of the central or local government or nominated by politicians.

Figure 9.1. Private Sector Participation and Regulation

	Concession	BOT
Assets		100%
■ % new vs. old ■ % scope	Systemwide	Single plant
Financing	← Corporate finance	Project finance →
Customer base	Diverse - Direct to final user	Off-take contract
Price control	← General principles	Fixed price formula →
Regulatory arrangements	Regulatory authority	Dispute resolution

In the Argentine cases, results have been mixed. This political relationship does not appear to have impeded the functioning of the Buenos Aires concession to date. There seems to be more of a risk of the regulator not being fully independent from the provincial government in the Santa Fe case. And in Tucuman, the combination of inadequate contractual arrangements and political intervention in regulation has led to a breakdown and rescission of the concession.

Colombia is still developing its national water regulatory agency, and a good part of the regulatory function is currently undertaken by the municipality through the contract. The Regulatory Water Commission is financially dependent on the government budget, and the responsible ministry has representatives on the commission's board, making regulation vulnerable to fiscal constraints and changes of government. Furthermore, the devolution of responsibility for water services to the municipalities means that they also have a regulatory role, which is not always clearly differentiated from that of the commission.

The establishment and administration of an effective economic regulatory system is a difficult and costly process. Even after such a system is established, it is unlikely to be effective unless the staff are adequately (and continuously) trained and supported for a period of several years. Remuneration has to be adequate to attract the right caliber of people, and directors must have the credibility to enforce their decisions. Although Argentina—and particularly Buenos Aires—has gone furthest in setting up an appropriate system of economic regulation, even here the lack of adequately trained staff has been a practical impediment to effective regulation.

Approach to price review. Although it has proved to be a successful concession in terms of delivery, the Buenos Aires case draws attention to a specific dilemma over the choice of approach to monitor investment and the use of price reviews during the life of the concession.

Monitoring investment activities in Argentina involves not only assessing whether the concessionaire is meeting its targets and levels of service, but also establishing whether actual expenditure is consistent with the expenditure plans that were offered in the original bid. There is, therefore, a presumption that all expenditure that was initially proposed must actually be spent. It is increasingly recognized that a better way of regulating a company is to concentrate on outputs (and targets) and to allow the company the freedom to find the lowest cost means of delivering them.

Monitoring investment spending is closely linked to the issue of price reviews. The Buenos Aires concession was bid for on the basis of the price at which the concessionaire would provide the level of services specified in the bidding documentation. The concession was based on the premise that this price level would remain in force unless changes in the contractually committed investment plans became required. In theory, apart from the provision for adjustment in response to defined categories of extraordinary events (such as changes in quality standards or devaluation), the price level should be capable of surviving for the full concession life. If circumstances do change, as is almost certain over this length of time, the concessionaire can call for periodic revisions at the start of a new investment plan period to reflect changes in the targets and capital investment envisaged from those foreseen in the original expansion plans. Critically, however, the concession does not set out any real guidance as to how such revisions should be made. Thus, although the short- to medium-term price levels have been well defined, there are uncertainties about the mechanisms for setting price levels in the longer term.

This contrasts with the typical process of periodic price review undertaken in the United Kingdom or Chile, where prices are revised at specified intervals within a reasonably well-understood framework. The revisions take into account the revenue requirements of the company, the need to finance new investment, and the likely increases in efficiency. Of course, the Buenos Aires concession could evolve in this direction, but the uncertainty in the concession framework leads to potential risks for both the private sector concessionaire (which faces risks to future revenue streams) and for customers (on whose behalf any price adjustment must be negotiated with the concessionaire).

The potential advantages of avoiding pre-scheduled price reviews, as in the Buenos Aires concession, are, first, a lower regulatory burden, if the need for a price review is not triggered by changes in circumstances that affect investment levels and priorities; and second, if substantial scope for efficiency and service improvements is visible in relation to pre-concession levels, a significant share of these gains can be captured for customers through effective competition for the concession. The failure to capture ongoing efficiency gains may be less important by comparison with this initial step change.

On the other hand, there are potential drawbacks of not providing a well-defined framework for periodic review of prices. First, it may restrict the potential number of bidders, with the risk that the initial competition for the concession will not be as effective. (That is, not all companies will take the type of risk that this uncertainty over future revenue setting mechanism implies, or will discount it heavily.) Second, it is more difficult to pass ongoing efficiency gains over the life of the concession to consumers (and these could be significant over a 30-year period). Finally, the regulator is in a weaker position to negotiate variations to investment commitments. (The concessionaire can drive a hard bargain if it is not obliged to deviate from the investment plan in its original bid.)

The circumstances under which advantages of not having well defined price reviews might outweigh the drawbacks are only likely to arise when there is good knowledge of the state of the existing system and customer base that the concessionaire will inherit, which will strongly influence future costs and revenues; a reasonable degree of certainty over the future investment plan and service obligations; scope for substantial improvements in service levels and for price reductions from current levels (so that there is less risk of political intervention at a later date that would threaten the concessionaire's financial viability); and difficulty in establishing regulatory institutions with sufficient autonomy and competence.

It is not surprising, perhaps, that in Buenos Aires the difficulties associated with the tariff objectives set out in the regulatory framework have resulted in the need to commission a consultancy study for the reform of the tariff regime.

Appropriateness of the Basic Approach to Private Sector Participation

This section reviews the basic purposes for which different types of private sector participation schemes would normally be employed, and summarizes conclusions concerning the suitability of the approaches actually chosen in the case studies to the prevailing circumstances and requirements.

Figure 9.2. Main Types of Private Sector Participation Schemes

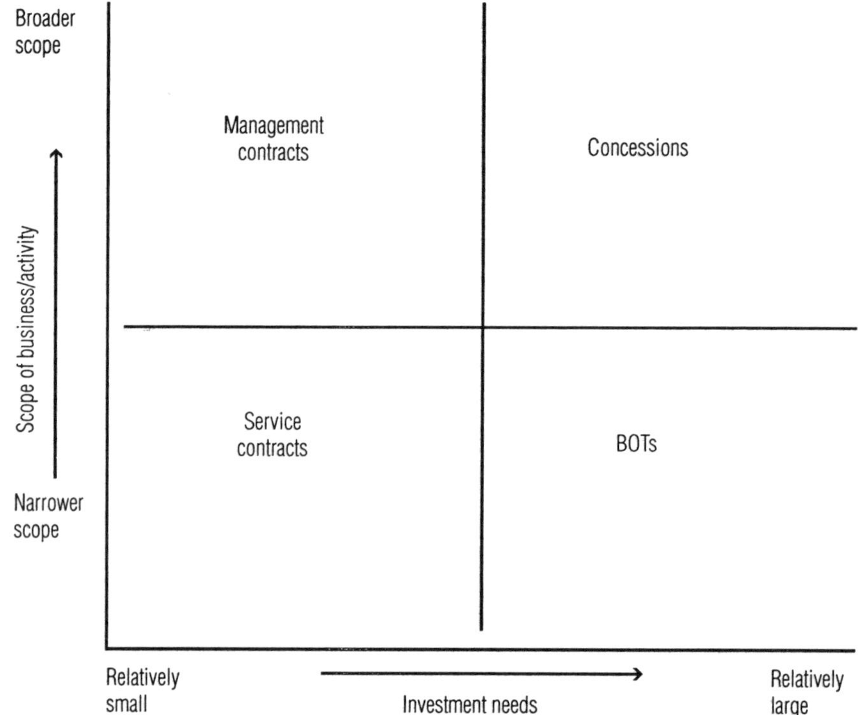

Figure 9.2 provides a schematic representation of the different forms of contracts found in the case studies. As the scope of business or activities for which the private sector is to be given responsibility increases, the preferred form of private sector participation shifts from service contracts or BOTs to management contracts and concession. Similarly, as investment needs increase, the preferred form of private sector participation shifts from contracts where little or no private sector investment is required (service contracts and management contracts) to contracts based on the private sector providing core investment finance (BOTs and concessions).

Some approaches to private sector participation are better suited than others to the particular conditions of a country and the specific circumstances of the case concerned. The more "advanced" the contract form selected, the greater the need for political support for privatization and for a wider range of reforms.

Full divestiture and concession contracts are the most advanced approaches to private sector participation, because they allocate responsibility for investment for the entire water system to the operator, while service con-

Figure 9.3. Approaches to Private Sector Participation

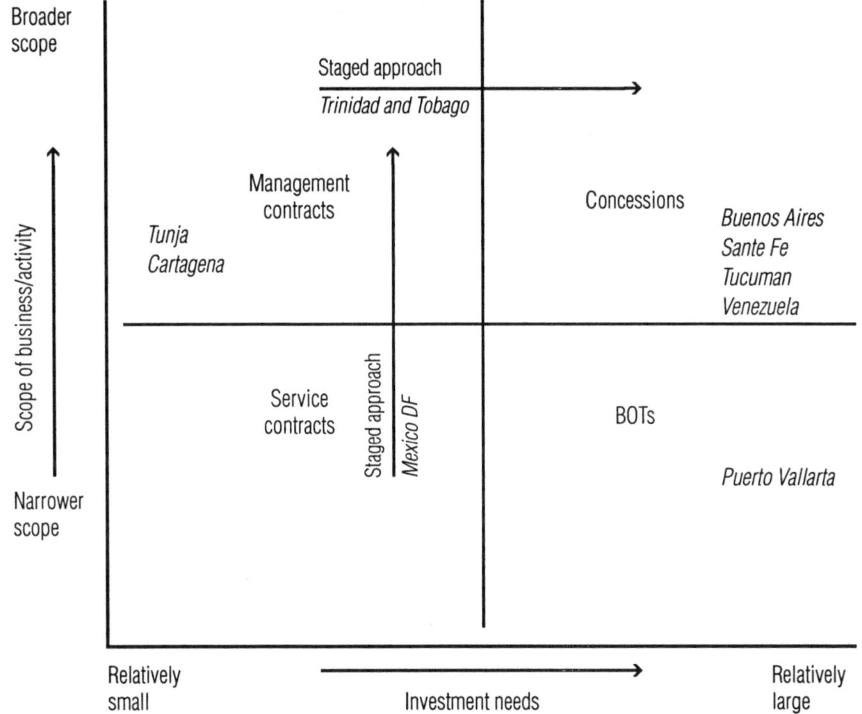

tracts and short-term management contracts have more modest scopes. BOTs stand somewhere in the middle. Although BOTs are less complex than a concession and tend to relate to single, self-contained projects such as treatment plants, their long-term nature means greater commitment is needed to privatization. Adequate regulation is also more important than for short-term management contracts in order to ensure the contractor is paid and to adjust tariffs to changes in circumstances. Figure 9.3 classifies the case studies by type of private sector participation scheme.

Case Studies

None of the cases studied involves full divestiture,[7] but four involve concession contracts—the three Argentine concessions (Buenos Aires, Santa Fe and Tucuman) and the contract in Venezuela.

[7]In fact, the only known significant case is privatization in England and Wales.

Concessions

Concessions are long-term contracts usually covering 25 or 30 years in which the private sector is responsible for operations, maintenance and new investment for service delivery. The awarding authority retains ownership of the assets, which are provided to the concessionaire with the stipulation that they be returned to the authority at the end of the contract. Concessions are particularly useful when one of the objectives of the government is to raise investment finance to improve service.

The failure to award the concession contract in Caracas, Venezuela is a clear illustration of a contract not suited to the conditions of the case. More subtle lessons can be learned from the problems faced by the Argentine concessions.

Venezuela. The failure in Venezuela had several causes. At the time, the country was undergoing an economic crisis and the government was losing public support. This meant that there was insufficient political support for privatization. In addition, the awarding body was not a single authority but multiple municipalities, each of which wanted to participate individually in the process. Their continuing disagreements created concern regarding the future relations of the concessionaire with its unpredictable counterpart.

Another reason behind the failure in Venezuela was the lack of a separate regulator. For a contract the magnitude of a concession, it is preferable to have a credible and independent regulator to ensure compliance, adequate enforcement of service standards, and a predictable and transparent process for tariff adjustment.

In addition, poor knowledge of the state of the assets, combined with the absence of any process to deal with this problem in advance of tendering, led to uncertainty among prospective bidders concerning the amount of investment needed to deliver the concession targets.

The case also presented a backlog of postponed tariff adjustments. The average pre-tender tariff was only \$0.04/m^3, which represented a small fraction of costs. Considering that the Venezuelan population has been notorious for demonstrating (sometimes violently) against tax and price increases, the burden placed on the concessionaire to be the first to increase tariffs to cover costs was excessive. This further contributed to the reluctance of potential operators to bid for the contract.

Finally, the exchange rate risk was not mitigated. Venezuela's currency is very much dependent on oil prices. Facing a decline in such prices and a critical economic situation, the exchange rate risk for investors was particularly high. The requirement in the bidding documents that the concessionaire assume the full exchange rate risk was unreasonable under these circumstances.

The result in Venezuela was that none of the five consortia that prequalified for the bid submitted one. Lack of political support for the process as well as an absence of profit guarantees adequate to the risks were cited as reasons.

Argentina. The situation in Argentina was more favorable to concessions. In the three cases, the first four conditions highlighted above were met: there was a clear commitment to privatization; the concessionaire had to deal only with a single authority (the provincial government); a regulator had been set up with clearly defined objectives, rights and responsibilities; and efforts were made to provide information on the state of the assets by contracting internationally recognized technical consultants to prepare reports. As a result, service improvements achieved under these contracts, especially in Buenos Aires, have been significant.

Service and Management Contracts

Both service and management contracts are suited to national circumstances where the private sector would judge it too risky to undertake major investment, where there is no credible independent regulation, and where there are no other satisfactory guarantees available to diminish the investment risk. The difference relates to the scope of activities involved.

Service contracts are used for contracting out specific activities such as bill collection, meter installation, meter reading and pipe repairs. They require careful specification of the tasks involved. Of the cases studied here, service contracts have been used only in Mexico City (first stage).

Management contracts are a more advanced form of contract. In this case, the operator also takes responsibility for the operation and maintenance of government-owned assets. These contracts are not, however, an effective way to raise private sector finance, since responsibility for investment is completely in the hands of the authority. Management contracts have been the chosen approach in Trinidad and Tobago (first stage), Mexico City (second stage) and, with some modifications, in Tunja and Cartagena in Colombia.

The contracts in Cartagena and Tunja are special forms of management contracts. Instead of a fixed fee or a performance-based fee, payment is based on the customer tariffs collected. Like a concession contract, the Tunja contract involves the contractor having responsibility for part of the new investment (the municipality for the rest) as well as for six five-year expansion plans to improve service. The Cartagena arrangement is based on setting up a mixed company with 50 percent participation by the Cartagena district.

The special forms of management contracts put in place in Cartagena and Tunja might be considered appropriate to the circumstances of the country, where service provision and regulation are mainly in the hands of the municipalities, although there is a separate central regulatory commission to regulate tariffs. The very nature of such decentralized provision has meant that contracts have had to be developed carefully to exonerate companies from the responsibility of not delivering agreed targets when either the tariff policy unexpectedly changes for political reasons or the municipality does not fulfill its financial obligations.

Efforts have been made in this direction in both contracts, although in both cases the municipality, in practice, is unlikely to have the funds to finance the investment promised under the contract. This can seem to be a major threat to the long-term viability of the two contracts.

In Cartagena, the establishment of a mixed company means that the municipality (district) is both regulator of the contract and a shareholder in the regulated company. As regulator, the municipality is required to be tough in its stance toward the company regarding the delivery of targets, quality standards and on maintenance of assets. As a shareholder, its interests lie in a much softer line, creating a conflict of interest. Furthermore, as part of the political process, the municipality will prefer to keep tariffs low to gain voters' confidence, while as a shareholder of the company it will have incentives to raise tariffs.

Staged Approaches

These newer forms of contractual arrangements involve starting from a relatively simple contract form in the first stage and subsequently moving to more advanced stages. Examples are the service to management contract in Mexico City, and the management contract to concession in Trinidad and Tobago. The staged approaches used in these two systems have much to commend in terms of suitability to local circumstances.

Mexico City. A decision was made to start the process of private sector involvement using service contracts, with full management contracts to follow at a later stage. This approach reflects the fact that Mexico is not fully ready for water privatization. In these circumstances, a gradual introduction of the private sector allows for airing possible political resistance to private involvement and gives time to the operators to demonstrate the improvements they can make, thereby gaining public backing for deeper forms of private sector participation in the future. This is an effective way of reducing risk for future contracts because it provides the initial operation with the opportunity to undertake tasks related to establishing the customer base and identifying the condition of the network. The initial service contract reduces the risks involved in the management contract to be entered into at a future stage. This risk reduction eases the task of securing finance and also reduces its cost.

One difficulty that arose in the case of Mexico City was that although bidders bid for the whole package (i.e., all the stages), the nature of the first two stages (service contract) was so different from that of the last stage (management contract) that it was difficult to establish an appropriate way to assess the whole package and obtain the most cost-effective overall solution. The result was that specific activities were carried out by the four companies at considerably different prices. In general, identifying the winning bid in this type of contract involves a complicated process that can lack transparency unless the evaluation methodology used is published in advance.

Trinidad and Tobago. The approach here has been a first-stage management contract of three to five years' duration aimed at improving understanding and management of the system, to be followed by a possible second-stage concession contract. The initial short management contract enables the operator to familiarize itself with the system and assess the state of the assets. This acquired knowledge reduces the risks when establishing the magnitude of the investment program that will need to be in place to deliver the expansion objectives set in the subsequent concession contract.

The Trinidad and Tobago contract has also introduced an innovative way to raise financing by asking bidders to offer a loan as part of the tendering process. Larger loans and lower interest rates resulted in higher points in the bid evaluation.

The main disadvantage of this staged approach is that the winner of the management contract will have a first option on the subsequent concession contract, despite the fact that its selection was based solely on the bid for the management contract (the first stage). This significantly reduces competition for the more important concession stage. In general, it is difficult to see how any concession that follows a management contract can be competitively tendered if the operator carrying out the first contract is allowed to bid. The operator will always have an advantage over the other bidders.

It could be argued that given the commitment to privatization in Trinidad and Tobago, a deeper approach from the start may have been more appropriate. Studies to assess the state of the assets and to understand the system could have been contracted to outside consultants. This is, however, a matter of balance. With the current approach, the reduction of the risk on the level of required expenditure to meet future targets leads to lower tariffs being offered in the bid for the concession by the incumbent. In the case of an initial full concession, all bidders will lack information concerning the state of the assets and will offer a less attractive bid, reflecting the higher risk involved. The contract will therefore be awarded at a higher cost than with the staged approach. Ensuring that the balance runs in favor of the staged approach requires a clear obligation on the incumbent to release relevant information at the time of the second stage.[8]

BOT Contracts

BOT contracts have been used in the municipalities of Puerto Vallarta, Cancun and Chihuahua in Mexico. They are suitable when specific and discrete projects are pursued, such as the building and operation of treatment plants, and where a long-term contract can be designed to deliver a secure revenue stream to the project company, either from a creditworthy customer or, potentially, through external payment guarantees to ensure payment by the local authorities. These projects depend also on a credible judiciary system to handle disputes.

Since the revenue stream for the project is secured on the demand from a single plant, rather than spread across a portfolio of projects, special care should be taken in assessing the capacity of the plants to meet short-term demand. This appears to have been an issue with the Puerto Vallarta project, for which the BOT approach can be seen to have otherwise been well suited. The project was built to treat 750 liters of wastewater per second (to be expanded to 1,000 liters per second in the second stage), but following the recession, actual municipal demand was only around 450 liters per second. Because the contract was on a "put or pay" basis, the municipality had to pay the contractor the minimum contracted amount of 600 liters per second (subsequently raised to 750 liters) despite being unable to recover an equivalent amount from users through charges. To face these financial problems, the municipality tried to raise tariffs. However, the newly elected government was initially reluctant to undertake tariff increases, and when it finally decided to do so, it found strong resistance from the hotel sector. The result was that the municipality was unable to meet some of the monthly payments due to the private company.

[8]This provision is in place in the Trinidad and Tobago contract.

Table 9.3. Appropriateness of the Contract Approach

	Type of contract	Appropriate approach to private sector participation	Government commitment	Precontract analysis
Argentina				
Buenos Aires	30-year concession	✓✓	✓✓✓	✓✓✓
Santa Fe	30-year concession	✓✓	✓✓✓	✓✓✓
Tucuman	30-year concession	★	★★	✓
Colombia				
Cartagena	30-year management contract mixed company	★✓	✓	★?
Tunja	30-year management concession contract	★✓	✓	★
Mexico				
Mexico, DF	10-year service/management contract	✓	✓	
Puerto Vallarta	BOT	✓	✓★	
Trinidad and Tobago	3 to 5-year management contract to end in concession	✓	✓✓	✓✓✓
Venezuela	25-year concession	★★	★★	★★

Key: ✓ = Positive
★ = Weakness
✓★ = Good in theory but not in practice

Despite these problems, the plant is up and running and has produced effluent of a quality that has consistently exceeded contractual standards. The plant has even served as a demonstration wastewater treatment plant in Mexico, known for its well-tested design and operation. Table 9.3 presents a summary of the appropriateness of the approach in each case.

Efficiency Incentives in Payment Forms

An important distinction between approaches to private sector participation relates to the different efficiency incentives placed on participants. Table 9.4 summarizes the efficiency incentives implicit in the different contract types associated with payment forms.

Each of the approaches to private sector participation differs in the incentives it provides to the operator to improve efficiency. The *concession contracts* of Buenos Aires, Santa Fe and Tucuman in Argentina provide the most extensive framework of incentives, both to reduce costs and to increase revenues. Operators are remunerated through the tariffs they collect directly from

Table 9.4. Efficiency Incentives in Payment Form

Argentina	
Buenos Aires	✓✓
Santa Fe	✓✓
Tucuman	✓✓
Colombia	
Cartagena	✓✓★
Tunja	✓
Mexico	
Mexico, DF	★
Puerto Vallarta	✓
Trinidad and Tobago	✓

Key: ✓ = Positive
★ = Weakness
✓★ = Good in theory but not in practice

customers, so that their "fees" are, in effect, the profits earned from operation of the service. Furthermore, because the concessionaires are also responsible for investment in service expansion, they have a clear incentive to minimize the whole package of operating and capital costs. As a result, the payment form implicit in the concession approach means that operators are more likely to reach overall cost optimization than when they are responsible only for operating the service, as under a management contract. The particular forms of *management/concession contract* in Cartagena and Tunja provide similar incentives in terms of revenue, since payment is based on tariffs collected from customers. In the case of Tunja, however, incentives for cost minimization are restricted to operating expenditure and only that part of investment costs for which the private operator is responsible. In Cartagena, because the operator is a mixed company with partial municipal ownership, there is some incentive to minimize investment and operating costs because they are ultimately reflected in the profits of the mixed company, part of which will be distributed to the private owners and part to the municipality. For more typical *management contracts,* where payment is a fee set independently of revenue collected from customers, efficiency incentives can be introduced by tying part of the fee to the operator's success in meeting key performance targets. Companies then receive both a fixed fee component and a variable fee component. The Trinidad and Tobago contract is particularly innovative in this respect. Companies were awarded higher points for offering a higher proportion of their fee based on performance. Bidding companies were then able to choose the performance-based component in their fee, ensuring not only that it would be actually achievable, but also, that the companies were fully accountable for their choice once the contract was awarded. The result was that it was possible to arrive at a high performance-based fee. The winning company, Severn Trent, offered to accept 61.4 percent of its payment on a performance-related basis.

The activity fees typical of *service contracts* such as that in Mexico City are less effective in providing efficiency incentives. Of course, once the fee is agreed to, the operator has the incentive to minimize the cost of the particular activity in order to improve profitability. A problem arises, however, whenever different methods can be employed to reach a given final goal. For example, the activities chosen by the contracting authority to undertake leakage control may not be consistent with an optimization program leading to overall least-cost solution. Had the operator been asked to perform based on achieving final targets and given responsibility for choice of program, it would have had a clear incentive to arrive at an overall least-cost solution.

The payment for *BOT contracts*, such as that for the wastewater treatment plant in Puerto Vallarta, Mexico, provides efficiency incentives for the operator, given that any savings from ongoing cost reduction are for its own benefit. From the customers' perspective, the benefits of efficiency incentives are captured in the bid price.

Tendering Process

Given the limited scope for introducing competition *in* the market to provide water services, there is a particularly pressing need to ensure effective competition *for* the market. This means that the tendering process must be organized so as to attract a significant number of well-qualified bidders.

This objective can be achieved in a variety of ways. At a basic level, bidders are more likely to be attracted to the competition if the private participation approach itself is well-suited to local circumstances and subject to appropriate risk mitigation. Effective marketing of the privatization process is also important, together with clear and specific terms of reference, adequate time to present proposals, and a transparent process for qualifying and evaluating the bids.

In most of the individual cases studied, privatization attracted significant interest from international firms (Table 9.5). Exceptions are Tunja and to a lesser extent Cartagena, which attracted only two and three consortia, respectively. In all the other cases, at least five consortia showed interest at the prequalification stage.

Table 9.5. Competition for the Market

	Tendering		
	Adequate number of bidders present expressions of interest	Adequate time to prepare proposals	Adequate number of bidders presenting proposals
Argentina			
Buenos Aires	✓✓✓	✓	✓✓
Santa Fe	✓✓	✓✓	✓✓
Tucuman	✓✓✓	✓	★
Colombia			
Cartagena	✓✓		✓
Tunja	★	★	★★★
Mexico			
Mexico, DF	✓✓✓	✓✓	✓✓✓
Trinidad and Tobago	✓✓✓		✓✓✓
Venezuela	✓✓✓	✓	★★★

Key: ✓ = Positive
★ = Weakness

When measured in terms of the number of companies actually submitting bids, success is lower. The least successful case is that of Venezuela, where none of the five prequalifying firms submitted bids due to the approach selected and the problems previously described. In Tucuman, there was no competition for the market, since only one company, General des Eaux, submitted a bid. In Tunja, there were only two bidders and in Cartagena, three. Competition was stronger in Mexico City, with six consortia bidding, in Trinidad and Tobago (five), and in Buenos Aires (four).

In the case of Tunja, it was argued by the unsuccessful bidder that the 45 day preparation period was too short to put together a complicated bid involving the specification of expansion plans and six five-year operational plans.

Buenos Aires did particularly well in marketing its concession internationally, seeking qualified assistance to prepare the terms of reference and evaluate the bids. The result was that six companies requested the terms of reference, five prequalified, and four submitted a bid.

Given the relative lack of experience in most countries and the difficult technical and economic issues that arise, it is clear that the most successful schemes have been those where suitably qualified technical assistance has been provided at the outset.

Dealing with Other Stakeholders (Customers and Employees)

Introducing private sector participation will often bring significant changes for both customers and employees. These changes may be both marked and abrupt when the scale of the investment and performance improvement programs built into contracts is large and ambitious in terms of the time frame. The way in which the stakes of customers and employees are managed can have important implications for the ultimate success of the scheme.

Handling Initial Tariff Increases

A major issue in several of the cases studied was the way tariff increases were handled soon after new private sector participation arrangements were put in place. The clear message is that, where significant tariff increases are required, it is best to introduce at least part of the increase before seeking to attract private sector operators. This will yield both a more financially viable baseline position and also provide the political and presentational advantage of distancing private sector participation from the tariff increases. In the case of Tucuman, poor handling of agreed tariff increases was the major factor behind the collapse of the whole contract. The successful consortium won the contract by bidding for the lowest tariff increase. This increase was nevertheless considerable, doubling existing tariffs for some users and requiring an average increase of 69 percent. The social impact was considerable and bill collection declined significantly as a consequence. Furthermore, three months after operations started, a new provincial government was elected and advised the rescission of the contract "for excessive guilt of the awarding body."

In Puerto Vallarta, Mexico, the resulting excess capacity required the municipality to increase tariffs beyond what was acceptable to some consumers in the hotel sector. Rejection of the increased tariff, coupled with a change of municipal government, meant that the municipality faced financial difficulties in meeting its contractual payments.

A similar situation has arisen in Mexico City, where increased charges due to the introduction of metering and measured billing has slowed achievement of targets. The newly elected mayor is opposed to tariff increases and is likely to intervene in favor of tariff reductions.

In Venezuela, low existing public utility tariffs (4 cents per m^3)—and the consequent need for the incoming private operator to increase them considerably to recover costs—was one of the main factors discouraging potential bidders from bidding for the contract.

In contrast to the above cases, the policy of advance tariff increases was followed in Buenos Aires, where nominal tariffs were increased twice in 1991: by 25 percent in February 1991 to compensate for inflation, and by 29 percent in April 1991 to enable the public sector company to operate without injections of capital from the state treasury. Similarly, in Trinidad and Tobago, tariffs were increased by 35 percent a year before granting the management contract.

Experience suggests that it is important to carefully analyze the population's likely reaction to tariff increases. When efficiency improvements are unlikely on their own to be enough to finance the service and its intended improvement, it may be better to delay improvement and expansion plans in order to soften the initial tariff impact. In some cases, low-income groups may need assistance through direct payments to cope with the high tariffs for connecting service. This has been the approach followed in Chile. There are benefits from timing improvements in service with tariff increases. The operator in Santa Fe made particular efforts in this respect.

Dealing with Redundancies

Improvements in staff management by private sector operators are likely to provoke adverse reactions from the former utility's employees. Appropriate redundancy packages have to be provided and training for those remaining has to be introduced to safeguard their jobs in the long term.

Benefits Achieved to Date

Commercial Management, Service Improvements and Efficiency

Achievements in terms of commercial management, service improvements and efficiency should be considered in the context of the relatively short period that has passed since most of the contracts were initiated, the particular objectives of the contract arrangements, and the difficulties faced with the selected approach to privatization (Tables 9.6 and 9.7). Furthermore, there have been more recent improvements, especially in the case of Trinidad and Tobago and Tunja, that are not reflected in the table for lack of information.

For the cases studied, private sector participation has been particularly

Table 9.6. Commercial Improvements

	Argentina		Colombia		
Achievements	**Buenos Aires**	**Santa Fe**	**Cartagena**	**Tunja**	**Mexico, DF**
Customer register completed	✓✓✓	✓✓✓	✓✓✓	✓	✓✓✓
Billing and bill collection	✓✓✓	✓✓✓	✓✓		✓✓
Customer relations	✓✓	✓✓✓	✓✓✓	✓	✓✓

Key: ✓ = Positive
★ = Weakness

Note: No information is available on Tucuman or Trinidad and Tobago. The commercial improvement issue does not apply to cases in Venezuela or Puerto Vallarta.

positive in improving revenues by simply identifying customers, introducing effective systems for billing and bill collection, and improving customer relations. Progress has also been made in improving continuity of water service and increasing coverage. Much less has been achieved, however, in extending sewerage connections, with the exception of Buenos Aires, and in treatment of wastewater discharges.

The Buenos Aires concession appears to be on target for all its performance measures for 1998 except wastewater treatment. Its achievements in terms of new connections have been particularly impressive: 300,000 new connections for drinking water and 100,000 for sewerage, involving network extensions of 4,200 km and 1,400 km, respectively.

Table 9.7. Service Improvements and Efficiency

	Argentina		Colombia		Mexico	
Achievements	**Buenos Aires**	**Santa Fe**	**Cartagena**	**Tunja**	**Mexico, DF**	**Puerto Vallarta**
Increase in water coverage	✓✓✓	✓		✓		
Increase in sewerage coverage	✓✓	✓				
Continuity of supply	✓✓✓	✓		✓		
Drinking water quality	✓✓✓	✓	✓✓			
Sewage treatment	★	✓				✓✓
Labor productivity	✓✓✓	✓✓			✓✓✓	✓

Key: ✓ = Positive
★ = Weakness

Note: No information is available on Tucuman. The experience in Trinidad and Tobago is too recent to expect much improvement. The issues in the table do not apply in Venezuela.

Table 9.8. Sustainability of Service

	Argentina		Colombia		
Achievements	Buenos Aires	Santa Fe	Cartagena	Tunja	Mexico, DF
Asset inventory	✓✓✓	✓✓✓			✓✓✓
Maintenance work	✓	✓	✓		
Leakage control	✓✓✓	✓✓			
Pressure		✓		✓	

Key: ✓ = Positive
★ = Weakness

Note: No information is available on Tucuman. The experience in Trinidad and Tobago is too recent to expect too much improvement. The issue is not relevant in Venezuela.

It is difficult to obtain reliable measures of cost efficiency. Nevertheless, figures on labor productivity appear to show that significant improvements have been made in systems management. Argentina reduced the number of employees per 1,000 connections from eight at the beginning of operations to three in 1997.

Maintenance

Activities related to maintenance of the assets needed to ensure sustainable service have helped by improving knowledge of the system, especially in relation to the state of underground assets (Table 9.8). This has been particularly noticeable in Mexico City, where an important part of the service contract was the assessment of the state of the network. In Buenos Aires, the introduction of leakage control programs, together with a better knowledge of the customer base, have resulted in a decrease in unaccounted for water from 45 percent at the start of operations to 31 percent in 1997. There have also been improvements in pressure control. The contract in Tunja has asset maintenance as one of its key priorities, given the geographical position of the town in a hilly area, which results in large variations of pressure and consequent pipe bursts.

Less has so far been achieved in network renovation, with the exception of the unblocking of sewerage networks in Buenos Aires.

Conclusions

Competition and Completion

Of the nine case studies examined in this chapter, eight have achieved contract award and seven are in operation. The failure of the attempt to let a concession for Venezuela involved a wide range of difficulties relating to inadequate design and preparation and to difficult macroeconomic circumstances. The rescission of the Tucuman concession in Argentina in the year following its award involved a combination of political changes that occurred shortly after the contract award, at the same time as an initial tariff shock. In the other cases, private sector participation arrangements are operating broadly in line with the spirit of the original intention, and they appear to be delivering real benefits in those cases where enough time has elapsed to form a judgment.

Competition *for* the market, as embodied in the private sector participation contract/concession, is particularly important because there is little or no scope for competition *in* the market once the contract or concession has been awarded. The case studies show that there has been no difficulty in attracting bidders for the prequalification stage, but more of a problem in some cases of taking bidders through to the final tender. For example, the Tunja project had only two bidders and the Tucuman project became noncompetitive, with only a single bidder.

Experiences that have been less successful than they might have in establishing effective competition and completing the transaction have reflected a range of factors, including inappropriate forms of private sector participation given prevailing circumstances; lack of clarity of contract terms and the bidding process; inadequate preparation; and poor knowledge of the asset base.

Information Deficiencies

In many cases where existing assets and operations are to be included under a form of private sector participation, there are significant deficiencies in the existing level of information about the asset and customer bases. In such cases there is a real risk that the resulting uncertainty would have threatened the ability to let a concession or contract on reasonable terms. Two approaches have been followed to address these concerns. First, qualified technical assistance has been brought in to survey the system and its assets. Second, a staged approach has been chosen, under which a key focus of the first stage is to address information difficulties, thus providing a foundation for a more ambitious form of private sector participation in stage two.

The second approach has been followed in the staged approach process adopted for Trinidad and Tobago (from management contract in stage one to concession in stage two) and for Mexico City (from service to management contract). The reasons for following the staged approach in Trinidad and Tobago went beyond the need to find out more about the system—there was also a need for sufficient time to develop a regulatory regime that could support a full concession, combined with an immediate need for assistance from a private sector partner to help address severe operational problems. These staged approaches provide a way to make real progress even where more ambitious private sector participation approaches are not immediately feasible. There is a residual concern, however, that subsequent stages of a multistage approach will not be subject to the same degree of effective competition as in single-stage cases. The potential downside of this lack of competition needs to be weighed against the benefits of earlier private sector participation. This balance will depend on the circumstances of each case, and care needs to be taken to mitigate the consequences of reduced competition in subsequent stages through the terms of the initial award.

Benefits Achieved

Although a number of the private sector participation cases are still in their early period of operation, and thus provide limited evidence, the general picture appears to be one of substantial improvement in a number of areas:

- *Efficiency.* The number of staff per 1,000 customers has been reduced by more than half in Buenos Aires, Santa Fe and Cartagena;
- *Commercial management.* In most cases, customer registers have been created or improved and customer payment has improved. The number of bills issued in Mexico City has increased from 1.3 to 1.7 million, and from 80 percent to 97 percent in Buenos Aires.
- *Service.* In most successful cases, continuity of service has improved in the Argentine concessions and in Cartagena and Tunja, and quality has improved in Buenos Aires and Cartagena.
- *New connections.* Buenos Aires has added 300,000 new water connections and 100,000 new sewerage connections.

Raising Finance

Attracting private sector capital has been a key reason for undertaking private sector participation projects and is an inherent part of full concessions and BOTs. By making the provision of a loan a part of the bid, the first stage of the Trinidad and Tobago management contract adopted an innovative approach to securing finance where conditions are not right for a full concession.

In other cases (Cartagena, Tunja) the private sector participation arrangements have been set up within a framework that relies on municipal budgets to support new investment. Although it is too early to judge the effectiveness of these approaches, there may be difficulties in the future if the municipalities fail to deliver on their investment commitments. This approach is only likely to avoid complex renegotiation if the areas for which the municipal funding is to be relied upon are well defined and capable of being ring-fenced (e.g., free-standing projects), so that any shortfall in funding does not impact on the core performance of the private sector's involvement.

Price Impact

In a number of cases, there have been problems resulting from significant tariff increases that come into force shortly after the start of private sector operations (e.g., Tucuman, Mexico City). In general, the need for price rises tends to reflect circumstances where tariffs may have been too low originally, or where the investment plans may have been overly ambitious.

The consequences may threaten project viability because of the political risks associated with the price rises. This underlines the need to make realistic forecasts of tariff increases needed to deliver service improvements and to assess the viability of implementing such increases.

The options for mitigating this risk include:

- Increasing prices in advance of private sector participation if the existing level really is too low by comparison with the costs of an efficiently operated company (as was done in the Buenos Aires case).
- Timing price increases to coincide with identifiable improvements in service levels (in Trinidad and Tobago, prices have been increased, but customers have benefited from major improvements in the continuity of supply).
- Modifying ambitious time scales or targets for service extension and wastewater treatment if the resulting investment needs would lead to politically unsustainable price increases.

Regulation

The need and type of regulation depends on the approach selected for private sector participation. Service and management contracts do not require independent separate regulation at the outset. Where the investment commitments are clear throughout the life of the contract (BOT), it is possible to regulate by contract, using a fixed price formula. Where investment finance is provided by the private sector and there is uncertainty about the future investment requirements (divestment, concessions), clear principles to deal with new requirements are necessary, and these are better stated and enforced through separate regulatory bodies.

In the case of concessions, the use of periodic price reviews is a key issue. In the Buenos Aires concession, the initial tariff is implicitly intended to survive throughout the full life of the concession, subject to tariff adjustments based on indexation, extraordinary events or target changes. If, as seems likely over a 30-year period, the investment and service needs alter from those implied in the original bid, then there are no real criteria to determine how to handle the necessary price changes. This presents material risks for both the concessionaire and the regulator/customer. There is no single answer as to what is the right balance to strike between a predetermined price mechanism, with no real rules to govern a review, and one that allows for periodic revision.

A predetermined price mechanism for a full concession period is only likely to have advantages where major improvements in the operation and service are such that their benefit can be captured for customers through effective competition at the outset; the impact of private sector participation will be to reduce prices rather than increase them; there is reasonable certainty over the likely levels of future investment; and where it might be difficult to create an effective regulatory institution to administer a price review. In general, an approach that involves price reviews would seem to be more appropriate.

Institutional and Structural Reforms

Less emphasis has generally been placed on appropriate reform of the structure of the industry and the environmental aspects of regulation in the context of private sector participation. Only in Argentina, and to a lesser extent in Colombia, has the introduction of private sector participation been accompanied by institutional reforms in the water sector. Structural and institutional reform can deliver significant benefits in that an optimal industry structure could yield savings (both monetary and environmental) and promote efficient competition (treatment plants).

A key issue related to reform is the devolution of responsibility to local (or even regional) government. Devolution has a number of advantages relating to increased local accountability, but it also has drawbacks with respect to the need for regulation in the context of private sector participation. High professionalism and adequate budgets and training are essential for adequate functioning of newly created institutions. This may be more difficult to achieve when responsibilities are devolved to local governments where fewer professional staff are available. In addition, devolution of responsibilities to municipalities may make regulation more vulnerable to political interference. Finally, there is a risk of losing economies of river basin management with excessive devolution. These tradeoffs represent an area where careful thought is required in private sector participation design.

Appendix 9.1

Analytical Framework

This appendix sets out an analytical framework intended to assist countries in Latin America and the Caribbean in designing water sector reforms. The analytical framework covers the industry structure; institutional arrangements, including economic and environmental regulation; approach to private sector participation; and design of the tendering process.

In each case, the analytical framework has two main components:

- A theoretical framework that sets out the main principles and constraints that should be taken into consideration, together with possible means of mitigating such constraints;
- A process flowchart, which aids in applying the theoretical framework to practical situations.

Analytical Framework for Industry Restructuring

A key area for consideration in sector reform is the basic organization of the sector in terms of the size and scope of the operational entities responsible for service provision.

Appendix Figure 9.1 illustrates the key principles and constraints that have to be taken into account in order to establish the most appropriate industry structure.

1. The *principles* that guide the restructuring reforms; for example, new structures have to aim to achieve economic efficiency.
2. The *constraints* that may hinder following those principles; for example, administrative reforms that grant powers to the municipalities, some of which are small units of production (below 100,000 people) where economies of scale are not realized.
3. The possible *scope for mitigating such constraints*; for example, the amalgamation of municipalities.

Appendix Figure 9.1.
Key Principles and Constraints in Industry Restructuring

(1) Principles and criteria

Promotion of economic efficiency through:

- Economies of scale in production, management and finance
- Scope for efficient competition
- Introduction of management expertise and technical knowledge

Promotion of higher environmental standards through:

- Incentives/controls on environmental externalities
- River basin scope

(2) Constraints

Constraints on structural options include constitutional reforms granting powers to municipalities and geographical considerations such as distance and logistics

Establish appropriate industry structure

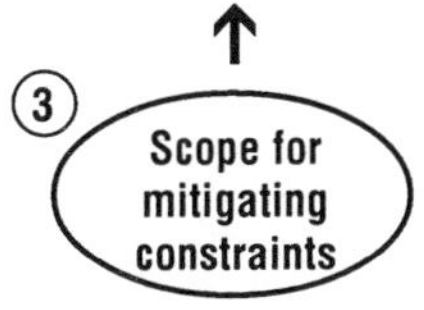

Will for reform embedded in legislation and backed by political support

Possibility of amalgamating units c.f. economics of separating units

Process for Design of Industry Structure

Appendix Figure 9.2 builds on the framework set out in Appendix Figure 9.1 to outline a process by which the approach can be applied in practice. The steps involved are to:

1. Review the size of operations under the current industry structure.
2. With the information on potential economies of scale, assess the possible cost reductions (productive efficiency) resulting from expansion or contraction of operations to arrive at the optimal economic size.
3. Assess the benefits of focusing on river basins and establish whether the scope of operations should be changed to achieve environmental objectives.
4. Use the combination of (2) and (3) to provide a theoretical optimal size and scope in relation to the scale of operations and the relationship with the appropriate management of river basins.
5. To see whether this new structure is viable, check the institutional and political constraints that are currently limiting the restructuring towards the best theoretical model.
6. Assess the possibility of mitigating such constraints.
7. Deal with the constraints to the extent possible.
8. Arrive at the appropriate new structure within the circumstances of the case.

Appendix Figure 9.2.
Process to Establish Most Appropriate Industry Structure

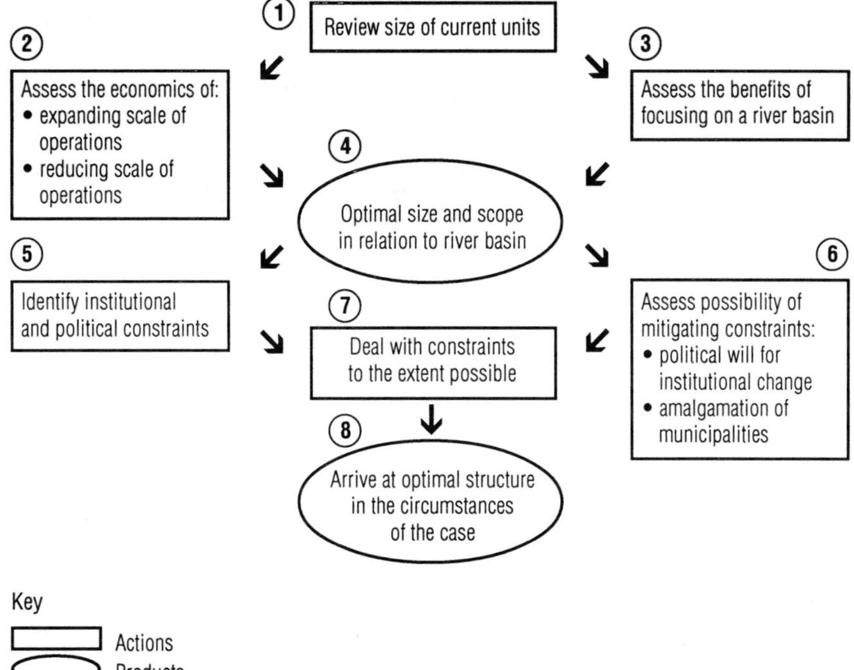

Appendix Figure 9.3. Theoretical Framework for Institutional Reform

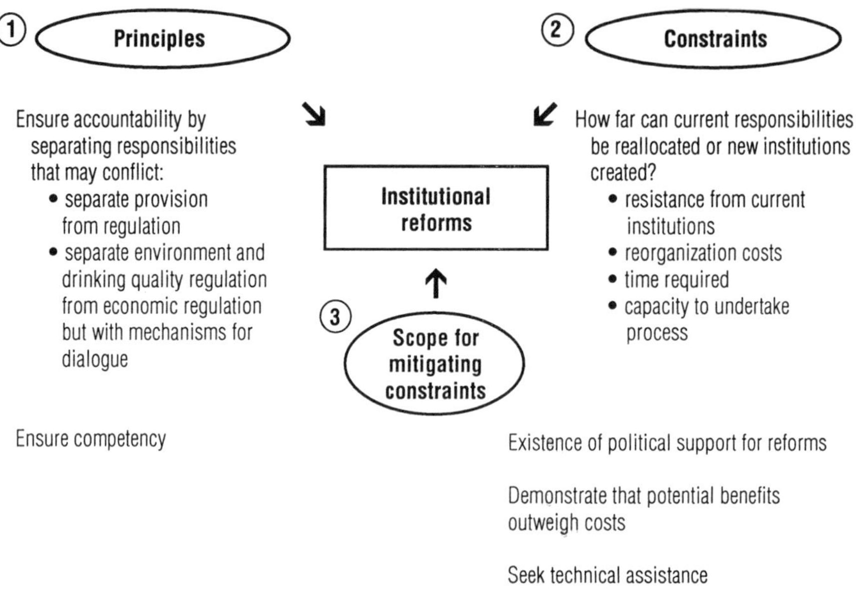

Analytical Framework for Institutional Reform

Appendix Figure 9.3 summarizes the theoretical framework (principles and constraints) to be taken into account in institutional reform. The figure shows:

1. The principles behind the reforms needed to establish appropriate institutions, particularly ensuring accountability and competency, and avoiding conflicts of interest by separating conflicting responsibilities.

2. The constraints reforming such institutions, such as resistance from employees of current institutions and reorganization costs.

3. The scope for mitigating the constraints; e.g., political support for reforms.

Appendix Figure 9.4. Process for Designing Institutional Reforms

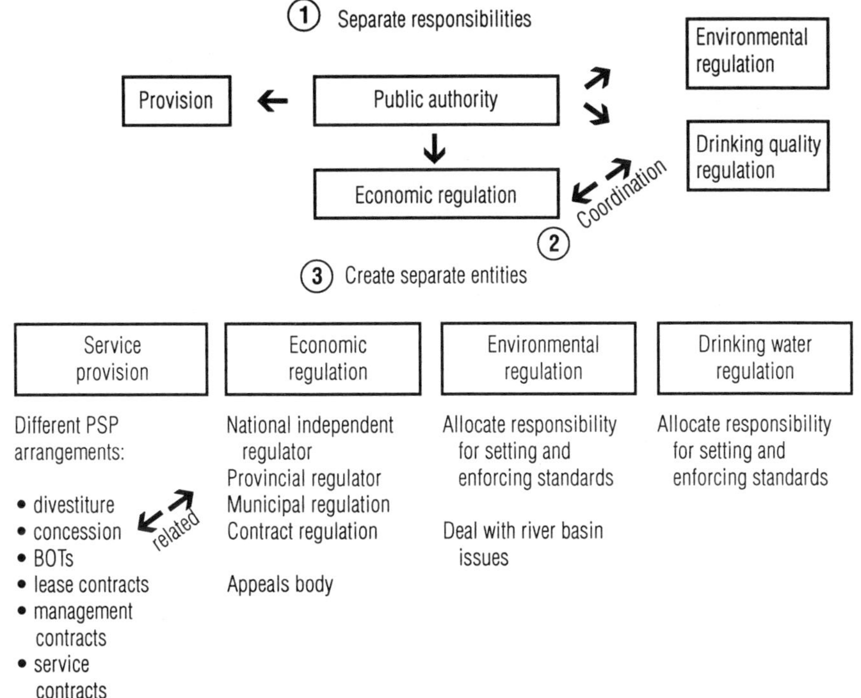

Process for Design of Institutional Reforms

Appendix Figure 9.4 is a process flowchart to aid in the design of institutional reforms in practice. The steps involved are:

1. Separate conflicting responsibilities that are currently in the hands of a single authority (municipal, provincial or central), including separating service provision from its economic and environmental regulation and from drinking water quality regulation.

2. Facilitate coordination between economic regulation and environmental and drinking water quality regulation to ensure that standards are consistent with the higher tariffs that may result when the cost of implementing such standards is taken into account.

3. Create separate entities to deliver each of the functions mentioned above, and allocate their responsibilities.

Appendix Figure 9.5. Theoretical Framework for Selecting Appropriate Private Sector Participation Approach

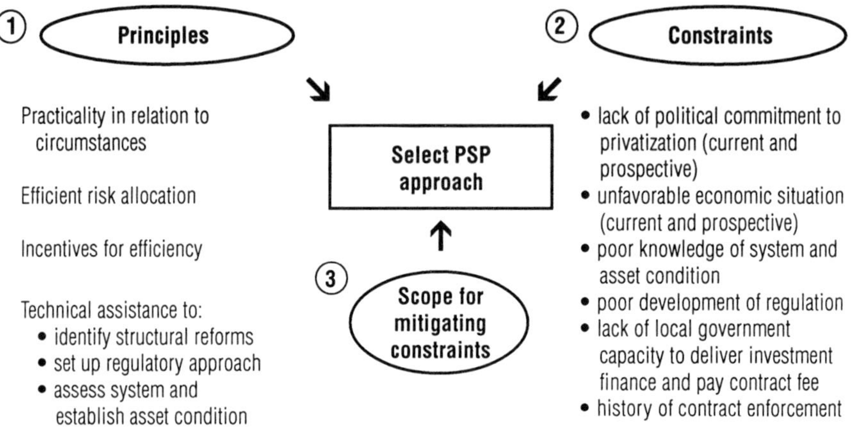

Analytical Framework for Identifying Approach to Private Sector Participation

Appendix Figure 9.5 summarizes the theoretical framework to be taken into account in selecting the appropriate private sector participation approach. The figure shows:

1. The principles behind the selection of an optimal private sector participation approach are to ensure significant scope for service improvements; establish practicality in relation to circumstances; and introduce incentives for efficiency/service level improvement.

2. The main constraints that can arise include a lack of political commitment to privatization (current and prospective); the economic situation; weak development of regulatory structure; and poor knowledge of system and asset condition.

3. Ways to mitigate such constraints include providing technical assistance to set up regulatory reforms and establish the state of the assets; and improving guarantees on investment finance.

Process for Identification of Appropriate Private Sector Participation Approach

Appendix Figure 9.6 is a process flowchart for selecting the most appropriate method of private sector participation. The steps involved are:

1. Assess the current water situation in order to identify priorities for service improvements.

2. Having identified priorities, define the specific objectives and the level at which they should be achieved.

3. To deliver the objectives, establish the primary role of private sector participation in terms of provision of investment, expertise, and better incentives to improve efficiency.

4. Assuming all these objectives are desirable, assess divestiture or concessions of preferred private sector participation approaches.

5. Check whether the necessary conditions for divestiture or concessions are in place in terms of political commitment, knowledge of system and asset condition, and regulatory arrangements.

6. If the conditions are adequately met, choose concession or divestiture; if not, use alternative approaches such as service or management contracts and staged contracts.

Appendix Figure 9.6.
Selecting the Appropriate Private Sector Participation Approach

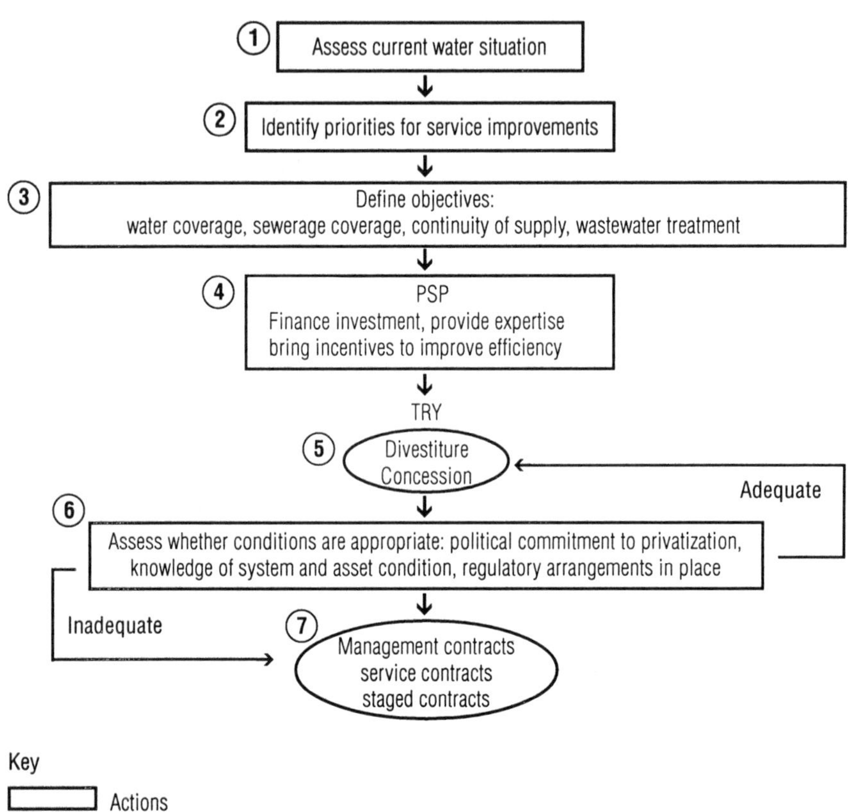

Appendix Figure 9.7. Theoretical Framework for Selection of Appropriate Tendering Process

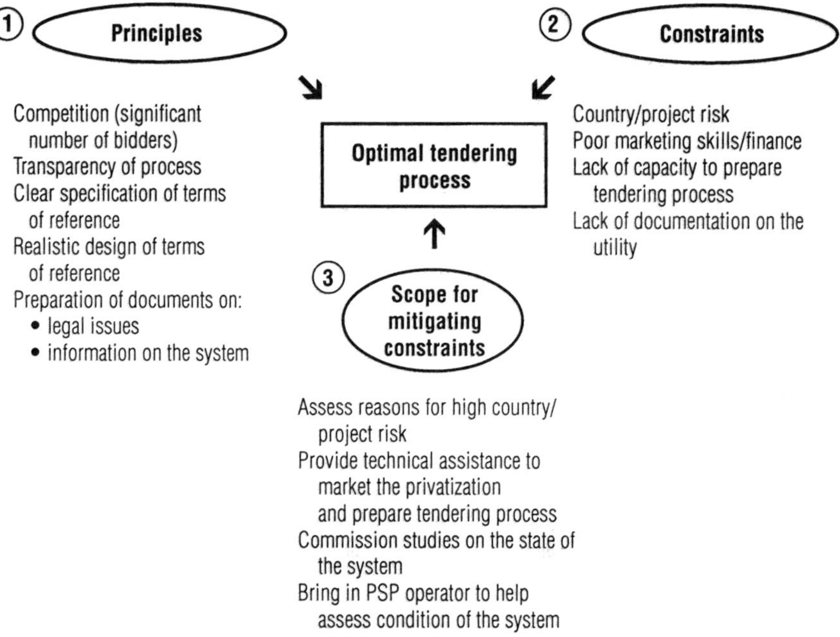

Analytical Framework for Design of Tendering Processes

Appendix Figure 9.7 presents the principles and constraints involved in implementing an optimal tendering process, and the scope for mitigating such constraints. The figure shows:

1. Key *principles*:
   - Competition;
   - Transparency;
   - Realistic design of terms of reference.
2. Key *constraints*:
   - Country/project risk that may be too high to attract private sector participation;
   - Poor marketing skills;
   - General lack of capacity to prepare the tendering process.
3. Once the constraints are identified, the *scope for mitigating those constraints* should be analyzed. The options include providing technical assistance to market the privatization, and carefully preparing the early stages of the tendering process.

CHAPTER 10

Private Participation at the Subnational Level: Water and Sewerage Services in Colombia

Rubén Avendaño and Federico Basañes

Historically, Latin America countries have dedicated significant amounts of human and financial resources toward improving drinking water and sewerage services. Nevertheless, these services are characterized by low coverage, large losses, poor quality and reliability, and high costs. In addition, the systems depend heavily on central government transfers for investments. To tackle these problems, several countries have launched extensive reorganizations of their potable water and sanitation sectors, including measures to foster private sector participation.

The reform process is spreading from cities like Buenos Aires, with the longest experience, to the Dominican Republic, where reforms are just beginning. Experiences to date show different results in improving management efficiency and coverage. Overall, success seems to be directly related to the extent to which countries carry out the institutional and regulatory reforms essential to attract private participation.

Providing drinking water and sanitation services is a complex process because of characteristics peculiar to the sector: high sunk costs, economies of scale and scope, massive consumption, and externalities. High sunk costs—that is, fixed costs that have little or no alternative uses—imply that firms will have incentives to stay in operation when operating costs are below operating income, even if this is not enough to recuperate investment. Economies of scale and scope make the industry a natural monopoly; that is, the cost for the relevant range of production is such that no combination of firms can produce as cheaply as a single provider. The nature of the product implies that it is massively consumed and that everyone should have access to it. Finally, there are externalities associated with the consumption of this service, since it has a high impact on public health and the environment.

These peculiarities—particularly sunk costs and asset specificity—create room for opportunistic behavior by the different actors involved in the sector. To serve the short-term interests of consumers and win some political support, the government may disallow recovery of investments by setting prices at a level that will only cover operating expenses. Firms that foresee this behavior will not be willing to commit resources to the sector or will try to commit them in a way that will not necessarily be efficient. For their part, private providers have incentives to use the natural monopoly power to increase prices, decrease quality, and disregard the effects on the environment.

Unless conditions can be created to limit opportunistic behavior, potable water and sanitation will continue to rely heavily on the public sector as the service provider and the source of investment. Although in principle services could be provided efficiently by the public sector, experience shows that factors like political interference, multiplicity of objectives, and lack of market pressures often have a negative impact on public provision. Such has usually been the case in Latin America, where for the last three to four decades service provided by public utilities was subject to considerable political interference. This translated into extremely inefficient operations.

To change these conditions, different schemes are now being tried in the region under diverse economic, legal and institutional circumstances. The reforms generally are designed to tackle the problems generated by the characteristics of the sector, so they include elements to eliminate opportunistic behavior and promote efficiency. The first element is to establish credible regulatory frameworks to limit discretionary power, as well as regulatory institutions that can enforce them. The second element is to pursue different forms of private sector participation to introduce efficiency in management and investment, as well as to include other parties interested in eliminating the political manipulation of tariffs. The final element is comprehensive sector restructuring, which includes fragmentation and decentralization to ensure local responsibility for service delivery and multiple sources of political support for the process.[1]

Although decentralization (as a form of fragmentation) can have these obvious beneficial effects, it also presents new challenges to the process. It moves the reform to smaller, less-developed economies whose institutional capacity is weak and where separating tariff setting from politics (and therefore limiting

[1]Multiple operators in Chile and multiple operators and regulators in Argentina were important parts of the reform process.

opportunistic behavior) may be harder. Decentralization can also create companies of inefficient size that do not take advantage of existing economies of scale and scope in the sector. These factors can, in turn, make it difficult to encourage low-cost private sector participation and restrict private participation to intermediate contracts for the management of services without major investment commitments. Even worse, they can make private participation impossible.

Different measures can be taken to mitigate these problems. First, a national regulatory framework (with a centralized and independent regulatory institution to enforce it) could help create commitment to a credible long-term scheme and therefore provide assurance to investors. Second, mixed firms that involve equity participation of the local government could help reduce political meddling in setting tariffs.[2] Third, provision of the service by conglomerates of municipalities could help reduce the problem of small size in a decentralized environment.

The reform process of Colombia's water and sewerage sector provides an excellent example of these issues. Colombia moved from a centralized state-owned model of provision to a highly decentralized model with responsibility at the municipal level. The process also included a regulatory framework for the sector at the national level, a national regulatory institution, and legislation to promote private sector participation.

At the beginning of the century most of the utilities in large urban centers in Colombia were privately owned. Outstanding examples included the water distribution enterprises operating in Bogota and Barranquilla, which were privately owned until the 1920s. This period of private participation ended in the 1950s, when the government, given the precarious conditions in which the services were provided and the lack of investment, purchased most of the private enterprises in the sector. The limited institutional framework at that time made the public sector the only one willing to assume the risk of investing.

The next period was one of centralized state provision through a public entity attached to the Ministry of Health. This entity became responsible for the administration, operation, financing and maintenance of water distribution and sewerage, as well as for planning and regulation. This centralized structure was characterized by political interference and lack of accountability and became highly inefficient. Centralization ended in the late 1980s, when inefficiency in the sector became intolerable.

[2]Although this can also create conflicts of interest for the local government.

In response to the crisis, the government decided to decentralize sectoral responsibilities. This action was part of an extensive decentralization program under which responsibilities for the provision of services considered local in nature were transferred in 1987 to the municipal level. Decentralization per se did not solve the difficult situation that the sector was going through. Attempts were made to solve the problem at the local level but, in general, the process was constrained by the lack of a proper legal, regulatory and institutional framework.

A second wave of private participation in public utilities started in the 1990s. Private participation was encouraged by a new Constitution in 1991 and the enactment of the Residential Public Utilities Law (Law 142) in 1994. The new Constitution abolished the government monopoly on public utilities and opened the way for private participation. Law 142 was intended to create a modern institutional structure and legal framework.

Despite the newness of the process, over 100 municipalities (roughly 10 percent of the total number in the country) now have private sector participation in the sector.[3] The sections that follow analyze and compare the experiences of five of those municipalities with private sector participation in potable water and basic sanitation services.

Located on Colombia's northern coast, *Barranquilla* is a city with over 1.8 million inhabitants. Beginning in the mid-20th century, it became a major industrial center and today is the country's fourth largest city in terms of population. The city began to administer municipal public services under a private management mode in the 1920s. In 1950, local political pressure forced the creation of municipal public enterprises that were subsequently taken over by the local political class. Administrative and financial neglect, however, eventually led to their liquidation in 1991. This, in turn, led to the creation of a mixed enterprise, the Sociedad de Acueductos, Alcantarillado y Aseo de Barranquilla S.A. (informally known as "Triple A" of Barranquilla) to manage the assets of the water distribution system under a 26-year contract. Its private capital stock was initially acquired by local businessmen and industrialists. Although Triple A was able to successfully exclude local political intervention, it did not have sufficient financial capacity to make the investments necessary after so many years of inefficient operation. Thus, in a second stage, the municipality sold a

[3]Private participation is understood to be any type of nongovernmental participation. For example, even though a co-op or neighborhood committee may be operated on a not-for-profit basis, these entities are nevertheless private in nature.

portion of its capital stock to the Spanish group, Aguas de Barcelona, which currently operates the system.

Cartagena is the country's most important tourist center, with a population of 800,000. Cartagena operated a utility that was also controlled by the local political class for almost 30 years until it was liquidated to make way for the creation of a mixed enterprise, Aguas de Cartagena S.A. (Acuacar). Unlike Barranquilla, private participation in Cartagena did not involve an intermediate phase of a mixed enterprise with local capital. Instead, the utility marketed its shares of capital stock directly to qualified international operators, with the transaction eventually made with the Aguas de Barcelona group.

Although located in one of the country's wealthy cattle-raising regions, *Montería* (population 272,000) has faced serious problems involving both left- and right-wing political groups for more than 15 years. Montería liquidated its municipal public enterprises for much the same reasons as Cartagena and Barranquilla, replacing them with a mixed enterprise where former workers were allowed to participate as shareholders or subcontractors. This effort was unsuccessful in attracting investor capital to meet the accumulated demand for investment resulting from years of public sector neglect. Accordingly, the municipality is conducting a second phase of privatization in which it expects to grant a concession contingent on commitments of private capital with support from the central government.

Marinilla and *Apartadó* are two cities in the region of Antioquia. The former is a major agricultural center and the seat of the banana-exporting region of Urabá, bordering on Panama, while the latter is located near the city of Medellin. Apartadó has had the unfortunate distinction in recent years of being at the center of an armed conflict between various political factions with significant influences from guerrilla and paramilitary groups.[4] Even under these difficult circumstances, local private sector operators have provided services to these communities for the past year. Since foreign capital and operators were explicitly excluded from participating in the process, sanitary engineering consulting firms joined with construction firms to provide the service.

Each of these municipalities has encountered the difficulties of a reform process in a highly decentralized country with a fragile regulatory environment. Overall, private sector participation has generated gains, primarily in terms of systems management efficiencies. However, the lack of a strong regu-

[4]Paramilitary groups operate outside the framework of the law and wage war against traditionally leftist guerrilla groups.

Table 10.1. Key Data from Case Studies

	Marinilla	Montería	Cartagena	Barranquilla	Apartadó
Population	43,656	271,952	765,685	1,832,245	82,000
Users	5,954	35,000	87,573	187,000	9,173
Water system coverage (%)	94	71	72	81	56
Sewerage system coverage (%)	44	23	60	68	52
Unbilled water (%)	25	55 (est.)	54	48	35
Micrometering (%)	65	0.07	50	48	65
Average rate ($/m^3)			383	243	
Annual billings ($ millions)	0.535	2	12,186	na	0.68
Actual collections (% of billings)	73	68	85	67	58

latory environment that limits discretion, and the highly decentralized structure of service provision, have limited private participation to management contracts, without major commitments for additional investments.

Institutional Transition Toward Private Participation

The history of the potable water and sanitation sector in Colombia during the second half of this century can be divided into three periods.

• An initial phase when management was the responsibility of the National Municipal Development Institute *(Instituto Nacional de Fomento Municipal, INSFOPAL)*, a central government entity charged with providing and financing services, planning investments and regulating services from the financial and rate-setting standpoints. This stage covers the period from about 1950, the time this organization was chartered, until its closing in 1987.

• A second phase characterized by a transition toward municipal decentralization.

• A third stage beginning with the passage of the Constitution in 1991 and Law 142 of 1994, when the concepts of regulation and private participation were incorporated into the potable water sector.

In the initial stage, INSFOPAL was responsible for the administration, operation, financing and maintenance of water distribution, sewerage, and garbage collection and disposal systems. It also issued norms, enforced proper compliance, and established criteria for the recovery of investments. In addition, it was charged with issuing technical design norms and performing other regulatory functions.

INSFOPAL was at once both judge and party in regulatory affairs. In addition to issuing norms establishing mandatory compliance applicable to system operators, it was also the country's principal operating entity. This, together with the political environment in which INSFOPAL evolved, which was characterized by a clear lack of accountability, eventually spelled the end of this model.

The crisis that befell INSFOPAL led the government to undertake a far-reaching reform by virtue of which responsibilities for the provision of services considered to be local in nature were delegated to third parties. The country's decentralization process led to the popular election of mayors and provided the municipalities with the authority to collect taxes at the local level. In this second phase, responsibility for the provision of water and sanitation services was transferred to the municipalities.

The final phase has been characterized by a new perception of the role of the government in management. The 1991 Constitution introduced the foundation for a more modern state. With regard to residential public services and private sector participation, the Constitution established a number of basic principles in the form of constitutional rights:

- *Competition.* Free competition is a right within Colombian territory, but one that presupposes responsibilities. The state is required to ensure that economic freedom is neither obstructed nor restricted and to prevent or monitor any abuse committed by individuals or enterprises deriving from their dominant position in the national market.
- *Efficient provision.* As regards the history of inefficient provision in the area of public services, the 1991 Constitution takes a transcendental step forward in requiring the state to guarantee[5] the efficient provision of public services to all the country's inhabitants.
- *Solidarity.* Laws must establish an appropriate system of rates, which must take into consideration, in addition to cost factors, criteria related to solidarity and redistribution of income. Toward this end, the law must define appropriate entities for setting rates and authorize the central government, de-

[5]To guarantee is a new obligation that replaced direct participation by the state in the monopolistic provision of service, as it had been doing up until 1991. Although the Constitution does not preclude the possibility that the state might continue to provide services, it does impose restrictions.

partments, districts, municipalities and decentralized entities to provide subsidies to enable low-income individuals to pay fees for residential public services that would cover their basic needs. In addition, the law must define the rights and duties of users, establish a system for ensuring their protection, and determine the ways in which they may participate in the management and oversight of state enterprises charged with providing the service.

• *Fundamental objective of state activity.* The overall well-being of the population and the improvement of its quality of life constitute goals of the state. A fundamental objective is to satisfy unmet health, education, environmental sanitation and potable water needs. To that end, public expenditures for social purposes take priority over all other allocations in the plans and budgets of national entities.

In order to implement the 1991 Constitution, the National Congress in 1994 enacted Law 142, known as the Residential Public Utilities Law. The law has the following objectives:

• To create a new category of "enterprise" within the Colombian corporate structure, i.e., the residential public utility enterprise. The aim is to establish the business unit as the center of activity for providing residential public services.

• To define the contract as a key element in the institutionality of residential public services. Until the law was enacted, activities associated with the provision of public services were governed by informal relationships not subject to contractual formalities.

• To create conditions that will enable public service enterprises to operate in an environment of competition as a way to promote efficiency.

• To promote private sector investment and management in order to strengthen competition and encourage the identification of new sources of capital.

• To incorporate regulation as the exclusive responsibility of the state (government) for monitoring monopolistic public services in order to protect service users. Toward this end, the law creates regulatory commissions as independent government agents charged with preserving competition and preventing abusive practices by monopolistic providers.

• To rationalize the tariff structure by establishing economic and financial criteria for assigning prices, and to guarantee transparent administration of public service consumption subsidies.

• To create a system of state oversight that will ensure respect for laws and norms, guarantee the proper management of the enterprises providing the public services, and prevent practices that restrict free competition.

In short, the new Constitution and the Residential Public Utilities Law attempted to create conditions to limit opportunistic behavior and therefore promote efficiency and investment. In particular, Law 142 created a centralized regulatory framework that protects producers by limiting the discretionary power of the authorities, and protects consumers by limiting the monopoly power of providers. It also created the Potable Water and Basic Sanitation Regulatory Commission (*Comisión de Regulación de Agua Potable y Saneamiento Básico—CRA*) to enforce the regulatory framework. All the reform cases analyzed in this chapter were initiated either before or right after Law 142 was enacted, and as a result could not take full advantage of the new institutional and regulatory environment.

Case Studies

Barranquilla

Barranquilla's first water supply system was built and administered by the city's businessmen in 1880. To that end, they chartered a corporation to be responsible for providing both water service and street lighting. However, inadequate coverage levels impelled the municipality to take over the systems in 1920 in order to assure that coverage would be sufficient to satisfy demand at a time when the city was experiencing significant growth.

During negotiations in 1925 for a loan from the Central Trust Company of Chicago for construction of the new water system, the municipal corporation underwent a series of reforms. Representatives from the City Council, the local Chamber of Commerce and the Chicago bankers were appointed to sit on the company's Board of Directors, and these directors were subsequently assigned responsibility for managing the firm. However, after the withdrawal of the Chicago bankers in 1945, the company went into decline for several decades, until it was finally liquidated in 1960 upon the creation of the Municipal Public Enterprises of Barranquilla *(Empresas Públicas Municipales de Barranquilla—EPM).*

The return to a public sector-based scheme in 1960 served only to further accentuate political meddling in decisions involving the firm, which gradu-

Table 10.2. Municipal Public Enterprises, Barranquilla, December 1990

Operational	
Losses	70%
Water system coverage	65%
Sewerage system coverage	55%
Personnel	7.6 employees/1,000 subscribers
Financial	
Accumulated deficit	$9.2 million
% collected	65% of billings
Revenues/Year	$13.2 million
Rate of indebtedness	92%
Liabilities	$60 million
Personnel costs/Revenues	86%

ally extended to the workers' union as well. Municipal Public Enterprises became a sort of bureaucratic fortress, a major source of financing for political campaigns, and a system of payback through the awarding of contracts. In addition, it fell prey to the excesses of the labor union (which in late 1990 succeeded in increasing the worker benefit ratio to 4.5 times the average salary, while the same ratio in the Colombian public sector was 2.23, and in the private sector 2.7).

By the end of 1990, water service coverage was still only 60 percent of the total population of Barranquilla (with periods of rationing that decreased effective coverage to 50 percent), while sewerage service reached only 55 percent. The enterprise at one point had as many as eight workers for every 1,000 water system subscribers, when in fact a maximum of only three was needed. For each peso invested by the enterprise in service provision, it received a return of only 20 percent in revenues from the sale of service. Liabilities reached $75.6 million,[6] which made it impossible to meet commitments to creditors. This placed the enterprise by the early 1990s in a situation of technical bankruptcy.

The Triple A. By early 1991, local pressure to change the existing situation was building. Such deficient service in the country's fourth largest city, along with the bleak management outlook in the EPM, prompted the national government to support a process of institutional transformation that concluded with liquidation of Municipal Public Enterprises and the creation of the Socie-

[6]Consisting of foreign debt of $18.2 million, debt contracted with national entities of $10 million, local bank debt of $18.7 million, and labor obligations amounting to $13.6 million.

dad de Acueducto, Alcantarillado y Aseo de Barranquilla, S.A. (Triple A). The District of Barranquilla[7] kept 89 percent of class A shares ($9.5 million) of the newly created firm, and 11 percent of class B shares ($1.1 million) were subscribed to by the local private sector.

Triple A and the District of Barranquilla signed a contract giving the former the right to use the assets assigned to service provision for a period of 20 years, in exchange for payment of a royalty. The contract stipulated that the mixed enterprise would only be responsible for administering the assets assigned to the provision of water, sewerage and garbage collection services, which would continue to be owned by the municipality. The mixed enterprise would have no obligation to invest in system expansion, leaving this important responsibility with the district.

The District of Barranquilla also assumed liabilities of Municipal Public Enterprises of more than $70 million. In exchange for the city's agreement to assume these costs and commit itself to a process of institutional change leading to the creation of a mixed enterprise, the national government assumed responsibility for the enterprise's external debt of $24 million and, in addition, transferred $34 million during the five-year period to the resulting investment plan.

The change from a model based on local political cronyism to one designed to reduce political interference, in which management was technical in nature, had some clear positive effects on internal efficiency. The mixed enterprise posted improvements in management indicators (Table 10.3) and made investments of close to $30 million, 70 percent of which were financed with nonreimbursable funds from the central government budget.

One key element was the participation of local civil society. The business community and other forces in the city were successful in imposing a different management model, even over the initial objections of local authorities. The model adopted was important, as it opened the way for civil society and the public sector, working together, to rescue public service provision from the inefficiency to which it had descended.

Private sector participation was negotiated through the creation of a mixed enterprise responsible for administering the assets of the system owned by the

---

[7]In this chapter, references are made to the "Districts" of Barranquilla and, later, Cartagena. In Colombia, the classification of municipalities includes a special category for purposes of the applicable fiscal regime. There are four districts: the Central District (Bogotá), the Cultural and Tourist District of Cartagena, the Port and Tourist District of Barranquilla, and the Port District of Buenaventura.

Table 10.3. Comparative Analysis of EPM and Triple A: Management Indicators

Indicator	EPM 1991	AAA 1993	AAA 1995
Collections/Billings (%)	65	70	71.3
Employees/1,000 users	7.6	4.3	3.3
Personnel costs/ Collections (%)	85	40	
Unbilled water (%)	70	67	
Operating expenditures/ Operating revenues (%)	> 100	77	73
Water coverage (%)	60	67	83.3
Sewerage coverage (%)	55	62	68.6
Total employees	1,800	917	

municipality. This stage represented a transition from an inefficient structure, with considerable meddling by local politicians who had effectively taken over the firm, to one that attempted to decrease political influences. However, the characteristics of the particular model adopted were not sustainable over the medium term, for the following reasons (among others):

• Private investors entered the new structure in association with the local government mainly to guarantee support to a scheme whose principal objective was to correct what was a chaotic situation. Private participation was not really designed to introduce an experienced operator to the sector, nor to contribute with risk capital for investment. In fact, the new firm was the outgrowth of a precarious management scheme and therefore established a "new" operator with no other experience in the sector. Moreover, the new system left the burden of investment to the national and local treasuries.

• Private sector contributions of fresh capital were only $1.2 million, while investment requirements were more than $60 million. Thus, while the change in the administration of the system was achieved, the much needed injection of funds was not. Central government contributions totaling $14.5 million, together with $18.6 million in municipal loans, covered only some 50 percent of total investment needs.

• The mixed enterprise model with public sector control provided no clear incentives for efficiency, since it combined the local government and private sector interests. This led to ongoing negotiations within the Board of Directors, since the objectives of the various members differed. This was a disincentive to risk capital into the system and, ultimately, to making long-term improvements in efficiency.

Consolidation of the private participation process. Deficiencies in the adopted model led authorities to adapt the scheme to favor incorporation of an internationally experienced operator that would also increase the capital of the firm. In 1995, a capitalization process was launched through the sale of shares of Triple A. A condition to their sale was that shareholders contribute know-how in addition to capital. Accordingly, a closed sale was held among enterprises having experience in operating water and sewerage systems similar in size to that of Barranquilla. The municipality would retain 50 percent of the ownership of the company, while the local private sector would decrease its participation from 11 percent to 6.69 percent and the international qualified partner would hold 43.31 percent of the capital of the Triple A Corporation, which was not modified.

The process was designed in two stages involving prequalification of firms by means of a direct invitation, and selection from among the preselected firms on the basis of technical criteria (20 points) and economic criteria (80 points). Although invitations were extended to 23 firms with experience in the operation of water and sewerage systems, the only ones seeking prequalification were Aguas de Barcelona, Lyonnaisse des Eaux, Canal de Isabel II and Ogden Yorkshire. Only Aguas de Barcelona met the prequalification requirements. The firm was called to negotiate the equity package directly, and negotiations were finalized in October 1996.

The process adopted to select the new partner created controversy regarding the transparency of the mechanism and the extent to which the city of Barranquilla got the best deal possible. An evaluation by the central government stated: "[While] this process was well conceived and advised, some of the conditions for prequalification and adjudication limited competition and restricted participation by international operators. The requirement that the operator have a minimum micro metering percentage of 80 percent excluded the English companies, while the requirement involving the provision of service to populations in excess of one million inhabitants prevented the participation of Genèrale des Eaux. The requirement involving service to a total of more than one million subscribers prevented the participation of Empresas Públicas de Medellín. There is still no logical explanation as to why Triple A should have imposed conditions that prevented the price per share from being bid up."[8]

---

[8]Ministry of Economic Development, National Planning Department, "Evaluation of Private Sector Participation in Water and Sewerage Provision," Bogota, August 1996.

The role of the central government in solving the city's potable water service crisis was key. The central government provided:

• *Political support* to the reform process and to the local civil society in its campaigns against the traditional politicians who "owned" the public enterprises.[9]

• *Technical assistance* to the municipality to help identify ways to improve management efficiency in public service provision.

• *Appropriate incentives* to successfully implement the transition, in the form of financial resources to cover the cost of the transition and funds made available for a new investment plan, with disbursement contingent on the municipality's liquidation of the public enterprises and its orchestration of a new form of management based on a non-public formula.

• *Compensation packages* for the retirement plan. Workers' compensation was handled with extreme care in order to ensure that all rights acquired, no matter how extravagant they might appear, were at all times respected.[10]

The restructuring effort solved two of the problems that originated in the first stage; it introduced an experienced international operator and injected some capital into the firm. Nonetheless, the other problems remained unsolved. Although the new structure contemplates a higher percentage of shares in the hands of the private sector, it was not clear that the private operator could take technical decisions without interference. There was an internal agreement within Triple A to have Aguas de Barcelona in charge of administering the system, but the original contract between the municipality and Triple A was not modified. Moreover, the burden of investment remained on the national and local treasuries.

In view of the financial difficulties being experienced in Barranquilla, the next steps in the process will likely involve an increase in the capital of the corporation, enabling the qualified partner to assume complete control over Triple A.

---

[9]In the critical phase involving the decision to liquidate Municipal Public Enterprises, support was provided directly by the president of Colombia.

[10]During the life of the old public enterprises of Barranquilla, the labor union managed to establish a payment known as the "carnival bonus," which was to be paid for no other reason than to recognize the carnival festivities carried out in the city every year in January.

Cartagena

Unlike Barranquilla, Cartagena made a direct transition from public enterprise to a mixed enterprise by means of an association with an experienced international operator responsible for managing the service. The transition, like in Barranquilla, did not require private agents to put up risk capital for investments and limited their participation to management of the system.

Cartagena turned over all public services to the state in the 1960s, with disastrous results. After more than 30 years of management by the Municipal Public Enterprises of Cartagena (EPMC), administrative neglect reached critical proportions in the early 1990s (Table 10.4).

The enterprises accumulated a net deficit of roughly $33 million, the result in part of staffing of close to 1,300 employees for a market of approximately 78,000 registered subscribers. When employees pertaining to services other than water and sewerage are excluded, this indicator totaled nine workers per 1,000 subscribers (excluding contract employees).

The enterprise was also hindered by political meddling in decisionmaking, particularly with regard to the appointment and removal of personnel, and consequently by a lack of procedures for staff selection and promotion as well as high levels of staff turnover, appointments and removals. Staffing levels were far greater than what was needed.

Creation of Aguas de Cartagena S.A. Following completion of a study contracted by the National Planning Department,[11] it was concluded that if the management model were not modified, public service provision in Cartagena would continue its steady decline. The City Council comanaged the enterprise, and beneath a formal model of business management was a second model of political management that handed out jobs and contracts and waived the collection of user fees in order to obtain benefits at election time. The results were obvious: the financial situation became unsustainable in the early 1990s. This led in December 1992 to the passage of Decree 1540 (issued by the Office of the Mayor of Cartagena), which modified the legal structure of the Municipal Public Enterprises of Cartagena by transforming it into a municipal-based industrial and commercial public service enterprise.

This decision to implement the reform, which led to the creation of enterprises devoted exclusively to providing water and sewerage services, was an

[11]Jaime Enrique Varela, "Alternatives to Water and Sewerage Service Provision in the City of Cartagena." Konsultorías Ltda., November 4, 1992.

Table 10.4. EPMC Management Indicators, Cartagena, 1989-92

Indicator	1989	1990	1991	1992
Water system coverage (%)	77	78	80	72
Sewerage system coverage (%)	62	61	65	59
Subscribers, water system	68,151	71,814	74,731	78,199
Subscribers, sewerage system	54,786	56,482	60,796	64,469
Micrometering (%)	66	65	63	47
Losses (%)	43	N.A.	52	52
Employees	1,451	1,576	1,334	1,290
Employees per 1,000 subscribers	12	12	10	9
Billing, water system ($ millions)	3.6	4.9	6.5	7.6
Billing, sewerage system ($ millions)	1.3	1.7	2.3	2.4
Operating expenditures ($ millions)	2.6	3.5	4.5	4.9
Net profit (loss) ($ millions)	(336)	57	(1.7)	(3.0)
Collection efficiency (%)	50		48	50

Source: Rubén Avendaño, Gabriel Piraquive and Bibiana Vásquez, "Colombia—Assessment of the Performance of the Potable Water and Basic Sanitation Sector." DNP, August, 1993.

important first step and opened up the potential for immediate private sector participation. In May 1994, the District Council of Cartagena approved Resolution 05, which eliminated the public enterprises from the district's organic structure, approved their dissolution and liquidation, and authorized the mayor to contract out to third parties—either individuals or legally established public or private organizations—for the total or partial operation of public services, and to create a mixed enterprise.

The mayor then ordered the liquidation of the firm. Public tender was opened, with the participation of international enterprises from France, England and Spain. In December 1994, the contract was awarded to the winning bidder, Aguas de Barcelona. Aguas de Cartagena S.A. (ACUACAR) was subsequently created in accordance with the Colombian Comercial Code and the Residential Public Utilities Law (Law 142). Its equity structure was as follows: District of Cartagena, 50 percent (class A shareholder); Aguas de Barcelona, 45 percent (class C partner); and the private sector, 5 percent (class B partner). Capital equity was $4 million, of which $2.4 million represented cash contributions made by the operating partner and $1.6 million contributions from the district. The bylaws granted management authority to the operating partner Aguas de Barcelona.

The enterprise signed a contract with the district for a period of 26 years. The operation and integrated management of the services are the responsibility of the private partner, which receives a premium based on total revenues of the enterprise. In addition, beginning in the sixth year of the contract, the private partners will receive an amount equivalent to one-twentieth of the total capital contribution, including profits or payments for shares of stock, with the understanding that such recovery does not assume any amortization of shares, decreases in participation in equity capital, and reduces the rights of the partners.[12]

The district assumed all regulatory and investment risks, while ACUACAR assumed all business and operating risks. In addition, the district agreed to "provide the capital and obtain the financing necessary to cover the costs for which it is responsible in order to comply with the objective of the contract" (clause 6), and to "design and implement such investment works as may be necessary for the expansion and improvement of the service, with the understanding that ACUACAR has no responsibility whatever in this regard" (clause 20).

In its first year of operation, ACUACAR was able to record positive results in terms of improving the quality of water distributed and in its business management and user service. However, there was considerable uncertainty with regard to the source of financing for the investment program (the Master Plan has an approximate cost of $88 million).

The reform process in Cartagena represented the transition from an inefficient structure with interference by local politicians to a system managed by an experienced operator isolated from political influence. Yet, the Aguas de Cartagena model was extremely fragile in terms of one of its objectives, which was to achieve an appropriate institutional structure that would make it possible to finance the investment plan. Thus, the benefit of private participation was limited almost exclusively to the improvement in management.

The district is deep in debt and faces difficulties in obtaining the required resources for investment. Different alternatives are being considered to solve this problem. The objective is to identify a partner able to finance the investment plan. To this end, it will be necessary to modify the original corporate structure and the management contract signed between the municipality and the provider, which assigns all the responsibility for investment to the municipality. The new contract should clearly establish the investment commitments and the increase in capital to be made. These modifications will in fact represent a shift from a management contract to a concession contract and there-

[12]The firm will pay annually to class B shareholders (local private entities) and class C shareholders (the operating partner), after a period of five years beginning as of the date of subscription and payment of shares, an amount equal to one twentieth of the total contribution, not including profits or losses generated in each fiscal period, with the understanding that such recovery does not assume any amortization of shares, decreases in participation in equity capital, or reductions of the rights of the partners (art. 20 of the Bylaws of ACUACAR).

Table 10.5. Improving Potable Water and Sewerage Services, Cartagena

Ratio	1992	1997
Water system coverage (%)	72	75
Sewerage system coverage (%)	59	61
Collection efficiency (%)	50	85
Employees/1,000 users	9	4
Unbilled water (%)	52	45

fore will radically change the rules established for the process won by Aguas de Barcelona. Accordingly, a new bidding process will probably be required for award of the concession.

As occurred in Barranquilla, the roles played by both the central government and multilateral institutions were key to resolving the potable water service crisis, as these entities were the only ones with the ability to pressure local politicians to seek out different alternatives.

Montería[13]

The city of Montería has a population of 272,00 and its principal economic activity revolves around livestock. Although located in one of the country's wealthy cattle-raising regions, most of the population lives in extreme poverty and lacks access to essential public services. Montería has had serious problems involving both left- and right-wing political groups for over 15 years.

Municipal Public Enterprises of Montería was created in 1955 as a public institution charged with providing services for water distribution, sewerage, garbage collection and disposal, firefighting and the administration of marketplaces. The highest corporate authority was the Board of Directors, which was presided over by the mayor and made up of city councilmen. The management of the enterprise answered to the Board of Directors and was headed by a manager appointed by the mayor. The manager was appointed to ensure "political peace" within the municipality. As a result of such coalitions, the individuals appointed had enormous political obligations.

[13]Information for this section was provided in part by the consortia Chemonics International, Selfinver, OMI and IP3, current contractors involved in designing and implementing the concession of the water and sewerage utility.

This scenario of inefficiency was self-perpetuating. Given the almost exclusively political nature of the operation of the enterprise, its managers or members of the Board of Directors had a clearly defined interest in climbing politically, as a result of which their election campaigns were generally conducted on the basis of promises to not allow rates to be increased or even to not allow any more meters to be installed.[14]

Under such circumstances, the financial and operating situation of the company reached unsustainable levels. Nominal coverage was 71 percent for water service and 25 percent for sewerage service. Water service was intermittent. On average, water was supplied 21 hours per week (three hours daily). There was no planning of services, no inventory of networks or equipment, and no macro or micrometering. The poor management of the public enterprises generated permanent deficits that forced the municipal and national governments to make fiscal contributions to resolve critical problems in the city's water supply system. In addition, the national government was required to assume responsibility for making the required investments in the system, as no internally generated resources were available.

Creation of the Aguas de Montería Water and Sewerage Corporation. In 1992, the Montería City Council authorized the mayor to liquidate the old Municipal Public Enterprise and create in its place a mixed enterprise to provide water and sewerage services. The Montería Water and Sewerage Corporation *(Sociedad de Acueducto y Alcantarillado de Montería—SAAM, S.A.)* was created in 1994 as a municipal mixed enterprise with the exclusive responsibility for providing water and sewerage services. The subscribed capital is $300,000, divided into Class A and Class B shares for public and private shareholders, respectively. The bylaws provide for a limit on the power wielded by the public sector (a maximum of 49 percent of the shares can be held by the public sector, with the municipality holding at least 40 percent of them) and private agents (each private stockholder can hold a maximum of 5 percent of the shares). With a vote of 70 percent of the total shares subscribed, the Shareholders Assembly may modify the capital structure of the enterprise.

The enterprise created is in charge of "management, administration, implementation and provision of residential water and sewerage services for

[14]Montería was known for its sui generis system of buying votes with water: once the user received the bill for service, he would go to the political boss, who would sign the bill on the back if the user would agree to vote for him in the coming elections. Subsequently, the voter would go to the cashier's office of the enterprise with the bill and the "employee" of the politician who had signed the bill, upon seeing the signature of his boss, would eliminate the bill from the enterprise's commercial registry.

the Municipality of Montería" (taken from the bylaws of SAAM), toward which end it is authorized to conduct activities ranging from construction, expansion, replacement, restructuring, maintenance and conservation of infrastructure to the signing of contracts and collection of revenues for service provision. The enterprise does not own the assets of the system but rather was granted use of those assets in exchange for payment of an annual amount equal to 10 percent of the total amount of revenues from billings.

SAAM is affected by a critical financial-structural problem stemming from the low level of capitalization and the weak composition of the market. The low amount of capital contributed to the firm ($300,000) greatly limits its management capability. Also, approximately 80 percent of its subscribers are classified as low-income, requiring subsidization according to the terms of Law 142 of 1994.[15] Half of the low-income users pay nothing for service. On average, only 68 percent of the total amount billed is actually collected. The municipality, in turn, has not yet created the Solidarity and Revenue Redistribution Fund to compensate the enterprise for the subsidies it is required to pay.[16]

A significant element of the institutional transition from the old public enterprises to the new SAAM was the arrangement made with former workers. The environment was highly politicized, with violence by extremist groups that strongly influenced labor unions categorically opposed to privatization. Accordingly, the decision made by the national and local governments was to terminate any personnel involved in disruption, a decision carried out through payment of indemnification to workers and creation of a program to reinstate them into the workforce. This program involved creating cooperatives of ex-workers, to which SAAM subcontracted certain activities of the new enterprise. In addition, workers were allowed to purchase shares in the new enterprise.

The change in management model from a public enterprise to a mixed enterprise brought two main benefits to the management of services in Montería. First, like Barranquilla, the problem of the politicized management of public

---

[15]There are three industrial subscribers that generate 1.3 percent of all revenue and 2,090 commercial subscribers accounting for 9.9 percent.

[16]In Colombia, public services are financed for lower-income groups through the mechanism of the cross-subsidy between population groups. The operating form of the subsidy is based on the classification of income groups into six residential strata, plus industrial, commercial and official groups. The law requires that the intermediate stratum (stratum 4) be charged the mean long-term cost and authorizes the upper strata (strata 5 and 6 plus industrial and commercial) to be charged a surcharge of up to 20 percent of total consumption, which is used to subsidize the consumption of strata 1, 2 and 3. Funds collected in the form of surcharges are deposited into a "Solidarity and Revenue Redistribution Fund."

Table 10.6. Municipal Public Enterprise of Montería Prior to Reform

Operating ratios	
Unbilled water	55%
Water system coverage	65%
Sewerage system coverage	30%
Employees/1,000 subscribers	9.8
Financial ratios	
Accumulated deficit	$140,000
Collections	65% of billings
Annual revenue	$1.1 million
Indebtedness	54%
Liabilities	$2.2 million
Personnel costs/Revenues	56%

services was decreased significatively. Second, considerable reduction in the size of the bureaucracy affected operating costs.[17] According to statistics for Colombian enterprises, SAAM today has the lowest administrative costs of any similar enterprise in the country.

Still, the new model had some problems. First, investment needs of the water distribution and sewerage systems when SAAM was created totaled some $100 million, owing to the lag in investments and poor administration, operation and maintenance of the system during the years in which it was the responsibility of public enterprises.[18] The new institutional structure adopted did not deal with this issue—capitalization of the system totaled only $300,000. Second, the corporate objective and the geographic scope of operations of SAAM were poorly defined. Third, no contract existed to regulate the relationship with the municipality. Thus, there were no stipulated conditions for turning over the right to SAAM to use the assets, their value and the grounds for rescinding the right to use them. Fourth, the contractual arrangement with the co-ops of ex-workers may yet lead to problems and conflicts of interest, since the co-ops are both shareholders in the enterprises and subcontractors.

The reform did not address the system's large investment requirements and lack of management expertise. This is not surprising, considering that the

[17]The enterprise reduced staff from 277 active employees and more than 100 part-time employees to a total of 109 workers (26 permanent employees plus 83 from the subcontractor co-ops).

[18]Although 75 percent of the households in the city were connected to the water distribution system, only about 50 percent could actually receive potable water on a continuous basis.

Table 10.7. Comparative Analysis of EPM-SAAM, Montería

	EPM (1992)	SAAM (1997)
Employees/1,000 subscribers	9.8	0.3
Personnel costs/Revenues		
Unbilled water	55%	55%
Operating expenditures/Revenues	90%	
Coverage		
Water system	65%	75%
Sewerage system	23%	23%
Unbilled water	60%	55%
Total employees	277	26

process was carried out under unstable political conditions, without an appropriate regulatory framework, and with no contract to regulate the relation between the new firm and the municipality. Although the operation of the new enterprise did not significantly improve service, it was at least partially able to cut the inefficiency cycle caused by political interference. This was made possible mainly by the decision to involve former workers as shareholders and contractors of the new enterprise, thus introducing private participation in the firm while also decreasing opposition to the reform.

Specialized consulting services were recently contracted to structure a complete process for private participation in the system. The purpose is to carry out the technical assessment and propose an investment plan in order to best bring in private sector participation.

Marinilla and Apartadó[19]

Until the initiation of the private participation process in 1992, the municipalities of Marinilla and Apartadó in the Department of Antioquia were associated with the departmental water and sewerage enterprise, Acuantioquia, created in 1960. The various partner municipalities had a minority equity participation in the enterprise (27 percent), while the majority (73 percent) was owned by the Department of Antioquia.

At the beginning of the 1960s, Acuantioquia had fairly efficient manage-

[19]This analysis was prepared with assistance from Dr. José Fernando Cárdenas, Director of the Water Unit for the Department of Antioquia.

ment, which enabled it to secure significant regional economies of scale in terms of system administration. Since the department it served was one of the two richest in the country, the enterprise enjoyed a favorable situation thanks to unconditional transfers from the central government for carrying out investments in member municipalities.

This financial advantage became unsustainable over the medium term, since the lack of a budget constraint led to decisions that had no economic justification, particularly regarding collection of fees (which were less than the costs of service provision), ranking and prioritization of investments, and salaries and promotions.

Unlike in most of the municipalities in the country, the process of decentralization of potable water and basic sanitation services to the municipal level did not materialize. On the contrary, although the municipalities modified their participation in the enterprise, majority ownership continued to be held by the Department of Antioquia. The member municipalities accepted the regional model because this was the only way of avoiding the loss of the investment subsidy received from departmental treasury.

By the mid-1990s, Acuantioquia's inefficiency had become unmanageable. Also, many municipalities began to realize that independence could be more lucrative than association, especially in view of cross-subsidies between municipalities. The new departmental administration proposed the liquidation of the enterprise and creation of a scheme whereby any subsidies provided by the department would be based on economic considerations. Accordingly, the decision was made to transfer ownership of the systems to the municipalities, and administration (management, operation and maintenance) to the private sector. This liquidated the firm Acuantioquia.

At first, the department considered a mixed enterprise model with an international operator like the one used in Cartagena. This led to expressions of interest submitted by Thames International and Aguas de Barcelona. Neither firm, however, would make a substantial investment commitment to the system, leading the authorities to consider a different approach. The department decided that a contract would be awarded only to Colombian enterprises operating together as a consortium. That is, the new strategy deliberately sought to establish a link with national capital, fully aware that there were no private enterprises in Colombia with experience in the operation of such systems.

Remuneration was to be based on a single formula, equivalent to a percentage of monthly collections. In order to avoid "flat" contracts, the departmental administration decided that collections were the best way to compensate the administrator for the operation of the system and the most effective way to have the administrator assume the commercial risk.

The contracts were for 15 years, and it was understood that during this period the concessionaires would be able to amortize the investments required to place the system into operation and also obtain an appropriate return on the investment. The terms of reference required the invited bidders to submit an investment plan for placing the system into operation at an optimum level, as well as the proposed remuneration for implementing that system. Each contract was to be awarded to the bidder submitting the lowest remuneration offer together with a commitment to comply with the management parameters set forth in the terms of reference.

The bidder's technical ability, experience in its area of specialization, and financial solvency were to be assessed during the tender proceedings. In order to allow participation in this activity by firms with no experience in managing such services, the tender proceedings were designed on the basis of the experience of the personnel that would be involved, as opposed to the firm submitting the bid. The contracts were awarded to Presea Ltda. in Apartadó and to Conhydra in Marinilla, both made up of engineering and consulting firms.

One of the most interesting aspects of the Antioquia experience is the promotion of private participation by the department itself, which established as an obligatory condition the prequalification of local firms operating together as a consortium, thus eliminating competition from international firms. According to the governor, this promoted local industry by protecting it in its initial stages by facilitating the merger of firms specializing in other areas related to the provision of potable water service.

The department was able to introduce some incentives to operate efficiently with the management contracts awarded. The decision to exclude international competition eliminated having an experienced operator administering the systems, but helped reduce friction from the process. Eventually, it may also help create some local expertise. One pitfall of the model was that, because of the pressures placed on each municipality, full advantage was not taken of the economies of scale of administering the departmental system together.

Conclusions

Private sector participation in the potable water and basic sanitation sector in Colombia has been a process of trial and error that has evolved over the seven-year period from 1990-97. The cases evaluated in this chapter clearly show that private sector participation has generated gains, primarily in terms of systems management efficiency, which is one of the central arguments offered to justify private sector participation in providing such services. However, the Colombian experience also shows that the potential of private participation has yet to be exploited to the fullest. The strategy adopted by the central and local governments, along with the country's fragile regulatory conditions, contributed to limiting benefits from private participation.

Creating small systems where there is an enormous need for investment and little or no capacity to finance it with user fees minimizes the potential for private investment. In Colombia, this problem arises primarily because of the decentralized structure of municipalities. As a result, it is virtually impossible, legally and politically, to combine markets and privatize regional rather than local systems with their corresponding administrative and technical economies of scale.

The lack of a strong regulatory environment that limits discretion, combined with the problems inherent in small systems, results in private participation that is limited to management contracts. Although this may be appropriate for those cases where an existing infrastructure is available and where the efficiency gains from management are evident, it does not solve the problem inherent in most of the systems, that is, the need for additional coverage.

The primary objective when private participation started was to liquidate inefficient state enterprises and replace them with different management modes that involved the creation of mixed enterprises and the introduction of private sector participation in management. The new firms created had an obligation to administer the assets of the cities' water and sewerage systems, but had no obligation to invest in their expansion, as this important responsibility had been delegated to the municipalities. Private investors were invited to associate with local governments solely for implementing new forms of management for the enterprises, leaving the burden of investment to national and local treasuries.

Processes to involve private participation were carried out at the local level, with support and follow-up provided by the central government. This generated a sense of ownership and legitimacy about the solutions adopted. Because of the involvement of the central government, the processes enjoyed access to national budgetary resources, as well as to loans granted by the financial system to meet all of the transition costs, which in some cases involved layoffs and the liquidation of commercial liabilities, as well as the internal and external debt of a number of the enterprises. The political backing of the central government also helped counter the significant local political forces that had actually created the situations of inefficiency and had become firmly entrenched.

The new form of management—mixed enterprise—though creative in the way in which it evolved, does not provide clear-cut incentives for achieving efficiency, as it combines a social objective inherent in the nature of the state, with private sector profit-maximizing objectives. This could result in endless renegotiations that obstruct management of the firm.

In the strictest sense, the operating partners did not become involved with the systems as the result of a competitive process. Reports from the central government confirm that the structure of some agreements has not always been transparent.[20] Colombian legislation is not particularly strict about the selection of the partners to participate in mixed enterprises and, as a result, this mechanism has been used as a loophole to avoid competing for access to markets. The immediate effect is that the reform may not ensure the lowest prices for the consumers or the most favorable technical conditions, particularly considering the enormous asymmetry in the negotiating ability of local governments vis-à-vis experienced operating enterprises.

The way in which the businesses were valuated did not follow strictly defined financial procedures and, as a result, the values assigned to the shares of capital stock in the enterprises were estimated from accounting-type valuations. This led to an undervaluation of the shares, thus reducing the potential for obtaining capital to invest in the systems and leading to an unjustifiable transfer of income from the public to the private sector.

Except for Marinilla and Apartadó, none of the private operators had clearly defined goals or commitments before signing the contracts. Moreover, the adopted strategies did not take into consideration, in any of the cases, structuring contracts based on the establishment of clearly defined responsibilities regarding investments and compliance with management goals and, therefore, compensation was not generally linked to performance. Also, the innumerable contingencies not taken into account in the contracts may lead to future conflicts between operators and municipalities.

In Cartagena, Barranquilla and Montería, there was strong labor opposition to private participation. However, the orchestration of direct arrangements, in which frank and open discussions were held from the outset regarding the

[20]Ministry of Economic Development, National Planning Department, "Evaluation of Private Sector Participation in Water and Sewerage Service Provision." August 15, 1996.

implications and goals of the processes, was a determining factor in the successes achieved in the transition period. All of the rights that the workers had acquired were respected. By paying all legally incurred labor liabilities and, in particular, by specifically indicating from the outset the intent to liquidate the enterprises, it was possible to ensure a smooth transition. Apartadó is particularly instructive, since no major setbacks took place in an area where armed conflicts between extremist political groups forewarned of the potential for problems. Still more surprising is the fact that it is precisely these same groups who today defend the improvements achieved in terms of quality of service.

None of the enterprises had sufficient technical capability at the municipal level to address the evaluation, design and subsequent structuring and negotiation of the processes of private participation. As a result, Colombia now finds itself facing serious problems in terms of monitoring the performance of the private agents involved. Moreover, technical capability at the national level was also limited. In addition, there was no legal framework in place to structure such processes until July 1994, when Law 142 governing residential public utilities went into effect.

Efforts were made to redirect the reform after the establishment of the new legal and regulatory framework. The national government defined a strategy to support (by means of specialized consulting services financed with its own resources) the structuring of processes of private participation for those municipalities whose mayors indicated their desire to participate. The objectives of the reform were more clearly defined and superior technical capability was made available. Unfortunately, these efforts have been limited in most cases by the institutional arrangements made in the initial phase and by some uncertainties created by the implementation of Law 142.

As the government itself concluded in one of its assessments of the processes of private participation: "Although the regulatory system is only now in its development phase, the ongoing issuance of new norms creates uncertainty in private agents. The differences in terms of interpretation of the law between government agencies create distrust and transform the regulatory and control framework into a high-risk scenario. Some of these norms create disincentives to private sector participation. Such is the case of the resolutions handed down by the Potable Water Regulatory Commission involving management plans, discount rates and contracting standards."[21]

[21]Ibid.

In general, the interpretation and application of the norms developed by the Potable Water Regulatory Commission is variable and may be adapted to each particular case, thus constituting a significant source of regulatory risk. For example, the range established by the commission for the discount rate in the calculations of capital recovery (between 9 and 14 percent) does not reflect the conditions of the financial market or the level of risk of the sector. This has led to private enterprises attempting to seek adjustments through management rates, or by purchasing supplies from affiliated enterprises. In other cases, the norms are being created, and therefore there is no assurance as to how the law will be interpreted.

As a result of the reforms introduced by the 1991 Constitution and the Residential Public Utilities Law, Colombia has in place a complex institutional organization. This organization may become a significant source of regulatory risk for a number of reasons, the most important being that regulatory functions are not the exclusive realm of the Potable Water Regulatory Commission. Also involved are the Ministries of Development, the Environment and Health, as well as the Superintendency of Public Utilities and the municipalities.

The Colombian strategy clearly demonstrates that the processes of private participation do not eliminate the necessity of government, but rather redefines that role. Accordingly, these processes require strengthening regulatory, monitoring and control functions in order to ensure the government's ability to regulate and control private sector participants.

The enactment of specific legislation for the potable water and basic sanitation sector that imposes restrictions on regulatory discretion, and the existence of institutions capable of enforcing the law, are necessary conditions to consolidate private participation. This framework is recognized by the private sector as an important element in terms of investment security.

Unlike Colombia, many countries in Latin America have established processes of decentralization to the state, provincial or departmental levels, thus facilitating the structuring of regionally based concessions, which may be more advantageous from an economic standpoint. When this is not possible, it may be necessary to define strategies to group municipalities to achieve economies of scale, or to group services to achieve economies of scope in order to make the process of private sector participation successful.

The Colombian approach that led to the disappearance of public enterprises, without a clear definition of the objectives being pursued and without the necessary conditions to promote efficient private participation, has decreased the effectiveness of the private participation process and has now led inexorably to a second stage for restating the strategy.

CHAPTER 11

Private Participation in Water and Wastewater Services in Trinidad and Tobago

David Stiggers

This chapter examines the interim operating arrangement (IOA) of the Water and Sewerage Authority (WASA) in Trinidad and Tobago as a means of reviewing the country's experience in introducing private participation to its water and wastewater services.

The analysis is based on a general concept relevant to most cases of private involvement in public utilities. The concept, depicted in Figure 11.1, shows two main driving forces for private involvement: lack of funding and the need for effective management. Often this is a self-reinforcing cycle, with lack of income and funds starving capital investment, and lack of management skills resulting in poorer levels of service. This leads to a common political problem: until the levels of service are raised, it is not feasible to increase tariffs. Introducing private involvement is seen as a catalyst to break this destructive cycle.

Figure 11.2 shows the various types of contracts commonly used for private involvement in water and wastewater operations, along with their respective levels of investment and risk. This is drawn from the operator's viewpoint, but the implications for the client can also be easily seen.

Many current initiatives worldwide have followed the concession model. However, this can cause problems if private involvement is needed quickly but key project parameters are not yet in place because of a lack of enabling legislation or adequate tariff increases, or even, as is often the case, because of a dearth of sufficient quality information about the business.

Figure 11.1. Driving Forces for Private Participation

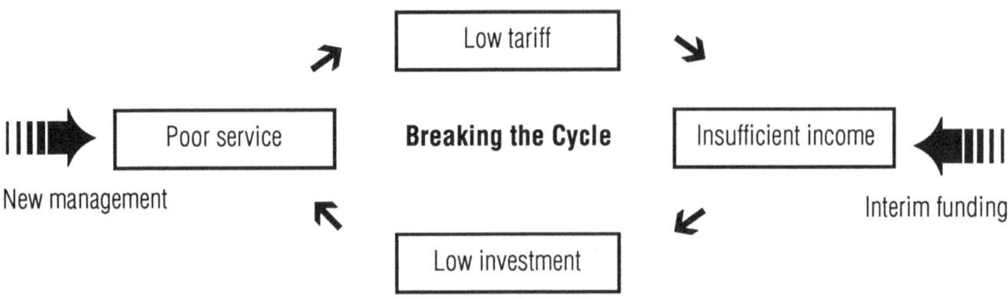

WASA and Trinidad and Tobago

WASA is an autonomous agency as constituted under the National Water Act, with a Board of Commissioners appointed by the government. The WASA management team is led by a chief executive officer, who has clearly delegated authority for overall management. The commissioners report to the Ministry of Public Utilities, which takes a direct and active interest in the continuing development of WASA. Although autonomous, WASA still operates within the constraints of public administration. The government, through direct negotiation, controls tariffs. Formal regulatory mechanisms for the sector are limited, in general, although this is being developed.

WASA serves the combined population of Trinidad and Tobago of 1.25 million with around 250,000 connections for water services. There is a mixture of urban and rural/agricultural demands, with an expanding industrial and

Figure 11.2. Types of Contracts

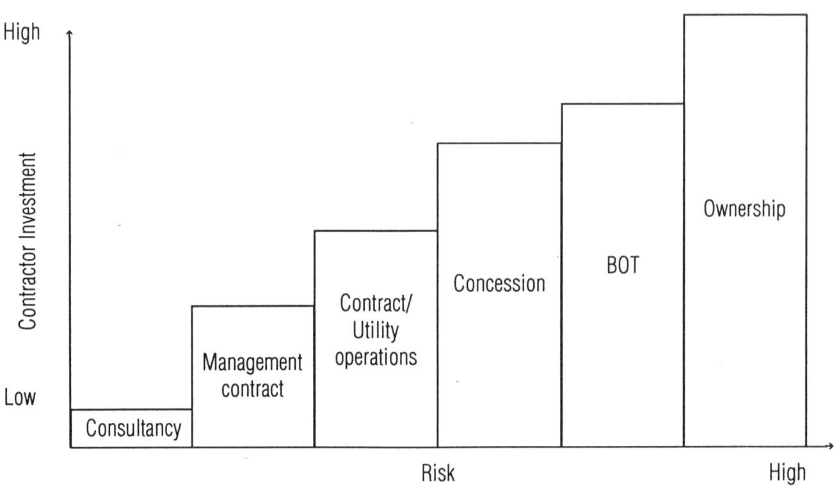

Table 11.1. Water and Wastewater Services in Trinidad and Tobago

	Water*	Wastewater*
Customers	250,000	40,000
Unaccounted for water	Over 50%	
Continuity of supply	24 hrs/day supply to 10% of customers	
Number of staff	3,450	
Employees/1,000 connections	16	

* Based on average family of four to five people.

chemical sector in Trinidad and tourism sector in Tobago. Much of the growing demand on the already overstretched water system is attributed to development of natural gas fields and to rapid industrial expansion.

The level of water and sewage services over the years in Trinidad and Tobago has been increasingly inadequate, despite the fact that WASA staffing levels of 16 staff per 1,000 connections are high compared to a regional "ideal" of 8 per 1,000, or levels as low as 2 per 1,000 in some European utilities (see Table 11.1). No major investment has been made in infrastructure since the oil boom years of the 1960s and 1970s, and, as one manager put it, "the whole water distribution system is leaking like a sieve."

The sector has also been a continuous and massive financial drain on central government funds, costing billions of dollars in losses over the last 30 years. Basically, costs have exceeded income and little money has been available for maintenance and capital investment. Overall annual costs of $46.9 million and revenues of $27.7 million have yielded an annual operating shortfall of $19.2 million. As a result, more than $600 million has been injected into WASA over the years, yet management had not improved and the level of service has continued to deteriorate.

True costs were not easily established, but as an approximate overall indicator the average cost of treated water into supply is approximately 19 cents (or TT$1.17) per cubic meter. However, the level of unaccounted for water was 50 percent and tariff collections were poor. The greatest share of cost was labor, accounting for approximately 65 percent of the total costs of WASA.

Before WASA can possibly meet growing industrial needs, water resources should, in theory, be adequate to meet current demands. However, as Figure 11.3 shows, there are massive losses within the system, resulting in inadequate supply to customers. Shortages at taps have resulted in a complex system of demand management, locally called "scheduling." This involves some 100 employees turning water distribution systems on and off throughout Trinidad on a daily schedule. The objective is to ensure at least some water supply to all

Figure 11.3. Demand for Water (Current production = 700 megaliters/day)

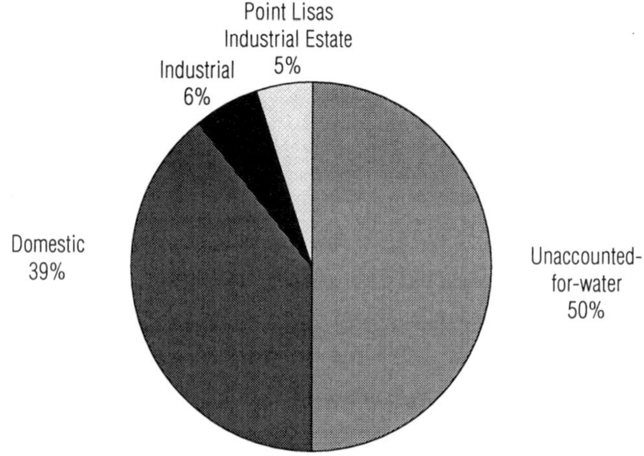

consumers, but in reality some consumers are said to go without services for days and weeks at a time.

Institutional Transition to Private Participation

Although water service was considered a major problem in Trinidad for many years, several factors influenced the decision for private involvement, including the role of the World Bank. Indeed, the decision to include some form of private involvement was a precondition of an earlier World Bank loan.

There was little accurate information available about WASA prior to studies of possible private sector involvement. Certainly, not enough was known to give confidence to investors about the agency's true commercial and operational situation. In 1993, the government set up a task force to review the situation. The review noted the continuing poor levels of service and the massive financial demands made by WASA, and proposed the introduction of private management and finance to reverse the situation. However, the government decided not to change current laws, so the process had to work within existing WASA legislation. This caused some practical difficulties later, particularly in the relationship between the private operator and the Board of Commissioners of WASA. The statutory responsibilities of the board did not change, and although the contract laid out the levels of authority of the operator, there was considerable debate on how these could be employed in practice. This resulted in a series of delays of decisions and approvals in the first two years of the interim operating arrangement, which in turn had an effect on implementation of operational and financial improvements.

There being no specific regulator for private involvement under the existing system, any regulation had to be covered by the contract for the new arrangement. There was a Public Utilities Commission, replaced later by a newly created Environmental Agency. Finally, only quite recently did the government enact legislation establishing a Regulated Industries Commission.

To accommodate the lack of available information and the desire not to change existing legislation, a two-stage plan was adopted to introduce private involvement. First, an initial three- to five-year IOA was to be put out to international tender. The successful bidder would manage WASA for the IOA period. Second, a long-term arrangement (20 to 30 years) would be developed during this IOA period, with the IOA operator given the preferential right to negotiate it.

Private Participation

The interim operating arrangement has many of the attributes of a management contract. However, the WASA Act limits the methods of delegation, so that in the end the IOA was adapted to work within this legal framework. The method chosen was for the private operating partner to provide key members of the WASA management team on secondments, including the chief executive officer, who holds key delegated powers under the WASA Act.

The contract is for an initial three-year period. The contract itself is very straightforward, stating the duties and obligations of all three parties: the government, WASA, and the private operator. In fact, the contract was only developed in detail during the negotiation stages. It is supported by a number of detailed commercial, technical and operational appendices, which provide parameters for its operation. A key area that took months of negotiation was establishing the exact levels of authority and delegation—practical yet within the law—of the WASA Board, the CEO and management.

Selection and Award Procedures. A major international consultant was appointed at the pre-bid stage and, with a government team, developed a detailed request for proposals (RFP). The RFP provided as much key information about WASA as possible. There was a short list procedure, and five world-class operators were invited to tender over a three-month period.

Figure 11.4 shows the timetable for the preparation, selection and negotiation procedure. During the evaluation process there were meetings and pre-

Figure 11.4. RFP Timetable

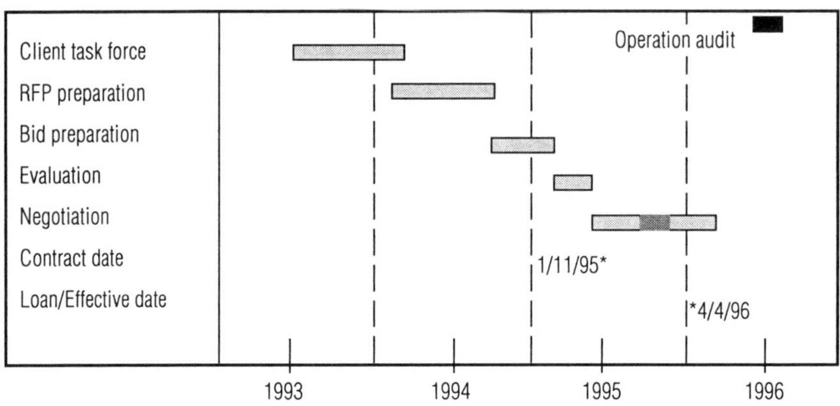

sentations to clarify the proposals, and then a preferred negotiator—the Severn Trent/Wimpey-Tarmac consortium—was called to negotiate and develop the final contract form.

Bids were evaluated on a three-envelope principle:

Envelope 1: Included details of the operational approach, the plan for putting WASA right, the CEO and staff secondment, and the form of new management information systems to be brought in. This was marked following a predetermined marking system.

Envelope 2: This envelope was only opened for those contractors who achieved sufficient "operational points" in Envelope 1. In addition to submitting a financial plan for WASA (evaluated on economic grounds), the operator had to provide a finance package that would cover the financial operating shortfall during the IOA period.

Envelope 3: This was to be a proposal to provide water to industry and to areas of the south. The operator was given a free hand both for developing this proposal and for any others it thought would be attractive to the development and operation of WASA.

The Severn Trent/Wimpey-Tarmac consortium produced the winning proposal. The financing was an innovative proposal funded by local institutions and syndicated by the local Citibank company on a nonrecourse basis. This funding was only required to address the operating shortfall, as funding for the capital works program was to be provided by WASA and the government, making use of international lending agency funds (e.g., World Bank, CDB and EIB). The consortium's Envelope 3 proposal for development and funding a number of essential projects was of particular interest.

Following the call to negotiations, teams from all parties to the contract and their advisers met and developed the final contract form. This process, together with the additional and lengthy process of setting up financing, took several months. The election of a new government and a new WASA Board resulted in further delays. Almost 15 months passed between submission of tender and the effective date of the contract (April 1996).

Variables Used in the Evaluation Process. As described previously, there was a predetermined marking system for various operational parameters. The value and form of the finance package was also given a weighting. Since this is similar to a management contract, tariff levels were not linked to the bids. Indeed, the government indicated there was a possibility that tariff levels might not change during the IOA period. Similarly, apart from Envelope 3 proposals and the operational deficit funding, no capital investment was requested from the operator. Finally, it was negotiated that over 60 percent of the operator fees would be paid against performance deliverables.

Flexibility of the Contract to Adapt to Changing Situations. Since the initial contract covered only three years and was defined in some detail, it was not envisaged that there would be a need for any drastic changes during the period. The contract assumes a cooperative approach between the parties. There are normal contract dispute resolution procedures, as well as an innovative mechanism called the Consultative Committee. Appointed at the ministry level, this committee has representatives from both WASA and the operating consortium's local company, Trinidad and Tobago Water Services, Ltd. (TTWS) and is chaired by a representative of government. The committee has proven to be a useful forum for discussing progress under the IOA, resolving conflicts, and helping to speed or support important issues.

Commitment by Government. The government of Trinidad and Tobago is fully committed to support for the IOA and to the development of WASA. The Ministry of Public Utilities takes a strong interest in the water sector and, having responsibility for WASA and the IOA contract, it expends a great deal of time and effort resolving problems that arise and ensuring that necessary support is provided. This ministry has responsibility for developing the full second stage of private involvement in WASA (i.e., concession or some other long-term arrangement). Preparation for this is ongoing, and negotiations are expected to commence with the current private operator during early 1999.

Financing Risks and Warranties. Since financing was provided on a non-recourse basis, no direct government guarantee was required. The loan was arranged on behalf of WASA, with a payment moratorium until after the IOA period.

Regulation and Reinforcement. Strictly speaking, the IOA is regulated through the contract. As indicated, WASA's operations (and hence the IOA) are regulated by the existing WASA Act and relevant regulatory agencies. In fact, both the WASA Board and the Ministry have paid close attention to operation of WASA and the IOA, resulting up until now in a continuing dialogue between all the parties to the contract.

Progress Under the Contract

Many management systems and processes were overhauled or put in place during the first 18 months of the IOA. The review at the end of the first year pointed to action and improvement in many areas. On the other hand, for various reasons, certain key elements originally envisaged under the fast track timetable at contract signature were not in place. These included, for example, delays in capital investment in infrastructure renewal, lack of approvals for a new industrial water supply, delayed agreement to establish a commercially effective Procurement Unit, and delay in procurement of specialized operational management systems. This has had a delaying effect on implementation of certain elements of the business plan. A key supposition had been that World Bank capital funding was almost ready for disbursement, when in fact funds were still not available 24 months after the effective date of the contract. This, in turn, has held up the vital rehabilitation program for water mains and associated infrastructure components, which is delaying key improvements in levels of service and revenues.

The lack of accurate information during the bidding stage has had ongoing ramifications. A major part of initial IOA activities was directed toward putting in place management systems to bring forward accurate and relevant information for daily strategic management needs. These systems have shown progress.

A cause of delay to the final contract signature was the appointment of a new board of WASA. Board members took their appointments seriously and reviewed their relationships with TTWS and WASA management under the IOA. The boundaries of delegation and authority between the Board and the CEO (and the influence of TTWS) continue to be the subject of many debates. One of the Board's concerns is to ensure its ability to act in its areas of responsibility under the WASA Act.

The operation of WASA under the IOA has shown a remarkable improvement, in spite of the various constraints mentioned here. These have resulted

Table 11.2. WASA Performance Measures

	Before private contract	Current/Predicted value
Financial measures[1,2]		
Operating ratio (operating costs: revenue)	During 1994: 1.31	April-July 1998: 1.15 (predicted less than 1.0 by March 1999)
Revenues	April-July 1997: $14.2 million	April-July 1998: $17.4 million
Operating expenditures	April-July 1997: $24.3 million	April-July 1998: $20 million (predicted annual total for financial year 98/99 is $54.7 million)
Bad debt		Reduced to 20 percent of its former value.
Liquidity	Overdraft 1994: $2.6 million	Overdraft 1998: 0
Hardship relief		Credits for reduction of water bills given to 7,415 old-age pensioners, and other deserving cases.
Operational Measures		
Total water production		Increased by 12 mgd since April 1996 (all users now receive an improved water supply)
Critical plant downtime		Reduced to four days, a reduction of 400 percent (resulting in a higher level of water into supply).
Business/Operational systems		Introduction of critical software and work processes (improved efficiency and cost-effectiveness, higher customer service, increased productivity).
Asset management		Database and management system introduced (more effective servicing, greater productivity).
Community outreach program introduced		Greater awareness and involvement of local communities of WASA operations, and wise use of water.
Staff rationalization		A voluntary early retirement plan introduced in 1998 (VESP) with staff reduction of 780 workers (reduced operating costs, more flexibility in deployment).

[1] Values in US$.

[2] Where definite values for representative measure for periods prior to the IOA contract are not available, examples of early figures available during the contract are given.

in the financial turnaround of WASA at the operational level, improved efficiency of operations, and an increased level of water supply to customers. Some examples of these improved performance measures are given in Table 11.2.

Conclusions

The approach to private participation in water and wastewater services being used in Trinidad and Tobago allows for rapid solutions when information is scarce, and gives some comfort to potential private partners, as some of the initial risks (particularly unknown risks) remain with the public sector during this initial period. While the operational and financial situation is improved, there is time to gather the necessary information and develop a viable and effective solution for the longer-term arrangement, which could be any of the different contract types.

At the same time, the problem of control and authority cannot be overlooked. The nature of this contract form dictates that the operator cannot have direct control over many of the key parameters, (such as major capital investment) and faces restrictions in other areas as well (e.g., potential for involvement by the board in day-to-day management matters). Yet the operator is measured by the overall success of the WASA operation. This was one of the most fundamental issues during contract negotiations, and the one to which careful consideration must be given during the contract drafting stage. The lack of immediate funding for capital works investments is certainly a negative aspect of this particular approach.

Finally, establishment of a Consultative Committee that includes representatives from WASA, the operating consortium and government has been a productive innovation that has speeded up contract implementation and made it more effective. The committee makes the best use of high-level strategic skills of the parties to the contract and provides a forum where problems can be solved jointly.

CHAPTER 12

Energy Reform and Privatization: Distilling the Signal from the Noise

Paul Hennemeyer[1]

This chapter examines Latin American experiences in energy sector reform, with special emphasis on electricity, in order to determine how to best proceed with reform and privatization. This is not a rigorous assessment based on quantitative analysis—the paucity of data and the relative newness of the reform in most countries make this infeasible. Rather, the chapter develops its framework and draws preliminary conclusions based on economic theory and supported by experiences to date.

There are a number of important factors that can greatly influence the outcome of reform efforts. These include macroeconomic conditions, social and cultural factors, climate and, most importantly, the political situation. While recognizing the importance of these variables, this chapter focuses on specific issues surrounding industry structure, policy and regulation and their roles in the reform of the energy industry.

The profound political and economic reforms undertaken across Latin America over the past 10 to 15 years have been as significant as any in the region's history. For many countries, they represent a fundamental departure from the political and economic model that prevailed for half a century and a transition to a new approach based on processes and institutions grounded in individual choice, both at the political and economic levels. As part of their macroeconomic reform efforts, Latin American governments have carefully examined the structure, function and performance of their utility sectors, and by and large found them wanting. Indeed, governments were well-advised to

[1]This chapter has benefited greatly from the comments and contributions of my colleagues at National Economic Research Associates, particularly Michael Rosenzweig, Andrej Juris and Carlos Pabon.

reevaluate their infrastructure sectors, given their importance in supporting economic growth and societal well-being.

The reforms are significantly changing the way in which electric power, natural gas and other infrastructure sectors are owned and operated. In the past, most Latin American energy sectors, along with telecommunications, water and transportation, had been nationalized and regarded as the domain of the public sector because of their natural monopoly characteristics and importance to the economy. Governments throughout Latin America assumed the multiple roles of owner, operator and regulator—a combination that has ultimately proven to be unsustainable. Indeed, government policies were characterized by excessive intervention into the operation of and investment in electric power and natural gas industries. Moreover, the habit of using the energy sectors for social goals (e.g., subsidized consumption and employment) increasingly collided with the need to efficiently invest in and operate these assets. Much of the resulting inefficiency was masked by continuing fiscal transfers to the energy utilities and toleration of the gradual deterioration of service and decapitalization of assets.

The inefficiencies rooted in infrastructure services were exposed during the 1980s as fiscal crises swept the region and governments' abilities to maintain existing operations, much less invest in new assets, were greatly compromised. There are detailed accounts of excessive wage bills, huge fiscal transfers to compensate for noncompensatory tariffs and insufficient collections, and spreading corruption. In the wake of the painful lessons of the 1980s, governments throughout the region understood and accepted the need to develop and apply a new approach to infrastructure service provision that redefines the role and responsibilities of the state, the firm, the investor and even the consumer.

Still, the reform experience is relatively new, and most Latin American countries have yet to embark on the difficult process of energy sector reform. Moreover, the process of reform is complex and affected by any number of variables (political, macroeconomic and even hydrological) that cloud the analysis and make it difficult to draw definitive conclusions.

Latin American Energy Sector Reform

Long before the United Kingdom White Paper was issued in 1989, a pioneering effort in electricity sector reform was well underway in Chile (1982).

Chile was the first country where commercialization and privatization were influenced by the notion that vertical disintegration could significantly improve the performance of the electricity sector. This occurred at a time when the prevailing wisdom was that economies of scale and scope required complete vertical integration within a monopoly utility. Chile's experience showed that commercialization and privatization, along with structural changes and the establishment of a regulatory framework, could produce significant improvements in the performance of the electricity sector. These improvements may have been further enhanced by the creation of a wholesale power market.[2]

This first experiment in serious electricity sector reform has now been followed by reforms in many countries in Latin America. Argentina, drawing from the lessons in Chile and the United Kingdom, moved decisively to restructure and privatize its electricity sector in 1991-92, producing one of the most dramatic turnarounds in the region. Subsequently, Peru (1992), Bolivia (1994), and Colombia (1994) embarked on reforms.[3] While the countries have different starting points and levels of progress in the reform process, they share certain goals and design principles. The two overriding objectives for the energy sector common to all reforming countries in the region are efficient operation and expansion of the electricity and gas systems, and reliable and secure service at compensatory yet affordable tariffs.

These goals are pursued by introducing important sector changes, including revision of the role of the state, regulation of the sector by an autonomous, technical body (or bodies), and a vastly expanded role for private operation and investment. The specific design elements have included:

- Recasting government to become a policymaker and to relinquish the conflicting roles of owner, operator and regulator that have so hampered sector efficiency and effectiveness in the past.
- Establishment, in lieu of government itself, of independent regulatory authorities to protect against monopoly abuses, and to advance "market-like" outcomes where markets themselves are not feasible.
- Vertical restructuring of the industry to permit generation, transmission, distribution and commercialization to operate as separate functions.

[2]Despite important changes introduced to promote the development of a wholesale energy market in Chile, in practice it has become a "generators' club" rather than a competitive market.

[3]The dates in parentheses denote the years when key reform legislation was approved.

• Establishment of access to transportation networks.

• Promotion of marginal cost pricing principles by employing competitive markets, such as in the case of wholesale power, and regulatory instruments for monopoly "wires" services.

• Introduction of commercial principles of operation in the sector that permit modern management of costs and require that consumers pay for their energy use.

• Introduction of private ownership and operation of new and existing assets.

These reforms, coupled with the increasing participation of the private sector in both gas and electricity, are producing improvements in infrastructure services. All the countries studied here have approved legislation that ushers in new reform models to govern their energy sectors.[4] While regional reform efforts are very much works in progress, some improvements can already be seen:

• Private investment has increased enormously. Total investment flows into the energy sector for the countries under consideration total more than $24 billion, and continue to rise. By the close of 1997, the Brazilian electric power sector had received nearly $13 billion in privatization proceeds, with the sale of large generators yet to come.

• The quality and reliability of service has improved. In Argentina, the quality of service as measured by the number of hours of forced outages per year has declined from 1,000 hours in 1992 to 300 hours in 1995, and continues to decrease. Availability of existing thermal assets has also increased considerably since 1992.

• There have also been substantial increases in new generating capacity. At the time of this writing, Colombia and Argentina were the largest beneficiaries of new capacity, with 1,600 MW and 1,700 MW, respectively, since the start of the reform.

• The natural gas sector has also benefited considerably, with increases in reserves and production as well as the development of important new infrastructure such as the Brazil-Bolivia pipeline and the trans-Andes facilities between Chile and Argentina.

---

[4]Argentina, Bolivia, Brazil, Chile, Colombia, El Salvador and Peru.

As indicated in Table 12.1, the seven countries under consideration here, which account for 60 percent of the total population of Latin America, have all passed legislation in recent years to restructure their electricity sectors, redefine the role of the state, and permit the introduction of the private sector and application of commercial principles. Countries with longer histories of reform—namely Argentina and Chile—are enjoying significant improvements in the quality, quantity and price of their energy services. More recent reformers, are witnessing large inflows of private capital via privatization and greenfield projects in both the gas and electricity sectors (see Tables 12.1 and 12.2).

There is enormous variance among countries and between the electricity and gas sectors in terms of level of development, progress in reform, and the approaches being employed. Argentina, with a fully developed gas sector, can pursue different policies involving greater levels of competition than a country such as Peru, where the principal objective is to develop a domestic gas industry and network starting from virtually nothing. Similarly, the experience of Chilean participants in the wholesale energy market may permit smoother transactions and the development of different contracts and terms than in other countries that have only recently launched their wholesale power market.

Variability among countries is only matched by the newness of energy sector reform. Is it possible, given the differences among countries, to make general observations about the process, or to draw conclusions regarding different reform approaches? An approach does exist that can improve the prospects for reform. While these conclusions have not been quantitatively supported for reasons outlined earlier, they do seem to suggest that the approach, when appropriately applied, can produce better outcomes.

The Approach

The approach to energy sector reform that will serve as the template for this chapter is comprised of four key elements: sector objectives, industry structure, rules of the game, and privatization. Each element determines the next and therefore the reform approach is sequential.

Sector Objectives

Given the energy sector's importance in terms of economic growth, social welfare and the national budget, government objectives for the sector generally in-

TABLE 12.1. Electricity Sector

	Argentina	Bolivia	Brazil	Chile	Colombia	El Salvador	Peru
Date of reform law	1991	1994	1995	1982	1994	1996	1992
Laws	Electricity Law No. 24065 Dec/91	Capitalization Law July/94 General Electricity Law No.1604 Dec/94	Act. No. 8987 Feb/95 Concession Law July/95 Regulation Law 1669/96 Electricity Law in Progress	Electricity Law	Electricity Law No. 143. July/94 Public Utility Law No. 142 July/94	General Electricity Law Sept/96	Electricity Concessions Law Nov/92
Time period of restructuring	1992-96 Major privatizations	In progress	In progress	1986–89	1994–present Privatization	In progress	In progress
% Privatized							
Generation	75	96 (1)	Minimal	100 (virtually all)	47	145 MW–IPP	51
Transmission	100 (virtually all)	100	na	100 (virtually all)	In progress (2)	0	0
Distribution	Appx. 70	na	(Ecelsa, Light, ERJ, Coelba CPFL, CEEE, Enersul) (3)	100 (virtually all)	Appx. 40	0	53
National regulatory agencies	National Regulatory Entity for Electricity (ENRE)	National Superintendency of Electricity (NSE)	Ministry of Mines and Energy (MME); National Dept. of Water and Electricity (DNAEE); Future: National Agency (1998/9)	National Energy Commission (CNE); Superintendency of Public Services; Superintendency of Electricity and Fuels	Electricity and Gas Regulatory Commission (CREG); Superintendency of Public Services	SIGET; General Superintendency of Electricity and Telecoms	Tariff Commission (CTE); OSINERG; Directorate General for Electricity; General Electricity Direction (DGE)

Privatization	na	US$40 mn/ transmission	Appx. $9.5 billion	na	$5.1 billion		$800 million +
Average change in prices since reform	-55% (4)	na	na Reform in progress	na Total price = +109%	Spot Prices 1996-1997 (5) Energy = +100%	na Reform in progress	na
Increase in capacity since reform (MW)	Appx. 1700	7 MW (Zongo)	na Reform in progress	na	1600 MW +	145 MW –IPP	500 MW +

(1) The "capitalization" process in Bolivia has meant that a minimum of 50 percent of the assets belong to private investors who have management control.

(2) The private participation in transmission lines includes the assets of the EEB, EPSA and 4 BOTs. ISA is in the process of selling shares.

(3) Including any generation.

(4) Prices for energy in the wholesale market for electricity have dropped from $45/MWh in 1992 to $20/MWh as of April 1997.

(5) Spot prices 1996-97; Source: ISA. In 1996, the spot price reached $.017/kwh and in 1997, $0.035kwh. The total price includes backup, penalties and restrictions. In 1996, it was $0.018/kwh and in 1997 (Sept) $0.037/kwh.

Table 12.2. Natural Gas Sector

	Argentina	Bolivia	Brazil	Chile	Colombia	Peru
Start of reform	1992	1996	1995	1980s	1994	1993
Laws	Gas law No. 24046 June/92	Hydrocarbon law April 96	Constitutional amendment No. 9 Nov/95 Law 8.987 Feb/95	na	Public Service Law No. 142/94	Petroleum Law 1993
Time period of restructuring	1992–93 Major privatizations and restructuring	1996-97 Major capitalization	Act. No. 9.074 July/95 1995-present New entry to the sector	1980s	New entry to the sector	In progress
% Privatized						
Production	100 (virtually all)	50% Capitalized	0	na (1)	0 (2)	na
Pipelines	100 (virtually all)	50% Capitalized	0	100	0 (3)	na
Distribution	100 (virtually all)	50% Capitalized	3 largest companies	100	na	na
Regulatory agencies	ENERGAS	SIRESE Superintendency for Hydrocarbons	National Petroleum Agency (ANP)	Energy National Commission (CNE); Superintendency of Public Services	Electricity and Gas Regulatory Commission (CREG); Superintendency of Public Services	PeruPetro
Privatizations	$7.6 billion	$836 million	$650 million	na	$105 million +	na
Greenfields	300 million +	$600 million	na	$350 million +	$2 billion +	$4 billion
% change in reserves 90–95	6.70%	–6.80%	34%	–59%	89%	No change
Increase/Decrease in production 90-95	30%	–25%	20.5%	17%	50%	–72%
Major pipeline transportation changes	1993–96 30% increase in pipeline capacity	Development of 2,000 mile Bolivia-Brazil pipeline	Development of 2,000 mile Bolivia-Brazil pipeline	New pipeline transport system built by Gasandes	1,250 new miles	Major pipeline project for Camisea-Lima system

(1) Most of the natural gas production in Chile is located in the extreme south in the region of Punta Arenas.

(2) The production of natural gas in Colombia is made using joint-venture contracts between Ecopetrol and private companies.

(3) The majority of the pipeline capacity is private. Law 401 creates ECOGAS, a public enterprise, as the main entity in charge of transportation.

clude safe and reliable energy delivery, expansion and modernization of the energy system, low-cost, affordable energy for consumers and even free energy for certain targeted groups, use of renewable energy sources, attraction of foreign investment, and high sales values for privatized energy companies.

While these aims are legitimate, policymakers must recognize that they often involve tradeoffs, and that not all can be achieved to the same degree or at the same time. Those reform efforts that have been more effective rest on a clear and comprehensive hierarchy of objectives that establishes priorities and embodies the tradeoffs that policymakers are willing to make. One important tradeoff is between efficiency and investment. In order for private entities to risk their capital, they must have a reasonable expectation of an adequate return for any given level of risk. Lacking this, they will simply not invest.

Most countries throughout the region are interested in attracting private capital to improve and upgrade their energy systems (as in the case of electricity) and develop infrastructure from scratch (as is more the case in natural gas). The high fixed costs and use-specificity of the asset (including immobility) pose important risks to investors. They cannot simply convert their facilities to other uses should the expected commercial projections fail to materialize, nor can they disassemble and remove the assets should customers default or the market become unprofitable.[5] In addition, investors in emerging markets face other important political, regulatory and judicial risks that may not encourage efficient investment. Therefore, they may seek additional arrangements that give them some comfort that these expensive fixed assets will yield an acceptable return. This can be achieved, for example, by building efficient plants or gas networks in underserved growth markets, or by securing guarantees from state purchasers or their government owners.

The question then arises as to how efficiency may come into conflict with the policy objective of large-scale investment in new energy assets. Efficiency is fully achieved in highly competitive markets where prices are driven down to marginal costs. Yet, in relatively high-risk environments, it is unlikely that investors will be able ex ante—given all the risks associated with uncertain regulation, weak judicial systems and immature markets—to calculate the right risk premium. Given that a marginal cost pricing system may not provide investors the information needed to reliably estimate an expected return that incorporates the appropriate risk premium, investors will seek to contract these risks

[5]The case of barge-mounted power plants is an interesting exception to this rule.

away. Moreover, most investors, given the choice, would rather not enter a highly competitive market, where arbitrage opportunities are few (since losing returns to competitors is not particularly appealing). This is important because reforming countries must effectively compete for investment funds with other investment alternatives.

After long years of neglect and underinvestment, many countries in Latin America are in real need of significant investment to develop, modernize and expand their electricity and natural gas systems. Such levels of investment may not materialize if a government is also seeking to achieve energy prices that are as close to marginal cost as possible (e.g., through the introduction of competitive supply markets for electricity and gas). Governments may, therefore, have to permit the signing of long-term off-take or supply contracts for electricity and gas that are of sufficient duration to allow developers to amortize the debt and provide their shareholders the expectation of real returns. Alternatively, governments may permit exclusive franchises (in essence a guaranteed market) for a certain period, with the requirement that a certain level of investment be undertaken.

Clearly, such arrangements can blunt the development of competition and therefore reduce the level of efficiency. However, in capital starved sectors characterized by significant country or regulatory risk, it may be necessary, for a fixed period, to allow arrangements that give investors the needed comfort that revenue flows will be sufficient to cover not only operating costs, but also to service debt and provide adequate return. There may be ways to limit the duration of contracts and franchises or to link regulated tariffs to prices in the market to inject some competitiveness into such arrangements.

This is merely one example where policy objectives may not be consistent—at least over the same time frame. Others that frequently arise are as follows:

- Maintaining or even reducing tariffs, while still seeking to attract private capital to the sector on acceptable terms (to the government).
- Maximizing the sale value of an energy asset while delaying the design and implementation of changes in structure and regulation of the energy sector; or alternatively, maximizing the sale value of an energy asset for fiscal reasons, while pursuing reduced or stabilized tariffs.
- Establishing independent and professional regulation of the sector and management of the enterprises, while still seeking to keep a range of interventionist tools in the hands of the government.

The point is that governments employ energy sector reform to reach a number of important sector goals. Yet, in most cases, many of these goals imply tradeoffs that are difficult to effect. Policymakers may find themselves constrained by macroeconomic conditions, sociocultural factors, climate and the political situation. And conflicts that are not resolved at the policy level merely resurface and undermine the reform objectives. An approach to policymaking that has internal inconsistencies can seriously disrupt the process of successfully implementing energy sector reform.

Governments are better advised to build their reforms on clear, comprehensive and internally consistent policy objectives. Priorities should be established and tradeoffs made at the outset and dealt with through appropriate sequencing of the reform, rather than trying to achieve multiple objectives at once. While it is plain that reform is a practical process that involves consistency as a goal rather than as an expectation, outcomes can nonetheless be improved by an aware and deliberate configuration of the necessary steps. Argentine policymakers decided early on that the sale of their electricity assets to qualified buyers through a competitive bidding process was more important than adjusting the rules of the game to seek maximum fiscal advantage for the treasury. Politically difficult matters, such as the sale of "national patrimony to foreign investors," may be better dealt with by first educating customers and designing policies that make them part of the pro-reform constituency. While there have been some difficulties in implementation, the Bolivian model of capitalization was ingenious in its dual aim of attracting significant new investment capital for existing energy assets, while moving to ensure that at least a part of the returns on that capital accrue to Bolivian citizens via their pension schemes.

Industry Structure

Once governments have developed an internally consistent and comprehensive set of policy objectives for the energy sector, they must turn to the question of how the structure of the sector can help them achieve these goals. This is not a purely linear process; iterations must be allowed. Policy objectives should be in the form of a template and, depending on the structural options that are available and feasible, the government may wish to adjust certain goals to ensure compatibility with workable structural choices.

Sector reorganization operates at two levels. One is the vertical restructuring of the industry into some or all of the four major components of generation/production, transmission/transport, distribution, and commercial operations/retailing. The other is the horizontal restructuring of the industry to break up the firm or firms that operate within each component to reduce concentration at each level.

The structural choices are driven by an economic assessment of where competition is economically feasible, what is technically feasible, and what is politically acceptable. The application of such thinking to energy utilities is relatively new and has not spread much beyond the 20 or so countries that have undertaken or are embarking on structural reform of their energy sectors. The notion that energy utilities should be integrated developed as a result of the underlying economies of scope and scale. Consolidation of the industry was promoted by efficiencies related to the size of the assets, not only (but primarily) in the central generating stations and the transmission and distribution networks, but also in planning, financing and central purchasing of supplies and equipment. Viewed as natural monopolies, governments accepted the integration of the industry and regulated it (or owned and self-regulated it throughout much of Latin America) to ensure that the public utilities provided safe power at reasonable rates. These state-owned utilities were also used as vehicles for a range of other social goals, often at the expense of reliable and universal energy services (Rosenzweig and Voll, 1997).

Advances in technology and shifts in ideology have led to rethinking the notion that energy services, particularly electricity, can only be provided through a vertically integrated utility operating as a monopoly. Rather, there is a growing body of evidence that generation and the supply and commercialization of electricity and gas can be provided on a competitive basis. Currently, independent power producers and wholesale power markets are features of the electricity sectors in Argentina, Chile and Colombia, and are emerging in Bolivia and Peru. Retail competition extends the choice of supplier all the way to the individual consumer and is being implemented in Argentina, and the Kw demand threshold for choice is progressively lowered. In addition, retail choice is currently being considered in El Salvador and is also part of the new structure proposed for Brazil.

While the transmission and distribution networks are still natural monopolies in the view of most commentators, competition can nonetheless be introduced at two levels. First, upgrading and expansion of the networks can be undertaken through a competitive bidding process. Second, operation and management of the networks can be opened to so-called franchise bidding, allowing different firms to compete for management of the networks under contract for a certain period. Both of these competitive tools have been introduced into the high-voltage transmission network in Argentina.

The option of structure is essentially a function of the question, "Who may sell to whom and what may be sold?" Structural models in the electric utility industry are differentiated by the degree of choice that buyers and sellers have in selecting one another and the services they wish to transact. In the most restrictive version, buyers have one choice of seller—the monopoly utility—and one choice of product—the bundled electricity service. Similarly, sellers have only one choice of customer (the ratepayer in their service territory) and the same single service to offer. Restructuring typically involves expanding the range of choices available to buyers and sellers.

This question, then, is mainly about the structural choices that are available. Four basic models can be identified:[6]

• *Model 1* is characterized by monopoly at all levels. A single company generates or produces, transports and distributes energy to all end-users. In some instances, the distribution function may be split off from generation or production and transport, but at each level there is only one service provider.

• *Model 2* (a single buyer or "monopsonist" model) introduces competition in generation and a single purchasing agency. The purchasing agency as the only buyer chooses among generators but retains the monopoly to supply all energy within the sector. There are also monopolies over the wires services and sales to the final consumer.

• *Model 3* introduces competition for wholesale supply. Distribution companies may purchase directly from energy suppliers (independent prower projects, utilities, marketers) over an open access transmission grid or pipeline network that provides such service. The distribution companies remain the monopoly providers of all distribution services and provide energy services to their captive franchise customers. Sufficiently large customers may be able to purchase energy directly from the wholesale market.[7] However, competition has been introduced at both the level of generation and wholesale supply. New trading arrangements, such as spot and contract markets, typically evolve at this stage.

• *Model 4* introduces choice of supplier and energy services all the way down to individual customers, no matter how small their requirements may

---

[6]See Hunt and Shuttleworth (1997).

[7]Demand thresholds are currently as follows: Chile, 2 MW; Argentina, 100 KW; and Colombia, 1 MW. These have, however, been declining.

be. Therefore, all customers choose their supplier and there is open access to both the transmission and distribution networks. These networks remain monopolies in their areas of service, but are open on a fair and comparable basis.

The principal policy question is what basic structure is best suited for the government's objectives. The economic answer is that competition should devolve to the lowest possible level to ensure that choice is present at every level—competition and choice being the twin drivers of efficient markets. However, there are two important caveats to this dictum, the first technical and the second political.

Technical constraints. As competition for energy supply devolves to ever lower levels, the systems for monitoring consumption and settling payment become increasingly complex and expensive. Wholesale competition introduces a considerable degree of complexity in the metering, settlement and clearing systems, as literally dozens and sometimes hundreds of large suppliers and customers are buying and selling energy "products" in spot markets and via contracts. The complexity is increased by several orders of magnitude once retail competition is introduced and all suppliers and consumers have access to the markets for different energy services. The simple fact that electricity cannot be stored requires that all supply and demand be "balanced" to ensure the integrity of the system and avoid a collapse of the network.[8] Competition can increase the technical challenge of maintaining system stability. Therefore, the level of technical and engineering sophistication may be an important constraint on the ability to introduce differing levels of competition into the system. Moreover, the metering, billing and collection systems, as well as the market clearing and settlement system (especially with retail competition), are extremely costly and may outweigh the benefits to be gained from greater competition at all levels.[9]

Political constraints. Governments have frequently used the vertically integrated model to meet various social objectives. These include rural electrification programs, subsidies for low-income users, regional development initiatives, and job provision.

---

[8]Natural gas can be stored, and therefore the instantaneous balancing and dispatch issues so crucial to proper electricity system operations do not apply.

[9]Cost/benefit analyses have cast some doubt on the value of introducing retail competition in the England and Wales system by 1998.

Table 12.3. Structural Models in the Electricity Sector

	Model 1: Monopoly	Model 2: Purchasing Agent or Single Buyer	Model 3: Wholesale Competition	Model 4: Retail Competition
Definition	Monopoly at all levels	Competition among suppliers, but single buyer of all supply	Competition among suppliers and choice of purchasers at wholesale level	Competition among suppliers and choice for purchasers down to retail level
Competing suppliers?	No	Yes	Yes	Yes
Choice of supply at wholesale level?	No	No	Yes	Yes
Choice of supply at retail level?	No	No	No	Yes

The private ownership and operation of energy assets and the introduction of commercial principles in the provision of a "public service" pose an important challenge for policymakers and elected officials. Private firms must be allowed to operate on commercial principles. However, the greater the degree of private ownership and competition in the system (e.g., more unbundling), the less scope the government may have to use the energy system to achieve social objectives. In addition, as part of their national development efforts, governments have frequently extended electricity systems to rural or remote areas that are not commercially viable. These so-called "stranded assets" have become a serious political issue in several countries as governments must decide how to treat the ownership of and return on assets that are apt to lose a large percentage of their value once they are required to operate in a competitive environment. Again, more competition, private ownership and customer choice limit the government's ability through cross-subsidies, franchises and the like to keep fundamentally uncommercial assets viable. In such cases as have been described here, governments must replace the hidden transfer that state-owned utilities provide with direct and visible transfers to those groups (e.g., the poor, farmers or utilities investors) who they believe are deserving of society's largesse.

Therefore, while the economic choice of structure is reasonably straightforward—greater levels of competition and choice are better—the technical constraints and political realities may limit a government's ability to introduce a more competitive industry structure. On the other hand, a structure that favors less competition and greater levels of concentration can produce economic costs that can be significant.

Rules of the Game

The choice of structure determines the requirements for regulation. Designing the structure of the energy industry will involve division into separable businesses (e.g., generation, transmission, distribution, and commercial activities); determining those separate businesses that are competitive (e.g., generation/production and supply) and those that have natural monopoly characteristics requiring regulation (e.g., wires and pipelines); and determining the requirements needed to promote competition in unregulated segments, which may include restrictions on cross-ownership and the degree of concentration within segments.

The rules of the game are comprised of economic regulation and trading arrangements. Both are applied in different arenas for different reasons, but with the same fundamental objective: the promotion of efficient outcomes.

Economic regulation is governed by the guiding principle that it should only be applied where competition and markets cannot function efficiently (e.g., market failures such as economies of scale and externalities). Therefore, regulation is developed to ensure that there is control over monopoly elements that remain in the energy sector. Under Model 1, the entire sector is monopolized by a vertically integrated utility and therefore the costs, operations, service and prices (i.e., tariffs) of the utility are regulated. In Model 2, there is competition among generators to supply a single buyer of output. The regulator consequently refocuses the regulatory scope on the activities of the single buyer, and the operation of (and access to) the transmission, distribution and commercial functions. The process advances with greater market operation of certain functions and regulation of the remaining monopoly elements of the industry. The regulatory function becomes increasingly more challenging with greater competition, as issues such as market power, network access and the performance of the firms providing the monopoly services (e.g., local distribution network operator) become more complex and nuanced.[10] Design of the regulatory function also entails a considerable number of issues related to legal authority, autonomy, precise scope, governance and funding.

Trading arrangements are the means by which the agents in the energy market may interact and replace the internal command and control functions

[10]However, even where markets are operating, some form of regulation is required to ensure that competition remains healthy and collusion and other anti-competitive behaviors do not emerge.

that once guided the operations of the formerly vertically integrated monopoly utility. There are essentially two basic trading arrangements: contracts and markets. Their number and complexity increase as the industry structure becomes more competitive. Model 2 may only entail contracts for fuel supply and energy off-take, whereas Model 4 (full retail competition) may involve the emergence of spot markets, hedging contracts and specific contracts tailored to individual consumers.

Therefore, the rules of the game must be designed around the *need for regulation* versus the *scope for competition* which, in turn, is a function of the choice of industry structure. While proper design of the rules can be challenging, it is weak implementation of the design that causes the greatest havoc on energy sectors around the world, including Latin America. The efficacy of reform and the ability to attract private investment is very much a function of regulatory risk. Investors and operators in energy sectors the world over recognize the power that regulators have to radically alter the nature and profitability of their investments. The following are the types of damage and inefficiencies that can be caused by inappropriate or uneven application of regulation, either by the regulator or his political masters:

- Raise the cost of capital by several percentage points;
- Allow significant efficiency gains to accrue to investors and not be passed along, at least in part, to customers;
- Eliminate all profits and force investors to either operate or sell at a significant loss;
- Cause or allow billions of dollars of uneconomic assets to be built unnecessarily;
- Indirectly permit the deterioration of service and decapitalization of assets.

Poor regulation is not alone in imposing great costs and raising the risks of operating in the energy sector. The judicial system can produce equal, if not greater, damage by undermining property rights and efficient trading arrangements. Increased competition in the energy sector can only be efficient if it functions in an environment where there is protection of property rights, sanctity of contracts, and, therefore, an impartial and expert judiciary. A history of a weak or politicized judiciary undermines the efficiency of markets and adds to risks in such a way as to produce a combination of higher costs and reduced investment.

In sum, structure drives regulation, but this is only the beginning. The appropriate application of regulation is a complex process, and the countries of the region are involved in an ongoing effort to "get the signals right" and seek to arrive at results that markets would produce were they able to function efficiently. Privatization, as part of the overall reform effort, is greatly helped by the development of a well-functioning and predictable regulatory and judicial regime. As newly formed regulatory agencies develop economic and technical capabilities to understand the issues with which they are confronted and to make decisions that are in the interest of all stakeholders, they improve not only the long-term prospects of the energy sector, but also make the sector more attractive to private participation.

However, no amount of regulatory capability can overcome a government intent on inappropriate and frequent intervention in the regulation and management of the sector, or a judicial system that does not uphold the commercial principle of property rights.

Privatization has fundamentally been regarded as the cure for ailing state-owned enterprises, although as a program it is often advanced for objectives beyond that of simply improving the efficiency of stagnant or deteriorating operations. Transferring enterprises to the private sector, it is argued, will imbue managers with an entrepreneurial spirit, motivate the workforce, create incentives to enter new markets and exit unprofitable ones, and improve corporate governance by subjecting the firm to the discipline of the market. At the same time, privatization is expected to:

- Improve public finance through the sale of assets, elimination of public subventions to deficit-ridden enterprises, and expansion of the base for corporate taxes;
- Reduce the presence of the public sector in the economy and relieve the government's administrative burden so that it can better focus its efforts on those activities it alone can do;
- Attract foreign investment;
- Harness domestic savings and develop wider share ownership, thereby creating irreversible public support for the reform efforts;
- Encourage economic growth.

These are among the many policy miracles that a wave of the privatization wand might be able to work under ideal conditions. However, no single element or tool of reform can accomplish a multiplicity of objectives, particularly if, as is often the case in privatization, it is not part and parcel of a well-designed and sequenced reform effort.

It is our view that changes in ownership of energy assets should occur only once the policies, structure and rules of the game have been determined.

However, there is a continuing tendency toward counterproductive substitution of privatization for the reform process, to the detriment of long-term development. Privatization is only one—though important—tool of energy sector reform, and should not be among the first measures to be implemented. Indeed, in general, countries that privatize their electric power or natural gas sectors with little prior attention to structural and regulatory reforms have experienced problems with a lack of competition and inefficient investment, nontransparent regulation, corruption, higher than necessary costs, and lower-than-expected sales prices.

Policymakers, however, argue forcefully to privatize as soon as possible, often citing the following:

• *Window of opportunity.* This view holds that politically, governments have relatively little time to undertake privatization before forces opposed to it mount effective counter-campaigns.

• *Fiscal boost.* When government finances are strained, governments search for assets (especially loss-making ones) to sell.

• *Investment now, efficiency later.* Where energy sectors have been deprived of new investment and become decapitalized, governments must rapidly seek alternative—namely private—sources of financing to improve the operations of energy infrastructure.

Each of these objectives as such certainly may be relevant and important in a given context. Sometimes, they may even trump a desirably deliberative process inasmuch as subtler debates may politically derail privatization. However, policymakers often place too little weight on the possibility that by proceeding to privatization before structures and rules are well defined, they run a real risk of undermining more important objectives. For example, governments that seek a quick fiscal fillip by selling energy assets as the first step in reform may ultimately receive low prices for their assets, as investors take into account the considerable uncertainties brought about by the lack of a defined structure and regulatory framework.

Similarly, private investors who enter into a poorly defined and regulated energy sector often require higher returns to cover the additional risks they perceive. Lenders, in turn, may demand very short amortization periods. To reduce these risks, governments may have to provide contractual obligations that commit it to ensuring a long-term revenue stream. From a policy perspective, such contractual obligations, especially overly generous ones, are an inadequate substitute for a proper regulatory regime, and can reduce the government's ability to inject real efficiency into the sector. Moreover, premature privatization may undermine other policy objectives, such as private investment in new assets or maintenance of tariffs at acceptable levels. These are among the tradeoffs that governments may not fully consider in the rush for private investment capital.

Privatization of energy assets ideally should take place only after governments have determined their primary objectives, defined the industry structure, and set up and implemented the rules of the game. Failure to do so adds risks that must be paid for and may also undermine other efficiency objectives that policymakers hold dear.

Summary

The main elements and sequence of a general approach to energy sector reform that raises the likelihood of long-run success include the determination of policy objectives, selection of structure, design and implementation of the rules of the game (both regulation and trading arrangements), and privatization. There are, of course, variations to these basic themes and operational issues in terms of when laws should be passed, regulatory authorities put in place, and assets sold. Moreover, the realities of a given context may greatly complicate or even render any given sequence of steps impractical. The next section explores the recent history of energy sector reform in Latin America. It illustrates why, we believe, this general approach would be most effective, and where feasible, cites examples and data to support that view.

Case Studies

Argentina Gets It Right

The story of electricity sector reform in Argentina is an impressive one. Within the relatively short period of time from 1992-96, the government designed and implemented a profound reform of the power sector that has produced, by virtually any measure, dramatic improvements:

- Prices for energy in the wholesale market for electricity fell from more than $45/MWh in 1992 to $13/MWh in January 1998;
- More than 1,700 MW of new generation capacity has been installed since 1993, with another 2,800 MW due to be commissioned by the end of 1998;

• The unavailability of thermal generating sets in peak hours fell from 60 percent in early 1992 to around 25 percent in 1996;

• The average thermal efficiency of thermal generating sets increased from more than 2,600 kCal/kWh to less than 2,400 kCal/kWh in 1996;

• The amount of unserved energy has dropped to almost zero from about 50GWh in 1991;

• The number of participants in the wholesale electricity market rose from less than 50 at the end of 1992 to more than 1,200 by December 1997, with most of that increase accounted for by the entry of large customers;

• More than 60 percent of installed generation capacity and about 50 percent of distribution (measured in terms of distributed energy) is now privately owned, compared with a wholly-owned state sector in 1991.

These important gains were largely the consequence of a well-designed and executed reform effort that was sequenced properly. Argentine reformers appear to have been clear from the outset that improving the quantity and quality of electricity service and guaranteeing reasonable tariffs were paramount goals. While also important, other objectives such as fiscal support or building domestic share ownership of the assets, were less of a priority. After careful analysis of the history of its own power sector and the reform efforts undertaken in Chile and the United Kingdom, the Argentine government determined that these goals could best be achieved by maximizing competition and private ownership into the electricity system.

The reform steps were implemented in an effective sequence. Following passage of the State Reform Act (1989), the government moved to design and incorporate, in Executive Order 634/91, the main elements of the intended electricity reform. The main features of the reform were thereby clearly signaled to participants in the sector. The key piece of legislation, the Electricity Law 24065, was approved in early 1992 roughly in parallel with development of the regulatory arrangements during late 1991 and early 1992.

The government initiated privatization once these important pieces were put in place. The bulk of the privatizations occurred from May 1992 through June 1994, although some generating assets (i.e., the binational hydro facilities of Salto Grande and Yacyretá, and the nuclear facilities), as well as some percentage of the provincial distribution and lower voltage transmission networks, are still in public hands. The process appears to have worked well, with multiple and credible bids being offered for both generating and transmission assets. Overall, the privatizations proceeded remarkably well and the number of players in the electricity market has increased substantially, thereby facilitating the development of a very competitive system. The government also implemented a radical horizontal disintegration, essentially dividing up the generation park into individual plants and privatizing them. This has created a highly competitive market in which more than 40 generators are bidding into the system. In addition, restrictions were imposed that prohibited any one shareholder group for owning more than 10 percent of the total generating assets. Clearly, the Argentine reformers had carefully examined the reforms in the United Kingdom and Chile, where the degree of concentration at the level of generation was considered by many observers to be too high.[11]

Reform of Argentina's electricity sector has not been flawless. There are a number of areas, particularly in transmission pricing and expansion, where the regulations seem to be producing inefficient outcomes. For example, the use of the "area of influence" method with the assignation of Buenos Aires as the swing bar has the net effect of not correctly identifying all of the potential beneficiaries of any transmission expansion; thus, the approach does not correctly align the costs and benefits of such an expansion.[12] The net result is that economically rational transmission expansion is not taking place. Another area of concern is that distribution companies essentially have no incentive to reduce the costs of the energy they distribute, as these costs may be completely passed through to captive customers.[13] In addition, regulation has not been accorded full independence from the government, since the Energy Secretariat is said to exercise considerable regulatory influence.

Nevertheless, the government, the National Regulatory Entity for Electricity (ENRE) and CAMMESA are in a continuous process of analyzing the operations of the electricity sector and seeking ways to improve their efficiency. Such fine-tuning efforts are encouraged. Indeed, because the broad approach to reform was correctly sequenced and implemented, the Argentine authorities

[11]Indeed, evidence of market power led UK regulator Stephen Littlechild to require that the two dominant generators (National Power and PowerGen) divest themselves of several thousand megawatts of capacity.

[12]The load flow studies attempt to identify potential beneficiaries of an expansion or upgrade of the network. Beneficiaries have the right to support or veto such investments and have an obligation to pay their share should the network improvements be made.

[13]Distribution companies pass through the "seasonal" energy prices, which are smoothed average forecasts of spot market prices. If the actual spot market prices diverge from the forecast, there is a true-up after three months. In addition, distribution companies may not pass on full contract prices unless those contracts were among the few that were signed during privatization to facilitate the sale of certain plants. The net effect is to greatly mute the incentive to sign contracts.

now have the "luxury" of undertaking relatively minor adjustments to the system rather than major changes that might well undermine the credibility of the sector regime.

The Argentine gas sector. Argentina has the most developed natural gas industry in Latin America, in part because of favorable climate and geographic conditions. Changing seasons with cold winters create demand for heating, population is concentrated in large cities, and large oil and gas reserves are located relatively close to demand. These favorable conditions have facilitated development of significant production, transportation and distribution infrastructure and high penetration of natural gas in the Argentine energy market. Natural gas represents about 35 percent of the energy consumed in Argentina, among the highest levels in the world.

The Argentine natural gas sector has undergone one of the most profound and rapid reforms in the world. Between 1992 and 1993, Argentina overhauled the industry structure, regulatory framework and ownership. The sector was divided along horizontal and vertical lines, privatized and exposed to competitive forces. The current government role is limited to regulation of transmission charges and retail tariffs, and enforcement of competition policy and environmental and safety standards. Although the gas market is still distorted by the apparent market power of YPF, a former state-owned oil and gas company, reform has yielded overall positive results, especially massive investment in the expansion of production, transportation and distribution capacity, and improvements in the quality of supply.

The aim of reform in Argentina was to reverse the industry's negative performance. Years of government ownership and management of Gas del Estado, a national gas monopoly, resulted in inefficient operation and heavily distorted retail prices. Low gas prices discouraged investment, which resulted in declines in reserves, production levels, and available pipeline capacity. Resulting pipeline bottlenecks limited service delivery in peak periods and caused service interruptions and gas shortages. For example, gas prices were generally 35 percent below actual costs of gas production and supply in the late 1980s. The size of proven gas reserves in Argentina fell by almost 20 percent between 1985 and 1990.

The government seized a unique opportunity brought on by widespread public discontent with failing public services in the 1980s and early 1990s and radically reformed its infrastructure. Gas sector reform had four main goals: attract private and particularly foreign investment; raise revenues from privatization and eliminate government subsidies; introduce competition; and improve overall efficiency and the quality of services. The design and implementation of reform closely followed these goals. The government formulated the overall strategy with a well-specified structure and sequence. Structural and regulatory changes were introduced first and were followed by the privatization of natural gas companies. The government was able to withstand substantial political pressures during the implementation of reform and, except in one case, it succeeded in achieving the desired goals. The main failing was insufficient competition in the production segment.

The current structure of the gas industry is relatively disintegrated along vertical lines. The natural gas exploration and production segment is separated from transportation and distribution and vertical integration is prohibited.

There are more than 30 gas producers in Argentina, but the production segment remains concentrated. YPF holds about a 48 percent share of total production and the 10 largest producers account for almost 83 percent of total gas production in Argentina, based on 1995 data. Pipeline transportation consists of two pipeline companies, Transportadora de Gas del Norte (TGN) and Transportadora de Gas del Sur (TGS), which are geographically separated but compete in the greater Buenos Aires area. Both companies are unbundled and operate under a 35-year concession that can be extended for an additional 10 years. Pipeline companies offer firm and interruptible transportation services under the open access regime to all eligible users. Initially, distribution companies were awarded 10-year transportation contracts that were gradually phased out up to 60 percent of initial capacity. At present, all participants in the wholesale gas market can purchase transportation services.

Argentina created a wholesale gas market where all producers, distribution companies and large end-users (with consumption above 10,000 cubic meters per day) can trade natural gas. Trading is also facilitated by marketers, agents who purchase or sell natural gas on behalf of other market participants. This increases market liquidity and serves to remove arbitrage opportunities created by price differentials.

The supply side of the wholesale market is dominated by YPF. Although its share is decreasing over the time, YPF controls about 80 percent of the gas contract market where large end-users purchase natural gas. Since wholesale gas prices are deregulated, YPF possesses market power in wholesale natural gas supply.

The distribution segment comprises eight regional distribution companies that operate under 35-year concessions with the option of an additional 10 years. The distribution companies have an obligation to supply small end-users, while they compete with each other and with producers and marketers to supply large end-users. Distribution companies are required to provide open access to distribution networks to large end-users if they chose to purchase natural gas on their own.

The regulatory framework in the Argentine gas sector was radically changed between 1991 and 1993. Gas companies were traditionally regulated by the Ministries of Economy and Finance. This was changed at the outset of the reform, when the government adopted several important legislative measures. Between 1989 and 1991, the Argentine government issued eight decrees that opened exploration and production of oil and natural gas to private companies, introduced competition in oil and petroleum product markets, commercialized YPF and Gas del Estado, established a new taxation and trade regime for oil and gas, and defined guidelines for restructuring the gas industry. In June 1992, President Menem signed Law No. 24.076 that defined the privatization of Gas del Estado and established a new regulatory framework for the natural gas industry. Decree No. 1738/92 in September 1992 developed in greater detail the application of the Law No. 24.076.

Under this legislation, the Argentine government established the Ente Nacional Regulador del Gas (ENARGAS) as a new regulatory agency for the natural gas industry. The role of ENARGAS is to protect consumers, promote competition in the gas market, and ensure provision of open access to transportation pipelines. ENARGAS defines technical and administrative regulations and procedures, formulates the bases for tariff calculation, and determines conditions for awarding concessions. The agency is financed through a fee that all firms have to pay in proportion to their shares in total industry revenues.

Prices for transportation and distribution are based on long-run marginal costs and regulated under the price cap regime. These are adjusted every six months according to the U.S. Producer Price Index and every five years by efficiency and investment factors. Well-head prices of natural gas are deregulated, while retail tariffs for small end-users are regulated.

The privatization of Argentina's natural gas companies was a success. The government privatized YPF and all 10 successor companies of Gas del Estado. Privatization of these companies raised more than $7 billion in mainly foreign investment. The government succeeded particularly in attracting foreign investors who brought the capital and knowledge needed to upgrade and expand natural gas facilities. Major investors were British Gas, Nova Corp, Enron, Italgas and several private Argentine companies. Investors were reportedly attracted by the well-defined concession contracts, open industrial structure, and an option to pay for assets in the form of Argentine foreign debt. Long-term concessions and supply and transportation contracts that defined price formulas and business operation conditions were attractive to investors because they minimized regulatory and market risks. The structure of the gas industry was also clearly defined, as all major structural changes had already been implemented. Investors used about $1.5 billion cash-equivalent of Argentine foreign debt to pay for privatized assets.

The Argentine gas industry has performed relatively well under the structure and regulations set up over 1991-92. Production levels increased by 30 percent between 1990 and 1995. Pipeline companies expanded transportation capacity by more than 30 percent in the first four years following privatization. The gas industry also benefited from the presence of world-class transportation companies. Modern metering and load management and balancing technologies were installed to optimize the operation of pipelines and transactions in the wholesale gas market. For example, TGN installed real-time telemeters in practically all of the gas injection and delivery points.

The open access regime allowed distribution companies and large end-users to diversify their gas supply. For example, TGN sold transportation capacity to about 23 clients in 1996, up from five clients at the beginning of the reform.

Large end-users, represented mainly by industrial customers, extensively use their right to contract natural gas directly. For example, 38 percent of total gas sold to large users is directly contracted with producers and 18 percent of gas destined for large users is directly contracted with transportation companies.

Distribution companies have invested more than $300 million in expanding distribution networks and removing bottlenecks. This has reduced service interruption and improved reliability. Polls indicate that customers have not experienced major supply restrictions in the last two years.

The major flaw of the Argentine gas reform seems to be a lack of restructuring of the gas production segment, where YPF remains a dominant player. Although its dominance is gradually decreasing, YPF still possesses market power in gas supply to the wholesale market. This seems to adversely affect wholesale prices and choice of gas supplies for downstream gas customers. Power generation companies and large industrial users are likely to suffer the most as they face fierce competition in their output markets.

The impact of YPF's power on the energy market is likely to be seen through an increase in spot market prices in the wholesale market. If YPF is able to exercise market power in the gas contract market, it will withdraw supply of natural gas to power generators and industrial customers in order to raise wholesale gas prices. Since gas-fired generation tends to set spot prices in Argentina, higher costs of gas will result in higher marginal costs of gas-fired generation of electricity. This will translate into higher spot price of electric power in the wholesale electricity market. YPF can employ various strategies to maximize wholesale gas prices, such as reducing the availability of natural gas during medium and peak load hours in the electricity market. However, YPF's market power is limited to some extent by interfuel competition in the Argentine energy market.

Another problem relates to regulatory policy and design. Concerns involve the Argentine regulatory framework, development of the capacity resale market, lack of time-differentiated transportation charges, regulation of retail tariffs, and the rigidity of regulatory procedures. The capacity resale market improves utilization of the pipeline system and can reduce the overall costs of pipeline transportation. At present, almost all firm pipeline capacity in the Argentine pipeline system is under contract; however, there seems to be a significant amount of unused pipeline capacity during off-peak periods. This capacity could potentially be used if there were a secondary capacity market where holders of unused capacity could resell it. Holders of capacity would recover some portion of their transportation costs through the resale of their firm contracts, while off-peak firm users would acquire firm transportation contracts for a lower price than the regulated rate.

Development of more flexible transportation markets seems to be hampered by a lack of appropriate time differentiation of transportation rates. At present, pipeline companies do not offer peak and off-peak rates, or low and high season rates, but, rather, essentially flat firm and interruptible transportation rates. This discourages development and use of storage facilities that could use low off-peak or interruptible transportation rates to inject natural gas when gas prices are low, and withdraw it during peak periods. As a result, power generation companies cannot take advantage of storage facilities to minimize the costs of natural gas.

In addition, ENARGAS attempts to regulate wholesale prices indirectly by disallowing the pass-through of gas acquisition costs to retail tariffs. This was initiated by ENARGAS's goal to limit YPF's market power in the wholesale gas supply. This approach may endanger cost recovery by the distribution utilities.

Finally, there is a need for a more flexible mechanism to allow the adjustment of concession terms. Concessions were formulated for a period of more than 35 years, and it is impossible to foresee all changes in the market environment. Actual operation in deregulated markets requires fast adjustment to changes in market conditions. Therefore, concession holders should have the ability to react to new situations and should not be unnecessarily constrained by concession contracts.

Successful Gas Reform in Bolivia

Bolivia successfully reformed its natural gas industry between 1994 and 1997 through deregulation, restructuring and privatization of Yacimientos Petrolíferos Fiscales Bolivianos (YPFB), the state-owned oil and gas giant. After a decade of declining production levels and under-performance in the sector, the government initiated the reform in order to attract private investment and technology, enhance competition and efficiency, create financially sound and internationally competitive gas and oil companies, and support development of domestic consumption as well as export of natural gas.

The Bolivian government was clear in formulating the goals and determining the correct sequence of the reform. The government decided to first introduce regulatory and structural changes to define the rules of the game needed to minimize the uncertainties faced by potential investors and operators in the gas industry. Once these were in place, the move began to privatize YPFB. The government was successful in pushing the agenda through the legislative and political process, with only minor alterations along the way.

Bolivia implemented the structural and regulatory changes relatively quickly. Adoption of the Hydrocarbon Law in April 1996 set the stage for the operations of private companies in both oil and gas. Natural gas and oil exploration, production, transportation and distribution were opened to private investment and operation, and blocks of potential oil and gas fields were auctioned to private companies.

The structure of gas supply was changed dramatically during the reform. YPFB was separated into two production companies of equal size (Chaco SAM and Andina SAM), a pipeline company (Transredes), and a residual refinery and marketing unit that kept the original name of YPFB. Chaco and Andina, together with about 17 additional private producers, are expected to form a competitive environment in production and supply of natural gas. There is great potential for more competition, as Bolivia plans to award additional exploration and production blocks in most of the remaining unexplored territories. All transportation pipelines owned by YPFB, including the stake in the projected Bolivia-Brazil pipeline, were transferred to Transredes, which was unbundled and required to provide open access to all eligible users.

In 1996, Bolivia profoundly changed its regulatory framework by creating the Superintendency for Hydrocarbons (SUPHY), an agency responsible for economic regulation of natural gas transportation and distribution, oil refining and distribution, and for enforcement of safety and environmental regulations in downstream oil and gas markets. SUPHY is a part of SIRESE, a multisectoral regulatory body that regulates electric power, telecommunications and other infrastructure sectors. Additional legislative measures introduced new investment, taxation and trade regimes that promoted private sector activities in all sectors of the Bolivian economy.

After the structural and regulatory stage was set, YPFB became the target of capitalization, a unique privatization program under which investors can acquire up to 50 percent of state-owned companies in return for a commitment to invest in the company. Three of the four YPFB successor companies were sold in December 1996, primarily to foreign investors, for a total of $835 million. Chaco SAM and Andina SAM were sold to Amoco and an Argentine-Bolivian consortium, while Transredes was sold to a consortium consisting of Enron and Royal Dutch/Shell. The fourth company, a residual unit of YPFB, remained under government ownership.

Capitalization of YPFB has been deemed an enormous success. Investors paid more than twice the book value of the privatized assets. The highest premium was accorded to Transredes; Enron and Shell paid $264 million for assets with book value of just $98 million. This particular transaction revealed the value of a strategic position of the Bolivian pipeline network in future intraregional natural gas trade. Transredes controls an export pipeline to Argentina and has a major stake in the Bolivia-Brazil pipeline currently under construction.

The success of the YPFB privatization signals that the overall reform of the oil and gas industry was well planned, although several years will be needed for more quantifiable measures of its performance. Despite fierce opposition from trade unions to the new Hydrocarbon Law and capitalization of YPFB, the Bolivian government firmly pursued its goals by breaking up and privatizing YPFB and introducing competition to both the gas and oil sectors. The root of this success seems to lie in the political will to design a proper reform process and the commitment to carry it out as planned.

The government has largely achieved its goals. It raised substantial revenues from YPFB's privatization and attracted private investors into the oil and gas sectors. In addition to the $835 million raised through the capitalization of YPFB, more than $600 million was invested in new exploration, production and transportation facilities in the gas sector. An important achievement was the agreement to build a transportation pipeline that opens new gas markets in Brazil for Bolivian gas producers. In 1996, YPFB finalized an agreement with the Brazilian counterpart Petrobras to construct a 2,000-mile pipeline from Río Grande in Bolivia to Porto Alegre in Brazil. The agreement, under which Bolivia will export about 280 million cubic feet of gas per day (MMcfd) to

Brazil, is expected to more than double Bolivian revenues from natural gas exports. The pipeline will also boost development of the country's vast gas reserves, and represents an important step toward an intraregional pipeline network linking Argentina, Bolivia, Brazil, Chile and Peru.

The government also succeeded in introducing competitive pressures in the industry by splitting YPFB's production facilities, encouraging production by independent gas producers, and introducing open access to the pipeline transportation network. This created favorable conditions for development of a wholesale gas market where producers, distribution companies and large end-users shop independently for gas supplies.

The gas reform was not flawless, however; the residual unit of YPFB still operates under an unclear status, is heavily overstaffed, and is uncertain in terms of financial viability. The unit remains a contractual party to the existing operations contracts concluded between the former YPFB and independent producers. Most staff who were not employed by new private owners were assigned to the residual YPFB. In addition, YPFB's obsolete marketing and technical services will have difficulty competing with market participants in new open markets. As a result, the future of the residual YPFB remains uncertain, as its only certain source of revenues is from the regulated refinery and distribution business.

The new regulatory agency in Bolivia lacks experienced staff and is vulnerable to political pressures. Effective enforcement and development of regulatory proceedings and rules can be impeded if SUPHY does not attract well-qualified personnel with a diversified mix of skills. Both natural gas and electricity sector reforms were heavily criticized in the recent election campaign, with the winning politicians promising to review capitalization deals and change all regulatory agencies into commissions. The idea of collective decisionmaking is a positive one; however, there is a great danger that the appointment of new regulators will be used to exercise excessive political control over regulatory policy and decisionmaking.

An important challenge for the Bolivian government will be to promote the development of a domestic natural gas market. Existing distribution networks are underdeveloped, since most end-users in the past were supplied directly by YPFB. In addition, final consumption of natural gas is small (less than 5 percent of total gas production), and most domestic consumption is by industrial users in three major cities, La Paz, Santa Cruz and Río Grande. Potential investors in distribution will have to spend large amounts of resources to develop the appropriate infrastructure, since most distribution pipelines are lacking. The government wants to attract investors by awarding exclusive 40-year distribution concessions. The most important issue in this regard will be whether regulatory policy will allow recovery of investment in an efficient, fair and equitable manner. This will depend both on the regulators as well as the government.

Chile's Electricity Sector—A Flaw in Structure

Privatization of Chile's electricity industry was part of the fourth stage of the privatization process initiated in 1974 to reverse the Allende government's determination to transform Chile into a socialist economy, in part through nationalization. Phase I (1974-75) consisted largely of returning nationalized enterprises to their original owners. Phase II (1975-83) involved more than 100 enterprises and had as its principal objective the generation of revenue for the state. The highly leveraged transactions that ensued set off a financial crisis that resulted in bankruptcies and the re-nationalization of many failed enterprises. Phase II firms were reprivatized during Phase III (1985-86), this time with wider share ownership intended to create more financially resilient entities. The fourth phase, which included the power sector, targeted the large core public enterprises created as joint stock corporations by the development institution CORFO.

Chile had reorganized and commercialized the enterprises owned by CORFO in the first years after 1973, with the goal of improving efficiency in order for the firms to be sources of profits rather than deficits to the Treasury. Favorable tax and import treatment had been eliminated, billing and collection procedures improved, prices drastically increased, and unnecessary assets divested. In the power sector, the two large state-owned integrated companies were divided into subsidiaries: CHILECTRA into a generation company and two distribution companies, and ENDESA into a series of distribution companies (two integrated companies to serve the southern regions [(SIC)],[14] a generation-transmission company in the north [(SING)] and two generation companies). In 1986, in order to make the sector more attractive to investors, the foreign liabilities of ENDESA were transferred to CORFO in exchange for the subscription of new shares, which were subsequently offered at discount to

[14]Currently, the majority of the transmission lines and substations in the SIC are owned by ENDESA (the largest generator) and leased and operated by Transelec, a wholly-owned subsidiary of ENDESA. However, a recent court decision has directed ENDESA to divest itself fully from Transelec.

employees and private investors (Saez, 1996; Bitran and Serra, 1996). The regulatory regime is comparatively well advanced and transparent, with an antitrust system created in 1973[15] and the National Energy Commission in 1978. The latter oversees electricity prices and guarantees the coordination of the companies in the interconnected system. Thus, like the British system, some of the success of the Chilean privatization is due to a longstanding effort to commercialize and restructure the sector.

The reform of the Chilean electricity sector has been rated an overall success. The introduction of a wholesale market, direct access for large customers, and economic regulation have been positive and pioneering features of the reform. Generally, prices have been characterized by a slow and stable long-run decline. Private investment has been active in all segments of the sector and, indeed, all of the distribution companies and most of the generating companies are in private hands. The quality and reliability of the system are high, and with a penetration of 94 percent, Chile provides access to electricity to a greater percentage of its population than any other Latin American country.

Nevertheless, the Chilean privatization process has been criticized for not going far enough to ensure a competitive framework, and for having an ambiguous regulatory regime. Industry concentration remains high: the privatized ENDESA, the dominant firm in the interconnected system, along with its affiliates, provides 65 percent of the country's power and controls the transmission system. The interconnected system is itself controlled by ENERSIS, which owns the system's largest (50 percent of sales) distribution company. ENDESA was not divested of its water rights, through which it can inhibit entry of competitive hydroelectric generators, and ENDESA currently is suing the National Water Commission after it was refused a request for additional rights. The antitrust system is viewed as needing much improvement, but major legislative reform has been successfully blocked. Recent rate-setting efforts demonstrate that regulators are having difficulties contending with problems of asymmetry of both information and technical expertise.

Without pressure from either a strong regulatory framework or a vibrant competitive environment, the savings from increased efficiency flow to investors in the form of monopoly profits rather than to customers in lower prices, and the incentives for sustaining productivity gains are diminished. The benefits of privatization to the state and investors may come at a cost borne by customers and the economy at large.

---

[15]Legislative reforms to strengthen antitrust have failed to pass.

The public prosecutor recently alleged that the vertical integration of the electricity industry is damaging for the country and brought a case to the Monopolies Commission. The commission ruled that the dominant position of the ENERSIS Group and its property structure were not prejudicial to free competition in the electricity industry. Despite the ruling, there appears to be evidence to support the public prosecutor's position. Private investors in the Chilean power sector have noted that rather than competing, ENDESA provides something of a "price umbrella" for other generators, and that there is no significant price competition.[16] Indeed, the wholesale market appears to be more of a "generators club" rather than a mechanism for true price competition. Moreover, ENDESA seems to be leveraging its market position to generate returns sufficient to permit it to fund a very ambitious acquisition program of electricity assets throughout Latin America. The matter of structure and industry concentration in Chile remains a serious concern for students of reform. If efficiency gains are to accrue to all stakeholders and not just shareholders, structural design must seriously address both vertical and horizontal disintegration in the sector.

Colombia—Uneven Reform and Unstable Rules

Colombia embarked on a reform of its energy sector in the early 1990s as part of an important reorientation of the role of the state in the economy. The view was that the prevailing pattern of distortions and fiscal transfers to the sector could not continue. In order to begin to appreciate the reasons for the rather confusing and patchy nature of the Colombian power sector reform, it is necessary to discuss the underlying problems that characterized the power sector prior to the start of the reform process.

Noncompensatory tariffs. Political decisions made in the early 1980s resulted in a tariff structure that was increasingly marred by subsidies, cross-subsidies and frozen nominal tariffs. These distortions, over time, began to undermine the financial health of the power sector, starting with the distribution companies and spreading back to generation. Similarly, such distortions garnered important political support from beneficiaries opposing their removal.

---

[16]This has also permitted small players (like Chilgener) to secure the resources necessary to acquire assets elsewhere in Latin America.

Self-regulation. The principal municipal utilities (Bogotá, Medellín, Cali), a regional company (Corelca) and a national company (ISA) historically operated as a pool for purposes of merit-order dispatch and reliability. Purchases and sales were made among the pool members to ensure reliability and the meeting of load requirements. However, poor development of the pool's incentive and governance structures, lack of enforcement of the pool rules, and weak regulatory oversight began to produce problems in the 1980s.[17] These included gaming of the pool arrangements, which undermined system integrity, substandard maintenance of the thermal plants, and even in some cases lapses in fuel supply. Facilities that were not dispatched were not maintained, and when poor hydrological conditions emerged in the early 1990s, many of the thermal plants were not available for dispatch. All of these circumstances undermined the ability of the system to respond to the drought caused by the "El Niño" weather pattern in 1992. The result was a forced rationing of power.

The mounting financial and operational problems in the power sector were masked for many years by massive fiscal transfers to the sector to support tariff subsidies and finance the construction of additional capacity (particularly hydro capacity).

By the early 1990s, it was apparent to power sector experts as well as to the incoming government that the prevailing arrangements were no longer tenable. Serious reforms initiated in 1990-91 were designed to eliminate the distortions and return the sector to operational and financial health. The new public utilities law was passed, tariff reform began, and the government began to convert its debt in sector enterprises to equity as a means of exercising control over the utilities and pushing them in the direction of reform.

However, these reform efforts were stymied by other factors over which the national reformers had only limited control. First, rationing (the result of poor hydrology and poor system management) made it extremely difficult to advance the tariff reform, the crucial first step in financially "sanitizing" the distribution companies.

Second, unlike the UK reform, where virtually all electricity assets were in the hands of the national government, Colombia's electricity assets were owned by national, departmental and municipal authorities. The local entities, in particular, had their own interests and rights to attend to, and could not be

[17]The other companies in the pool were the owners of ISA, which served as the interconnection company and dispatcher. The resulting self-regulation could not advert the companies' disincentives to distort the availability of their plants.

obligated to pursue a national program of reform without serious concessions from the national government. Only through negotiation with state authorities could the government move local authorities to adhere to its overall policy. For example, in order to restructure Empresa de Energía de Bogota, the Colombian government had to agree to capitalize 50 percent of the debt of the Guavio hydro facility held by EEB, sell Chivor, and take other steps to create the conditions necessary to privatize Guavio and unbundle EEB. Such negotiations—which appear to be inherent in the decentralized political context of Colombia—seriously complicated the design and implementation of reform, as local authorities sought outcomes that met their own needs, rather than those of the entire sector. In addition, significant resistance on the part of SOEs and trade unions proved effective in blocking efforts to restructure and privatize the industry.

Third, it is doubtful that the government could successfully reform the power sector and involve private capital without implementing a clear policy to resolve the debt burden of the distribution companies. Despite an attempt to subject the distribution companies to the discipline of "performance contracts," most distributors fell short of targets and many continued to accumulate substantial debts for unpaid energy. These arrears have moved back through the system, damaging the financial and operational health of major agents in the sector such as ISA and CORELCA. The government has since advanced a strategy involving capitalization of sector debts and continued to pressure for reform and privatization.

Disentangling the interlocking web of debt and cross-arrears, jurisdictional overlaps and subsidies has been extremely difficult. Moreover, the reforms were only partially completed when, in 1994, a new government assumed office. Despite privatization of some assets, the new authorities generally appeared to be less enthusiastic about power sector reform. It is apparent in the examples below that the reform process has unfolded unevenly, and with resulting difficulties, at least in part due to the concomitant crises and changes in the country's political life.

• From 1990 to 1994 the government enacted major regulations and laws to create a wholesale electricity market and rules for access to the network and to deregulate generation and supply. However, privatization and unbundling were left to subsequent governments. Long-term power purchase agreements were signed in 1991-92. They mitigated suppliers' risks of dealing only with state-owned utility distribution companies, while permitting the government to encourage needed private production in the face of uncertainty about future industry arrangements. However, the subsequent fall in market prices below long-term contract prices, and the introduction of supplier choice at the level of wholesalers and large users, has left utilities such as Corelca and ISAGen with significant liabilities.

• Private participants and potential investors in Colombia have voiced serious concern about the lack of clarity and stability of the regulatory regime. During 1995, for example, the start of the wholesale market was postponed for six months because a series of regulatory resolutions were being passed to establish and fine-tune the regulatory framework and basic commercial arrangements. An important goal of the reform was attracting large amounts of private capital to develop new thermal power sources to reduce system vulnerability to adverse hydrology. Private firms were encouraged to enter the sector but quickly encountered a series of obstacles: rules on the functioning of the energy market were not clear and frequently amended, and distribution companies were far from ideal customers for private power, as most remain in public hands, burdened by significant liabilities, exhibiting poor payment records, and having no clear incentives to operate commercially.

• The rules of the game were officially enacted in the last months of 1995, the pool started operating in 1996, and some rules were changed in 1997 by discretionary intervention of the central government. By 1998, the distribution companies were in the process of being privatized. Private investments in a number of generators have been delayed, perhaps pending these developments.

• The technical capacity and autonomy of the regulatory agency (CREG) is a serious concern. There have been significant delays in its decisions, and there is a perception of state intervention in the regulatory process—a perception that is aggravated by CREG's dependent relationship with the Ministry of Mines and Energy.[18]

The Colombian reform effort has not been without its successes. After some delays, the wholesale market is evolving and the number of buyers and sellers in the market is rising rapidly. The reform effort has also resulted in the privatization of roughly 60 percent of the sector. The recent successful privatization of EPSA and the Empresa de Energía de Bogotá (EEB) at sale prices significantly above the reserve prices are indications that the situation is

[18]Indeed, three of the eight members of CREG are ministers.

improving.[19] The privatization of CORELCA is planned for the near future, and investor interest appears to be significant.

Although the Colombian reform process is not over, the conclusion that is emerging is that it has been hindered by distorted tariffs, self-regulation, high indebtedness, and jurisdictional and ownership conflicts. These factors may have been a reflection or a result of shifting policy objectives and frequent revisions in the rules. The power of parochial local authorities, changing governments, and frequent shifts in political priorities have slowed and impeded consistent implementation of reforms.

Some observers counter that recent successes in privatization indicate reforms are proceeding well. Aside from the important observation that privatization is only part of the reform and cannot be equated with it, it is worth remembering that country risk in Colombia is lower, given its tradition of sound macroeconomic management. This is reflected in an investment grade rating from S&P and Moodys. In addition, the years 1996-97 have witnessed a very aggressive entry into Latin America by cash-rich foreign utilities anxious not to miss out on the current wave of privatizations. These factors seem to be fueling electricity sector privatization in Colombia and elsewhere in the region. However, it would appear that the Colombia privatization program would have been substantially more successful had the proper policies, structure and rules been in place and clear to all. Indeed, anecdotes from potential utility investors in the United States suggest that uncertainties and frequent changes in the Colombian regulatory regime have dampened their interest in becoming active investors in its power sector.

Brazil—Putting the Cart before the Horse

Until recently, the development of an effective reform process for the power sector in Brazil has clearly been subordinated to political and macroeconomic objectives. At the macro level, the government's priority has been to tame the inflation that has so long plagued the country. In doing so, it has had to de-

[19]However, the two successor firms to EEB (the generator and the distribution company) were acquired by the same consortium (Endesa de España and Endesa de Chile), with the real danger of abuse of market power.

pend excessively on monetary instruments,[20] as political factors have hampered its abilities to address underlying fiscal weaknesses. Privatization of national assets offered a relatively easy way of reducing the government's deficits and stock of debt. However, the recent privatizations of electricity assets have been less than optimal, largely because of the absence of a comprehensive reform program and continued uncertainty regarding the legal and regulatory arrangements.

Until 1993, Brazil's electric sector was dominated by Eletrobrás, the publicly owned holding company of most of the country's generation and transmission assets. The National Department of Water and Electric Power (DNAEE) was responsible for setting tariffs, although the Secretariat of Planning controlled investment decisions and intervened in pricing. Pricing was characterized by a failure of average tariffs to cover either average or marginal costs, discrimination by end-use, and uniformity across regions despite differences in cost. The power industry has suffered from overstaffing, mounting energy losses and underinvestment in system improvements, with concern mounting over the ability to meet load growth.

Brazil embarked in 1993 on a privatization program that included abolition of uniform tariffs and guaranteed rates of return for power companies; establishment of Sintrel, the national grid with open access for independent power producers and self-generators to sell either to distribution companies or end-users; a refinancing of Eletrobrás' outstanding debts; and privatization of both generation assets and distribution companies.[21] The government failed, however, to specify and implement a promised sector reorganization and associated national regulatory regime.

The sale of two distribution companies was marked by disappointing levels of participation, both in the number of bidders and the value of the bids. The privatization of Escelsa, which serves 690,000 customers in the coastal state of Espírito Santo north of Rio de Janeiro, attracted only two bidders, and neither had the desired electric utility experience. The winning bidder was a consortium of financial investors, leaving many observers skeptical as to whether the new owners had either the expertise or the long-term perspective to operate a successful electric utility. The winning bid was 15 percent above the minimum asking price, but included the use of "privatization bonds," which were counted

[20]These include improved tax collection and control of ballooning government liabilities in the areas of pensions and civil servant compensation.

[21]The National Privatization Plan was formulated and launched in 1990.

at face value for purposes of the bid but were discounted 40 to 60 percent in the market.

The sale of Escelsa was more successful than that of the Rio de Janeiro distribution company, Light, which was twice postponed while the government sweetened the financial requirements to allow use of 100 percent rather than 30 percent privatization bonds. Even so, it attracted only one consortium, whose bid reached the reservation price only after the development bank BNDES joined the consortium with additional funding. The auction of Nacional Energética failed altogether, as the expected buyers declined to bid when DNAEE refused to abandon the electricity tariff formula that adjusts with a cost-of-living index.

In both cases, observers cited the regulatory risks as the major stumbling block. The lack of a transparent regulatory regime, the infrequency of tariff adjustments and the reduced inability to predict an adequate stream of future revenue have deterred some private (particularly non-Brazilian) investors from making substantial investment in the Brazilian power sector.[22]

In July 1997, the government finally presented its blueprint for reform, nearly three years after the privatization program had begun. Already there are indications that the goal of developing a truly competitive power sector may be greatly delayed by decisions and transactions that have already occurred. First, the Brazilian government offered concession contracts as a substitute for (rather than a complement to) an appropriate regulatory framework. These concession contracts provided for full pass-through of inflation, fuel costs and any new taxes for a period of up to eight years, thereby casting serious doubt on whether consumers in Rio, Espírito Santo and Bahia will benefit from the efficiency gains realized by the utility for some years to come.

Second, the new structure of the electricity sector is likely to be a mixture of vertically integrated and apportioned companies. This is because some state governments have already sold large interests in vertically integrated state power companies (Light, Cemig), and it will be difficult to force private owners to divest their generation right after they have acquired ownership. More recently, following release of the government's new blueprint for the sector, the State of São Paulo appears to have reversed its original plan for vertical de-integration.

[22]Although there have been recent substantial acquisitions in the Brazilian power sector by major European, Brazilian and North American utility and business groups, larger sectoral and country risk issues have considerably dampened the appetite of potential acquirers of Brazilian electricity assets, as the cases of Metropolitana and Gersul suggest.

The original plan would have permitted real competition among suppliers at the wholesale level to deliver to large customers, free from the requirement to purchase from the incumbent utility. At the time of this writing, it seemed that with the planned signing of long-term contracts between the Eletrobrás generators and the state distribution companies, and the growing trend to privatize vertically integrated utilities, São Paulo has backed away from significantly opening its sector up when it appears that reciprocal access would not be afforded to its utilities. Vertical integration then raises concerns about efficient operation and exclusion of competition in the service areas of integrated companies. This situation does not only affect competition in the wholesale energy market, but also reduces the potential markets for new generators.

Brazil's blueprint is just that, and there remains a considerable amount of work to put into practice the market arrangements, the regulations at both the national and state level, the treatment of access to and operation of the federal and state transmission networks, and the rules and procedures for setting final tariffs. In the meantime, assets will continue to be sold, states will continue to pursue their own reform agendas, and one can expect continued uncertainty and ad hoc behavior.

One may argue that the reform approach employed in Brazil was the best possible outcome given the various contending forces at play. Indeed, given the highly decentralized nature of the Brazilian political system, this is certainly a strong argument. As has been suggested in the above examples, the uncertainty and unevenness of the approach has not been beneficial to the initial phase of the privatization process. Efficiency, too, has not been helped by the pattern of using concession contracts in lieu of regulation, permitting different industry structures to be privatized in different states, and leaving significant uncertainty as to how national and state regulation will develop and interact.

Brazilian gas. The case of gas reform seems to be unfolding in a way similar to that of electricity. Brazil initiated its reform of the gas sector only very recently. The natural gas industry is relatively underdeveloped, with minimal distribution infrastructure and low industrial and residential use. However, restructuring of the electricity sector and overall economic growth have created strong demand for natural gas. This has sparked an urgent need for expansion of domestic gas production and pipelines, and for securing sufficient gas supply from Bolivia. The gas reform has so far been limited to opening the gas sector to private operations and privatization of three state-owned distribution utilities. The major regulatory and structural changes have yet to be implemented.

The main goals of the federal and state governments are to attract private investment into the gas sector, develop transportation and distribution infrastructure, and support growth of natural gas demand. Designing the reform has been complex because of the federal system in Brazil. State governments enjoy relative autonomy and often pursue different goals than the federal government. So far, the reform has focused on attracting private capital into new and existing gas sector infrastructure. Little attention has been paid to the structural reform of the sector because of the economic and political might of Petrobrás, the state-owned oil and gas producing giant. As a result, gas reform is biased toward the privatization process, while structural and regulatory changes are being neglected or postponed. This has a negative effect on investment, as investors face uncertainty about the future regulatory environment.

The exploration and production segment is dominated by Petrobrás, which owns and operates vertically integrated production and transportation facilities and controls all supply of natural gas in the country. It enjoyed monopoly status in the oil and gas sector until November 1995, when constitutional amendment No. 9 ended its exclusive position. In addition, Law No. 8.987 of February 1995 and the subsequent Act No. 9.074 of July 1995 defined a concessions regime for provision of public services in oil, gas and other infrastructure sectors.

At the time of this writing, exploration and production of natural gas can be carried out by private companies, but so far entry has been limited. This is caused by the lack of legal protection and uncertainty about the future structure of the gas industry.

Pipeline transportation remains under the control of Petrobrás. There is an urgent need for expansion of pipeline infrastructure in order to serve increasing demand for natural gas. A number of pipeline projects are currently under development, but Petrobrás plays a dominant role in all of them.

The largest project under development is the Bolivia-Brazil pipeline. Brazil recently secured imports of natural gas from Bolivia that will almost double the country's supply of natural gas. The pipeline should deliver about 285 MMcfd in 1999, its first year of operation, and will double the output by the end of the 20-year contract. Petrobrás has a 51 percent stake in the Brazilian part of the project and 9 percent stake in the Bolivian part. Additional gas pipelines from Argentina and Peru are also under development.

The dominance of Petrobrás in production and transportation results in its dominance in gas supply as well. It is unlikely that a competitive supply of natural gas will develop any time soon because almost all capacity in the projected import pipelines is reserved for Petrobrás. The ownership of gas supply and transportation contracts in the Bolivia-Brazil pipeline illustrates this point.

Petrobrás purchased all available gas supply and transportation capacity on the Bolivia-Brazil pipeline, and it has an option to purchase more Bolivian gas up to the full capacity of the pipeline. Other project sponsors have an option to purchase additional pipeline capacity up to two-thirds of the Petrobrás quota, but this option must be exercised by the time of initial construction. Otherwise, Petrobrás can also purchase this capacity in full. It is unclear whether other project participants plan to exercise their options on pipeline capacity, because there is considerable uncertainty about availability of natural gas in Bolivia and adequate gas demand in Brazil that is in excess of Petrobrás' share, all of which cannot be resolved before the pipeline construction is initiated.

The distribution segment in Brazil consists of 16 state distribution companies and a gas distribution unit of Petrobrás. The most developed distribution systems are in the states of São Paulo and Rio de Janeiro, where the bulk of natural gas consumption takes place. Most distribution networks are underdeveloped. Strong demand for natural gas among power generators and industrial customers is creating a real need for modernization and expansion of distribution networks. For example, a distribution utility in São Paulo will need $300 million for expansion of its distribution system in order to accommodate an almost 200 percent increase in gas consumption over the next four years. Most investment will have to come from the private sector because both federal and state governments lack the necessary financial resources.

Regulatory changes in Brazil were introduced only recently, and the most important changes have yet to be implemented. This introduces great uncertainty for business operations and investment in the gas sector.

The gas and oil sectors are regulated by the Ministry of Mines and Energy and the Ministry of Finance. Most regulatory functions will be transferred to the Agência Nacional de Petróleo (ANP), a new regulatory agency responsible for the oil and gas sectors. The adoption of Amendment No. 9 to the of Brazilian Constitution and Law No. 8.987 of 1995 ended Petrobras' exclusivity in the oil and gas sectors. Private companies can engage in exploration, production and transportation of oil and natural gas after they obtain a concession from the government.

Ownership changes are at the forefront of policymakers' attention, but they were introduced only very recently. Privatization has been limited to gas companies in Rio de Janeiro and São Paulo, where distribution networks are the most developed. Other state-owned gas utilities are scheduled for privatization in late 1997 and 1998.

There have been three privatizations of gas companies so far in Brazil. The first transaction was concluded in January 1997, when the city of São Paulo sold a 19.5 percent share in Companhia de Gás de São Paulo (Comgás), a municipal gas distributor, to Shell for $74 million. The state and city of Rio de Janeiro privatized CEG and Riogas, two gas distribution companies, in July 1997. The winning consortium led by Enron paid a total of $576 million for a 56.4 percent stake in CEG and a 75 percent stake in Riogas.

The Brazilian gas reform is an example of an inverted reform model, where ownership changes occur prior to the implementation of the structural and regulatory ones. A lack of attention to structural issues in Brazil led to the loss of a unique chance to introduce an alternative source of gas supply to Petrobrás when the Bolivia-Brazil pipeline deal was structured. Unclear and undefined regulatory rules also increase uncertainty among investors and do not promote optimal development of the gas sector.

The recent privatizations of gas companies were carried out in an uncertain regulatory and structural environment. For example, privatization of 19.5 percent of Comgás shares represented the stake of the city of São Paulo. At the time of this writing, the remaining shares are still owned by the state of São Paulo and the Federal Ministry of Finance, which were, in essence, not consulted about the sale of Comgás. The state government indicated that potential buyers should be aware that the current statewide concession owned by Comgás might be divided in the future into several sections. This warning did not discourage Shell from buying a stake in Comgás, but it certainly affected the premium paid for the shares.

The main challenge in Brazil remains the structural and regulatory reform of its gas sector. Petrobrás' dominance in exploration, production, transportation and supply must be balanced with a large-scale entry of the private sector into new and existing gas operations. Brazil also must develop an appropriate regulatory policy for the oil and gas sector. ANP is likely, at least initially, to be inexperienced and underpowered to deal with a player of Petrobrás' size. The ability of ANP to protect consumers and other players in the gas sector from Petrobrás' market power will be limited unless the government clearly defines Petrobrás' role in the restructured gas industry.

Electric Power Reform in Peru—A Work in Progress

The 1980s saw a severe operational and financial crisis in the electricity sector caused by low tariffs, inadequate levels of internal financing, dependence on declining government outlays, and, of course, the serious domestic conflict in Peru. As a result, Peru pursued radical reform of its power sector. The government's four goals in electricity reform were to expand generation capacity and the transmission system; attract private investment; improve the quality and efficiency of electric power services; and make electricity companies into commercially viable entities.

The government decided to undertake structural and regulatory changes before privatization. In 1992, a new legal framework was established, the industry was vertically separated into generation, transmission and distribution systems, and competition was introduced at certain levels. Privatization of assets followed.

The Peruvian electricity sector is a hydro-intensive system (over 50 percent of capacity) with total installed capacity of approximately 4,600 MW. It is divided into two interconnected systems: the SICN (central and northern) and the SISUR (south). The former is the larger of the two and serves the principal urban centers and much of the central and northern Peruvian coast. The southern system is smaller, with about 650 MW of capacity, and supplies the important cities of Arequipa and Moquequa and large mining facilities. There is also a considerable amount of self-generation (about 30 percent of installed capacity), along with a number of isolated systems serving rural communities further east.

In a fairly short period, over half of all generation and distribution assets have been privatized. The principal investors to date have included Enersis and Chilectra (Chile), Endesa (Spain), Ontario Hydro (Canada), and Dominion Energy and Entergy (United States). The two transmission systems (ETECEN, with 2,300 km of lines, and ETESUR, with 711 km) are now state-owned share companies that operate the higher voltage networks in the two interconnected grids under concessions granted by the Ministry of Energy and Mines (Directorate General of Electricity —DGE). There are also some 4,300 km of transmission lines operated as secondary and feeder lines operated by generators and smaller isolated transmission entities. Distribution for customers in the northern and central areas of the country is undertaken by seven firms, three of which (Edelnor, Luz del Sur and Ede Cañete) are private. Some 350,000 customers in the south are served by three regional (i.e., publicly owned) distribution companies. In 1995, total Gwh produced and consumed was 12,744 and 10,683, respectively. Estimates are that production increased by approximately 14 percent in 1996.

A new legal framework was established in 1992 with the passage of the Electricity Concessions Law (Law 25844) and its corresponding regulations (Supreme Decree 009-93-EM). This framework required the vertical separation of the industry into generation, transmission and distribution, the introduction of competition at certain levels, and the privatization of public assets. The aim in Peru, as elsewhere, has been to create an efficient and commercially viable electricity sector.

Concessions awarded by the DGE are required for hydro or geothermal units of more than 10 MW. Thermal and nonconcessionaire hydro/geothermal units with installed capacity of more than 0.5 MW require authorization. There are strict prohibitions on cross-ownership to avoid anti-competitive behavior. Generators may not own all or part of interconnected transmission companies or distribution companies, or vice versa.

Sales to regulated customers (i.e., those with peak demand of less than 1 MW) are based on regulated busbar prices. Generators are remunerated for energy and capacity prices are set and approved by the Electricity Tariffs Commission (CTE) every six months. The frequency for resetting the prices reflects the seasonality of Peru's hydrology and the consequent effects on variable generating costs. The prices are based on projections for the subsequent 48 months, taking into account current and forecasted climatic conditions, fuel prices and trends, electricity demand projections, current supply and generation, and transmission facilities that are expected to come into operation. The bulk of this forecasting is actually carried out by the Committee for Economic Operation of the System (COES), but the costs and tariffs that result are reviewed and approved by the CTE. The busbar prices are then adjusted according to energy and capacity losses on the principal transmission system. Finally, the prices include a 12 percent return on investment for the generators.

Inter-generator sales are calculated at short-term marginal cost as determined by COES. Sales to the free market (e.g., those customers with peak demand in excess of 1 MW) are in accordance with contracts freely negotiated between the generator or distribution company and the large buyer. To date, some 40 percent of all energy sold is done so on the free market and bought by the approximately 190 large users in Peru who meet the minimum peak demand condition. The regulated busbar prices may not deviate by more than plus or minus 10 percent of the free market price for the same period within one zone of comparison. If they do, then the regulated prices are adjusted by the CTE so that they fall within this band.

The principles of open access and nondiscrimination govern the regulation and operation of the interconnected transmission system, which must be expanded to accommodate all requests for service. While the law states that third parties shall assume, when necessary, the costs of the required expansion, there are in practice differing views on who should assume this responsibility. A concession from the DGE is required to operate an interconnected transmission system, but these appear to provide relatively little in the way of specific rights, obligations and authority. The bulk of these matters are dealt with in the law and its accompanying regulations, as well as in the internal procedures of COES.

Remuneration for the principal transmission companies is regulated by the CTE on an annual basis and is for the use of the transmission lines and substations and all other ancillary services. The transmission tariff includes a fixed charge for connection based on the firm capacity of the generators connected to the system, and a variable income portion that is supposed to reflect the short-term costs of transmission (e.g., losses). The costs of expanding, operating and maintaining the transmission system are supposed to reflect those costs for a model efficient transmission firm. The total cost of transmission also includes a 12 percent annual return on investment. The entire transmission tariff for the principal system is then incorporated into the busbar prices.[23]

Distributors with average load greater than 500 KW require a concession from the DGE to operate. Concession contracts include the length of the contract, fixed physical area of service, and quality of service requirements. There is an obligation to serve. Prices for distribution customers with a peak demand under 1 MW are regulated and set every four years by the CTE. Distribution companies are required to have running contracts with generators to meet 100 percent of the needs of their load over 24 months. Prices to final customers reflect two important components that are recovered by the distribution company: (i) the busbar price, which covers the generation and transmission costs, and (ii) the VAD (or value-added for distribution) for a so-called "model distribution" company, which also incorporates an annual return.[24] Unlike the generation and transmission assets, for which the annual return is set at 12 percent, the return on distribution assets may vary within a band of 8 and 16 percent, depending on the value of assets calculated by the CTE. The distribution tariff recognizes distribution losses but only permits pass-through to final customers up to a certain level, which is being progressively lowered in order to provide incentives to combat theft.

---

[23]While there are conceptual distinctions between primary and secondary lines in the law, the basic difference appears to be that secondary lines have unidirectional flows from the generator to the principal transmission line or from the principal transmission lines to the distribution company. Secondary transmission lines are remunerated on the basis of a connection toll, which is set in an agreement between the parties involved, and a variable portion, which is based on marginal costs of transmission.

[24]There are three different categories of model distribution companies, which are differentiated on the basis of their systems and load characteristics.

There has already been some discussion of "model efficient systems." These are derived from two important methods that underpin the determination of costs and the setting of tariffs in the Peruvian electricity system. The first method establishes the "economically adapted system," which "is that electrical system in which an equilibrium exists between the supply and demand of energy resulting in the lowest costs of maintaining the quality of service."[25] This exercise is designed to define an optimal system in Peru for balancing supply and demand. Based on the determination of the economically adapted system, the CTE determines what the optimal capital investment is for each segment of the system (generation, transmission and distribution). This is set for each grouping of assets (e.g., a distribution company, or an interconnected transmission system) and is known as the new replacement value (VNR). According to Law 25844, "the VNR represents the cost of replacing the works and physical assets destined to provide the same service with the current technology and prices, also taking into account: (a) the financial expenses during construction; (b) expenses and compensation for the establishment of rights of way; and (c) expenses for studies and supervision"[26]

As of June 1997, however, this methodology had not been fully implemented. The CTE was still engaged in the process of determining the economically adapted system for Peru. This process has been hampered by the absence of a fully developed set of quality service and reliability norms for the electric power sector. As a consequence, the VNRs and the technical standards in use appear to be of a very provisional nature.[27] This does, of course, pose the question as to what VNRs will apply to the various assets in the power sector once the study on the economically adapted system has been completed. This may, in theory at least, significantly change the basis of remuneration for many owners of electricity assets. Moreover, the law provides for the economically adapted system and the VNR to be updated every four years, which again raises uncertainties for investors.

The Peruvian power sector is noteworthy in the degree of dispersion of regulatory authority governing the sector. There are four main regulating agencies: the Electricity Tariffs Commission (CTE), the Committee for Economic

---

[25]Electrical Concessions Law, Decree Law No. 25844, Annex VII.

[26]As was noted above, the return is, in fact, 12 percent on the VNR that has been set by the CTE, whether or not this VNR approximates the real investment costs that were incurred.

[27]The VNR for Etecen's system is based, for example, on a study carried out by the engineering firm of Black & Veatch in 1995.

Operation of the System (COES), the Directorate General for Energy, and OSINERG.

The Electricity Tariffs Commission is a decentralized technical agency principally responsible for setting electricity rates. It has five members representing the Ministries of Mining and Energy, Economics and Finance, and Industry and Tourism. It also includes representatives from the generation and distribution concessionaires. The commission's main functions are to set tariffs for electricity services and sales and serve as the final administrative authority on all disputes related to tariffs. It may also impose sanctions for noncompliance with its directives. It also undertakes the determination of the economically adapted system and the VNR values that flow from it.

The Committee for Economic Operation of the System is a technical, self-regulatory body comprised of representatives of the generation and transmission companies in any interconnected system that has more than 100 MW of installed capacity, and is a creation of Law 25844. Neither distribution companies nor large customers are members. COES is responsible for planning the operation (scheduling and dispatch) of the interconnected system and ensuring that its members operate accordingly. This also requires it to forecast supply and demand, schedule maintenance, calculate short-term marginal costs (guaranteeing energy sales at these costs if necessary), and determine the firm capacity rating of each generating unit. In addition, COES undertakes the analysis required for setting the new busbar prices in May and November of every year, which it then provides to CTE for review and approval.

As there are two such interconnected systems, SICN and SISUR, there are two corresponding COES. It is expected, however, that with the construction of the Mantaro line and the unification of the two interconnected grids, there will be one overall COES responsible for the entire grid.

The Directorate General for Energy (part of the Ministry of Energy and Mines) is responsible for overall regulation of the sector and enforcement of the Electricity Concessions Law and the accompanying regulations. Under the law, concessions and authorizations required for operation in the electricity sector are subject to the approval of the Ministry of Energy and Mines, which also supervises and enforces compliance with the terms of the concessions. The DGE has also developed a series of service quality and reliability norms for the power sector, although these are intended to be enforced by a newly established organization.

Finally, a new organization, OSINERG, was created in January 1997 to set and enforce service quality, reliability and other performance standards for the power system. This had been a serious gap in the development of the regulatory framework in Peru. At this writing, however, this organization has yet to become operational.

The Peruvian reform has certainly been a success when one considers the speed of the privatization process and the improvements in security of supply, although this latter achievement has much to do with the military successes against domestic guerrilla groups. The reform is still very much a work in progress, however, and several sources of concern have been cited by economists, investors and policymakers. These center on the following:

• Inter-generator sales are set by COES, which is a generators club that comprises only the supply in the system and not demand. Prices are calculated and approved by the CTE according to a pre-specified methodology and do not arise from any market interaction. Therefore, unless there is sufficient ability of generators to arbitrage their contractual obligations, such prices cannot truly reflect opportunity cost and may consequently send inefficient signals to agents in the market.

• Transmission may suffer from a lack of clear rules on rights and obligations for system expansion. Discussions with generators, transmission companies and distributors produce a consensus view that expansion of the high voltage system is "someone else's responsibility" and there seems, in practice, to be no clear incentives or mechanisms for system expansion.

• The general absence of performance standards and norms is a source of some uncertainty. Clearly, intelligent investment and operating decisions cannot be made unless there are clear rules on precisely what norms and standards should be met, what penalties are imposed for failure to do so, and what is the cost of compliance.

• Much of the uncertainty in the system stems from an undeveloped economically adapted system and the resulting new replacement values. Much of the system, particularly transmission, was justified largely on political as opposed to commercial grounds. It is unlikely that large segments of the system would be considered integral to an economically adapted system were they to be built today, and consequently they might be remunerated on a much more modest capital base, if at all. In addition, the fact that the VNRs may be reset every four years provides risks for investments going forward. This issue has surfaced in the case of the Mantaro interconnection, where analysts have noted that investing in a long-lived transmission asset (financed with long-term debt) becomes vastly more risky (perhaps even unbankable) if the capital base on which the tariff remuneration is determined can significantly change after four years following a re-evaluation of the economically adapted system and the transmission VNR.

• Finally, there is concern about the degree of regulatory fragmentation in the Peruvian system. Concessions, authorizations, load and cost forecasting, tariffs and standards, which are best (and most commonly in other systems) housed in one regulatory body, are spread through several regulatory authorities in Peru. For example, the authority in charge of setting and enforcing tariffs (CTE) is different from that which enforces standards (OSINERG). Moreover, the high degree of political representation in the CTE and its reliance on COES for load and cost forecasting may threaten its regulatory autonomy and credibility.

Although the Peruvian reform has as one of its chief aims the development of competition in the system, there is, in fact, relatively little. The priority seems to have been placed on ensuring a steady revenue stream to facilitate privatization and attract new owners, and to ensure improvements in the quality and reliability of supply. There is little doubt that significant progress has been made on these fronts. As Peru enters a more mature stage of reform, it may now be opportune to examine ways of expanding competition in the system, establishing clearer rules of the game (e.g., standards, transmission expansion, and the VNR), and reducing regulatory risks.

El Salvador—Off to a Good Start, So Far

The newest entrant to the electricity reform process is El Salvador. The Salvadoran approach to electricity reform provides a short but helpful illustration of how, in our view, the process of electricity sector reform should be pursued. The government has made it clear that its overall goals, in order of priority, are new investments, reduction of fiscal burdens, and promotion of efficiency in delivering power to all users. To meet these objectives, the government has laid out a fairly comprehensive and well-considered reform program that, interestingly enough, envisions an immediate jump to a Model 4 world—full retail competition. This will require a significant degree of both vertical and horizontal separation and the introduction of sophisticated metering, billing and clearing and settlement systems. While full retail competition is certainly an aggressive (some have argued unrealistic) objective, it appears that the government has given considerable thought to the means and ends of electricity sector reform.

Following initial analysis and design work in 1995-96, the government passed its new Electricity Law in September 1996 and established a multisector regulatory agency, SIGET. During the first half of 1997, the government issued its draft regulations and invited comments from various stakeholder groups. The government then undertook the restructuring of CEL, the vertically integrated state-owned utility, and also established an independent system operator. Finally, with most of the principle pieces in place—structure, regulatory agency and rules, and market mechanisms—the government moved ahead to privatize the assets and phaseout, in a programmed fashion, any remaining subsidies.

If process is any determinant of outcome—and it often is—El Salvador will be able to reap important benefits from the reform of its power sector. Much will depend on the ability of the new political configuration in El Salvador to maintain the consensus for reform and continue on the steady path of implementation. However, the process is still in its early stages in El Salvador. There are indications that the new political configuration may not support the planned trajectory of the reform. Moreover, past difficulties and commitments may resurface and inhibit implementation of what is a well-developed reform design.

Conclusions

The process of energy sector reform in Latin America is just beginning in some countries and has yet to start in others. Only one country—Chile—has a sufficiently long history of reform to begin to arrive at any definitive assessments. Therefore, the observations and views in this chapter are necessarily preliminary.

But while track records are not yet established and data are weak, economic theory and a growing body of examples suggest that there is an appropriate avenue for reform. This process begins with determining a comprehensive hierarchy of objectives for the sector and then moves to the design and implementation of an industry structure as competitive as technology and political constraints will allow. The two principal sets of rules—regulation and trading arrangements—are then built around the structure. Where competition is possible, it should be allowed to flourish; where it is not, economic regulation must be carefully designed and judiciously applied. Once the regime is in place, private capital should be encouraged to enter and to charge a price for its entry unencumbered by nonmarket risks and politically induced uncertainty.

The limited sample presented here shows certain governments have embraced this approach and, importantly, have had the political capabilities to implement it. Argentina and Chile have broadly pursued this approach and have benefited accordingly. El Salvador would appear poised to enjoy maximum reform benefits if it adheres to its well-laid plan. Policymakers in other countries, perhaps constrained by political factors, haste or a misunderstanding of reform and the role of privatization, have pursued approaches that appear, so far, not to have produced the best outcomes. This may persist in the longer term. Perhaps anxious for new capital or fiscal relief, Colombia and Brazil have encouraged privatization before the regime was completely set and have therefore paid a price in terms of higher capital costs, lower asset prices, reduced potential for efficiency gains to be passed along to consumers, or some combination of all three.

Not all countries or sectors may have the political scope to undertake energy sector reform in the sequence advocated here. They may be constrained by the political realities of negotiated consensus among parties, states or even individual ministers with differing or even conflicting agendas. It is important to state with complete clarity that nothing can substitute for the political will needed to develop and implement reform. Until such will is present, effective reform cannot occur. There are no silver bullets. However, once political will emerges, multilateral agencies and technical advisors can do much to inform and promote the most effective reform process, and to elucidate the consequences of failing to do so, thus helping governments at least to make informed decisions.

REFERENCES

Bitran, E., and P. Serra. 1996. Regulatory Issues in the Privatization of Public Utilities: The Chilean Experience. In *Privatization in Asia, Europe and Latin America*, ed. Jan Schuijer. Paris: OECD.

Hunt, S., and G. Shuttleworth. 1997. *Competition and Choice in Electricity*. Chichester, England: John Wiley & Sons.

Rosenzweig, M., and S. Voll. 1997. Sequencing Power Sector Privatization: Is Reform its Pre-Condition or Result? National Economic Research Associates, Washington, D.C. Unpublished.

Saez, R. 1996. Financial Aspects of Privatization in Chile. In *Privatization in Asia, Europe and Latin America,* ed. Jan Schuijer. Paris: OECD.

Vickers, J., and G. Yarrow. 1991. Economic Perspectives on Privatization. *Journal of Economic Perspectives* 2: 125-27.

CHAPTER 13

Incentives and Implications for Competition in Power Purchase Agreements in Central America

Richard Tomiak

Evidence is emerging from all over the world that the development and restructuring of energy markets is a slow and difficult process, highly politicized and invariably characterized by the need to reconcile a broad range of conflicting objectives.

What is also becoming clear is that each country or region pursuing reform needs to go through its own individual evolutionary process in order to establish a robust and workable market structure. Opportunities for shortcuts—that is, for moving straight to a "final" position based on the experiences of other countries—may appear attractive, but do not offer stable and lasting solutions.

However, it would be equally unrealistic to ignore the existence of an increasingly pervasive international energy scene. Inevitably, the reform agenda in any one country or region will be influenced to some degree by trends and events in others. There are benefits to be derived from sharing the experiences of the British experiment, started by Margaret Thatcher's government in the late 1980s, as well as the Latin American, Scandinavian and North American models, which will no doubt provide a number of salutary lessons for energy sector policymakers in Central America.

The Central American power market has several characteristics that merit special attention when considering the extent to which foreign experience can be applied in the region. The most obvious point is that the Central American countries are small, both in terms of their geography (area, population) and their power systems (installed capacity, per capita consumption). Any plans to develop their power systems would clearly benefit from implementation at a regional rather than a national level.

Table 13.1. Central American Power Capacity and Consumption

	Installed capacity (MW)	% Hydro	Nonindustrial consumption (kWh p.a.)	Industrial consumption as % of total	Electricity consumption growth, 1990–93
Guatemala	1,045	8.5	177	47	34
El Salvador	781	8.6	298	52	34
Honduras	541	6.7	207	78	36
Nicaragua	456	0.2	232	23	21
Costa Rica	1,009	5.4	919	75	23
Panama	987	6.8	846	56	16
Latin America & the Caribbean	164,928	4.9	625	61	49

Source: "Electric Power Sector Reform in Latin America and the Caribbean," Manuel I. Dussan, Infrastructure and Financial Markets Division, Social Programs and Sustainable Development Department, Inter-American Development Bank, June 1996.

Table 13.1 shows that in all the Central American countries, industry accounts for a much smaller proportion of total electricity demand than in Latin America and the Caribbean as a whole. However, the table also shows that, with one exception, growth in Central American electricity consumption in the early 1990s has been higher than the average for Latin America. This fact, coupled with a significant dependence on imports to meet energy demand, means that there will be increasing pressure for reform to produce a more efficient power sector.

In all the countries of Central America, state-owned monopolies dominate the electricity industry and the degree of vertical and horizontal integration is consequently very high. Institutional structures are weak and governments, either directly or through state-owned enterprises, organize and control most of the planning and investment processes that shape longer-term development. They also intervene in the operational side of the industry. Centrally-planned expansion strategies still tend to be imposed from above, and private sector participation in the process is negligible.

The financial condition of state-owned enterprises is correspondingly weak, and this can lead to problems once independent project developers come to regard them as potential credit risks. These enterprises then have to rely on the government to provide support in the shape of loan guarantees and debt service. As a result, it becomes relatively easy for governments to use the utilities to implement politically-driven pricing and fiscal policies.

Despite such problems, the process of economic restructuring and power sector reform in Central America is under way. It is epitomized by the Central American Electricity Market Framework Treaty signed in Guatemala in December 1996 by the governments of Guatemala, El Salvador, Honduras, Nicaragua, Costa Rica and Panama.

Implications of Power Purchase Agreements for Competition

Assessing the effectiveness of a power purchase agreement (PPA) requires being clear about what the contract was intended to achieve and over what time period. At the highest level, it is the government's responsibility to set the long-term strategy for reform and to define a clear overall vision of the kind of energy market it wants to see developed.

From the outset, one must distinguish between the two fundamental policies of privatization and liberalization, and recognize that each is undertaken for quite different reasons. Whereas privatization provides opportunities for changes in ownership and redistributes cash flows between public and private accounts, it is only the deregulation and liberalization of market structures that releases the competitive forces that can bring about improvements in economic efficiency.

Some countries have chosen to adopt these policies in tandem, whereas others have pursued one or the other. Whichever approach is taken, there is no guarantee of success. Pursuing a strategy of market deregulation—that is, facilitating competition—may increase perceptions of risk and actually drive potential new entrants away from the market. Similarly, privatization alone does not necessarily have any impact on competition. Transferring a monopoly from public to private ownership does not automatically improve the customer's position.

Interestingly, the role of PPAs in this context has been ambiguous. On the one hand, the emergence of independent power projects (IPPs) has forced competition on incumbent generators, but on the other, the long-term PPAs that support such projects tend to isolate them from competitive pressures.

Recent international experience shows that PPAs pose another conundrum for a reforming government; namely, how to resolve the contradiction between attracting private capital and facilitating competition. A successful privatization program requires that the government establish a relatively risk-free commercial framework that offers potential investors the prospect of an attractive return. In terms of financing independent power projects, the 15-year PPA has emerged as the mechanism that provides project developers with the secure, long-term income stream they need to participate in a new and uncertain market. Yet, it is exactly this long-term contract structure, which protects IPPs from market forces, that constrains the government's ability to achieve the longer-term objective of full competition.

The adverse consequences of failing to reconcile these conflicting pressures are now materializing in the United States and Great Britain, where, as the level of competition rapidly increases, the question of stranded IPP assets (sometimes called "legacy contracts") has raised concerns.

Evolution of PPAs

PPAs can be categorized as being either "technical" or "financial" contracts. Although the situation is changing, most PPAs today are of the technical variety. They manage the technical risk of building and then operating the plant, but they do not deal with market risk, that is, ensuring that the output of the plant can be successfully sold in a competitive market. In fact, technical PPAs are based on the premise of isolating the project from any market pressures and delivering to its owners a guaranteed long-term stream of income. If not exactly desirable, at least this is deliverable in a world of monopoly markets. But if it is the wish of government to create competition at all levels of the electricity supply chain, then such contracts are not the answer.

There are several consequences of entering into a long-term, low-risk, technical PPA. The first is that the generator becomes immune to market discipline, and payments flow on the basis of physical rather than commercial (i.e., competitive) availability. Subsequently, as escalation clauses are applied over time, the power purchaser faces the risk of the energy price becoming increasingly uneconomical as regulation becomes tighter, competition develops, and new and more efficient plants come onto the system. Thus, in the medium to long term there is growing pressure to break the contract, followed possibly by expensive litigation and court hearings.

There is probably much support in principle for the view that a long-term PPA should not be regarded simply as a fixed, legally binding contract, but rather as an ongoing, flexible relationship between two equal parties. Much can happen over the 15-year life of a typical PPA, so an effective purchase contract must be relatively easy and painless to revisit in the event of any fundamental changes to the basic parameters (e.g., fuel availability, fuel prices, new technological developments).

In the United States and Britain, the original tranche of independent power projects is now causing major financial problems for purchasers (supply companies), which face the prospect of substantial stranded costs. However, reaction to the problems that emerged with the early technical PPAs has gradually given rise to a number of subsequent developments.

Since the mid-1990s, there has been a move to more appropriate financial PPAs (structured as "contracts for differences"), which reduce future price uncertainty but are not technically focused and share risk more equitably between generator and purchaser. And despite everything that has been said by the banks about the need for guaranteed income, the British and North American markets are now seeing the emergence of "merchant plant" projects, that is, independent power projects with no PPA at all, and whose financial viability depends solely upon successfully competing to be dispatched into the "pool."

The emergence of the merchant plant concept in the more mature markets has significant implications for the future of generation projects everywhere. For example, energy companies are being established that manage price risk through active involvement in generation and trading; that is, tolling plants are built where the commercial risk is borne by the fuel provider.

A merchant plant necessarily represents a higher risk project than one backed up by a long-term fuel supply agreement and a PPA of equivalent duration. In addition, the structural problems are fundamentally different from those of a back-to-back deal. Such projects require a less aggressive capital structure than conventional generation schemes—they need more equity up front so that the debt service requirement is less onerous. Projects backed by PPAs and long-term fuel supply contracts have typically been financed at a ratio of 80 percent to 20 percent equity, but lenders to merchant plant projects want to see the operator commit more (perhaps up to 40 percent) of the capital cost.

Not all bankers are receptive to this concept, however, and many still seem to think they can invest in risk-free projects. However, the competitive pressures are such that the banks will have to get more comfortable with the idea of riskier projects, since to some extent the structure of a power purchase agreement will always reflect the relative bargaining power of the parties involved.

For example, in Great Britain during the years immediately following privatization, there were many potential independent power projects chasing a limited volume of funds. Negotiating strength was very much in the hands of the financiers who, quite understandably, insisted on long-term contracts that pushed most of the risk on to the power purchasers. In the last few years, however, the situation has reversed; there is now a lot of spare cash available, but not so many projects. Consequently, the balance of negotiating power has shifted discernibly, and this shift is clearly reflected in the changing nature of the new generation of PPAs that have recently been signed, with the banks being forced to pick up much more of the project risk.

Regulatory Issues

A utility can only afford to commit to a PPA whose long-term competitiveness is uncertain if it believes it has a secure customer base over an equivalent period. This truism suggests that governments ought always to be concerned about the extent to which existing supply companies are allowed to invest in generation projects that serve their own customers. Clearly, if a utility can pass-through output through an independent power project to capture customers at any price, there will be a serious conflict between its role as an investor in and a purchaser from that IPP.

To manage the problem of unconstrained pass-through in Great Britain, a regulatory requirement was placed on utilities to demonstrate "economic purchasing," i.e., that in light of the prevailing circumstances, purchasing from an independent power project under the terms of the negotiated PPA was the best option available.

While such a contrived solution may work quite well in a world of regulated and vertically integrated utilities, it is not consistent with the realm of competitive markets that the British government is endeavoring to establish, where adverse movements in escalation clauses can quickly render a generation plant uneconomical and where, after 1998, all customers will be able to vote with their feet by switching to a new supplier if they so wish. Despite this new free market, however, it seems likely that the regulator will abandon cost pass-through and enforce maximum tariffs to protect the smaller (<12000 kWh p.a.) customers who are unable or unwilling to exercise choice.

Regional Issues

In a mature economy, the government can focus on establishing independent, competitive markets, whereas in developing markets priorities may need to be quite different. For example, if the level of electrification and interconnection in a country is low, then a policy of providing incentives to investment in new generation projects may simply lead to overcapacity in isolated networks but a large, unserved demand overall. A more relevant policy in such a case might be to invest in the development and reinforcement of national distribution and transmission systems.

Security of supply in the United Kingdom is now regulated solely by the operation of the price mechanism. In less mature markets, it may be more appropriate for the security standard to be managed by government planning.

For example, in a system where there is a shortage of capacity, the immediate priority is not the introduction of competition but the expansion of supply.

However, this situation does not preclude privatization. Where supply lags demand, the first priority may be to invest in new capacity (through independent power projects) rather than develop a competitive market (i.e., privatize rather than liberalize). If the government has a defined expansion program, it can issue a "request for power" and invite bids from IPP developers to build additional capacity (competition "for the market" rather than competition "in the market"). In this case, the technical PPA is probably not an inappropriate model to use.

International Comparisons

There will always be strong pressure to adopt practices that have been established elsewhere, and this is already evident in some of the purchase contracts that have been signed in Central America. Similarly, in the early days of British privatization there was an influx of North American companies and consultants who insisted that only they knew how it could be done. It was true that in the context of a vertically integrated utility structure, these companies had built up impressive expertise in how to deal with the demands of the PURPA and PUHCA legislation. But in retrospect it is clear that this expertise was not particularly relevant to the British model. Lack of experience, accompanied perhaps by a lack of confidence, meant that British utilities became too dependent on the overseas project developers. Much of what was said to be impossible, particularly in terms of the allocation of risk between parties, turned out in the end to be quite possible indeed. Hence, it may be instructive to draw parallels between the British restructuring and the Central American reform program. (See Appendix 13.1 for a case study of the British experience.)

The Central American Experience

The key precondition for evaluating PPAs—an overall vision for the structure of future energy markets—already exists in Central America. The Central American Electricity Market Framework Treaty is a clear statement of intent to achieve efficiency through competition by creating an integrated, centrally dispatched regional market. Of course, a vision needs to be supported not only by the enthusiasm and commitment of all the parties concerned, but also by the creation of robust infrastructure that enables realization of the vision. At the highest level, this may well necessitate legal reform to support establishment of a regulatory framework and financial restructuring of the existing, publicly-owned utilities.

Such infrastructure also requires myriad detailed arrangements, including establishment of trading forums, agreement on membership criteria and the rules according to which they are run, creation of a range of financial instruments that can be traded on these markets, and nurturing of trading skills and a new approach to risk management. Work on producing an appropriate infrastructure is already well under way in the region, as evidenced by proposals to establish the El Salvador Energy Exchange.[1] A key element in this list of requirements must be the development of power purchase contracts that are consistent with and can deliver the global vision.

Central American Power Purchase Agreements

Many separate risks are involved in developing an independent generation project: the risk that construction of the facility will be delayed, that the plant cannot be run efficiently, that no electricity will be demanded, and that the plant will not be available to generate electricity. The assessment of who bears these risks depends on the structure of each individual project.

One way of analyzing project risks and rewards is to compare the positions of the participants before and after the project is in place in terms of the risks that have been assumed and their significance. The key point that emerges from an analysis of the PPAs and operating agreements currently being entered into in Central America is that they pass too much of the commercial risk (the price of and demand for electricity, the cost of fuel) back to the power purchaser. Since there is at present no competition in electricity supply in the region, virtually all the risk associated with PPAs can be passed on to the (captive) consumer, who has to pay whatever price is asked.

However, once competition is introduced, the situation will change radically and customers will be free to switch suppliers as they wish. If it is the government's intention to deregulate within the lifetime of existing PPAs, then this freedom to switch introduces major risks for power purchasers who could

[1]See "A Competitive Electricity Sector in El Salvador," Pablo T. Spiller, University of California, Berkeley and Law & Economics Consulting Group, Inc., October 1996.

be left with stranded assets (uneconomic contracts) on their hands. There are no mechanisms within these PPAs to manage such market risk nor to share the costs with the project developers. In other words, the power purchasers are underwriting the bulk of the project risk, and the prospect of economic loss for the other parties involved is relatively small.

Nonfirm Contracts

The Central American PPAs are all "nonfirm" contracts, in the sense that they only operate when the plant is physically available, thereby exposing the purchaser to significant market risk on two fronts. If the contracted capacity is available, the purchaser faces the prospect of being obliged to purchase the output, even if it is uneconomical to do so. If the plant is not available, then the risk is how and at what price the purchaser can make good the shortfall in his energy requirements.

This point provides a clear illustration of how business risks increase with competition. Some of these are "normal" business risks (e.g., credit risk, data collection and management), while others have their origins in the fact that electricity is a commodity, albeit a slightly unusual one because the demand for it is weather-dependent and inelastic in the short term.

Residential demand typically offers higher margins (customers prefer to avoid interruptions rather than save small amounts of money) in exchange for volatility in short-term volume. Under "traditional" monopoly arrangements, a forecasting error is not a significant risk, and utilities set tariffs and over time recover their costs. But in a competitive market the supplier cannot afford to be over or undercontracted. Because of supply side inflexibilities, the short-term variability of electricity prices can be very high. So, for example, a purchaser who suddenly finds that one of his PPAs is unavailable (or, conversely, who has underestimated the level of demand) may have to go to the market for more power at significantly higher prices than planned. In a low-margin business such as electricity supply, having to make forced purchases at the wrong time could reduce annual profits significantly.

Essentially the problem is one of buying short and selling long. In a volatile market it is risky to have a significant mismatch between purchase and sales contracts. (Box 13.1 quantifies a hypothetical scenario based on the British market.)

While they expose the power purchaser to major market risk, however, these PPAs actually reduce the degree of uncertainty for the project by defining

Box 13.1. Nonfirm Contract Risk Scenario

The information listed below—based on 1995-96 data for one of the British Regional Electricity Companies—is an example of the risks associated with nonfirm PPAs. The annual operating profit of $22.1 million (current cost accounting) represents a real operating margin of below 1 percent. Such a narrow margin, typical of electricity supply, means that a power purchaser faces significant exposure to sudden price rises at times when he is short of volume.

Assuming that an independent power project that is contracted to supply 10 percent of a utility's energy requirements suddenly becomes unavailable, the example shows that an increase in price of 16c/kWh (quite plausible at peak during a winter cold spell) could result in over $200,000 of additional costs being incurred over a four-hour period. If the plant is then unavailable for another five days and the cold spell persists, a utility in this position could see around 5 percent of its annual profits wiped out (assuming prices during the rest of the year remain at "normal" levels; if not the impact could be even more serious).

Total annual volume supplied	30.5 TWh
Annual operating profit	$22.1 million
Average revenue	10.1c/kWh
Operating margin	0.7%
Average hourly volume	3.48 GWh
Hourly PPA volume	348 MWh
Average daily profit	$60,500
Assumed extra price	16c/kWh
Additional cost	$56,000/hour
Additional cost over 4 hours	$224,000
Additional cost over 5 days	$1.12 million
Additional cost as % of full year profit	5%

in advance exactly what costs, prices and penalties will be incurred under various default conditions. This enables project developers to estimate their potential exposure with a high degree of precision.

Technical Contracts

In practice, only the technical risks (construction, availability and efficiency) are being carried by the developers. The project's exposure to these risks tends to be limited by putting the burden of proof onto the power purchaser and by including loose force majeure clauses. In some cases there are even contractual provisions for the power purchaser to become involved in the construction and operation of the project.

The tendency for power purchasers to participate in the physical operation of the plant—making decisions about the timing of maintenance programs, arranging for availability and other station tests, and so on—is potentially risky because it extends purchasers' involvement into areas that lie outside their basic expertise. For example, if there is some doubt as to the technical condition of a piece of equipment, the purchaser must not be involved in making decisions about whether or not the plant should be shut down. Once the purchaser starts taking responsibility for technical decisions, its position is compromised. The physical operation of the plant is entirely the responsibility of the project, and should not be referred to in the power purchase contract.

The tendency towards technically-based contracts is reflected in many other ways. For example, the PPAs define contracted capacity at different temperatures, times and voltage levels. They include complicated procedures for measuring capacity and mechanisms for delivering reactive power, and they specify procedures for resolving disputes. None of this detail should be necessary.

While it could be argued that deep involvement in the technical side of a project may be relevant if the generator contracts to deliver energy to a single bulk purchasing agency, it is not relevant in a competitive situation where the generator only runs the operation if he can deliver output at a lower cost than his competitors.

Financial Contracts

Where a pooling arrangement based on the British model exists, there is no need for physical contracts, since all energy is purchased from the pool and not from individual generators. The generator may have a contract with a purchaser, but the contract then simply deals with transfers of cash relating to the cost of notional volumes, not physical volumes. The reason a generator would want to have a contract is that it reduces his risk; he is guaranteed a certain revenue by the purchaser, no matter what the price in the market. However if the market price is higher than in the contract, then that generator must refund the difference to the purchaser. If he hasn't been dispatched (and therefore hasn't earned the high pool price), then the generator must find the cash for the refund elsewhere. (Appendix 13.2 contains a fuller description of financial contracts, such as contracts for differences.)

It is the generator's risk to manage (a purchaser contracts for a volume of energy at a given price over a specified period) how to deliver energy that is of no interest to the purchaser. It is up to the generator to ensure that his plant is running efficiently, that fuel is available at the right price, and that the plant is run so as to make an acceptable return. In the event that the plant is not available to generate, with the exception of predefined force majeure events, the project must make alternative arrangements to honor its contractual commitments.

Force Majeure

The force majeure provisions in Central American PPAs are invariably loose and favor the project developer. A common feature of the contracts is a clause stating that force majeure "includes, but is not limited to" a list of defined events. There are also the usual vague references to "acts of God," sometimes accompanied by a list of specific exclusions or by a partial list of inclusions. From the purchaser's point of view, this is unsatisfactory because it leaves too much open to retrospective negotiation and interpretation.

Indeed, some of the PPAs state that the burden of proof falls onto whichever party is raising a dispute, which is unacceptable. The power purchaser has entered a contract to buy power and the generator must honor that commitment. Should the plant fail to run, the generator is still obliged to find alternative ways of supplying his contracted volumes and the purchaser is indifferent as to how the generator achieves this. Only if a force majeure event occurs is the PPA suspended, and it is then up to the generator to demonstrate that this is actually the case.

Although it may require a lot of hard work, contracts need to be negotiated so as to unambiguously define what constitutes a force majeure event, instead of listing what does not. If an unplanned outage then occurs, the onus falls on the generator to prove that a force majeure event has taken place, rather than on the purchaser to prove that it has not. The issue rests on agreeing as to what events or circumstances are genuinely beyond the control of the project developer. Local strikes, for example, may not be, and all but the most extreme weather conditions should be accounted for, reducing the definition of these vague terms. To date, the Central American PPAs have not tackled these issues.

However, in the same way that technical considerations are of no interest to a power purchaser, the inclusion of force majeure provisions is ultimately irrelevant in a financial-style contract. Indeed, in the British market, the trading instrument known as the Electricity Forward Agreement contains no force majeure clause and yet has come to be accepted by most generators as an acceptable contract form.

Price Indexation

In general, the standard Central American PPA stipulates that the project will earn capacity payments simply on the basis of demonstrating availability, and that payments will then increase according to a specified schedule or move in line with a (usually fixed) escalation clause. Similarly, the cost of energy is linked to input fuel prices. Sometimes these are world market prices as reported in, for example, *Platt's Oilgram Price Report,* or they may be the prices paid at the local port of entry. In addition, there are often further adjustments applied to O&M costs based on the prevailing inflation rate. In any industry trying to reduce costs, there can be no justification for agreeing to provide a project developer with the luxury of an ever increasing revenue stream.

These arrangements ignore the reality that in a less than perfectly free market, electricity prices are no longer set by traditional input cost drivers, but instead are increasingly determined by strategic and behavioral factors, as companies attempt to outmaneuver their existing and potential rivals. Under such circumstances, pricing behavior is better explained by reference to game theory than by traditional economic analysis. By linking PPA prices to irrelevant indices, the generation project is effectively insulated from local market pressures.

Figure 13.1 shows how pool prices (time-weighted PPP) have moved in Great Britain since 1993 relative to the prices of generation fuels and to a fixed escalation of 3 percent per annum. It is clear that for the power purchaser, an inappropriate form of price escalation makes the effective PPA price uncompetitive, while leaving the generator with a profitable and safe investment. It is essential in a competitive market that incentives be provided so that IPPs can be as responsive as possible to end-user prices.

Foreign Exchange Risk

Most of the PPAs entered into by Central American utilities pick up foreign exchange risk. Typically, contract prices are either expressed in U.S. dollars or

Figure 13.1. United Kingdom: Indices of Energy Prices

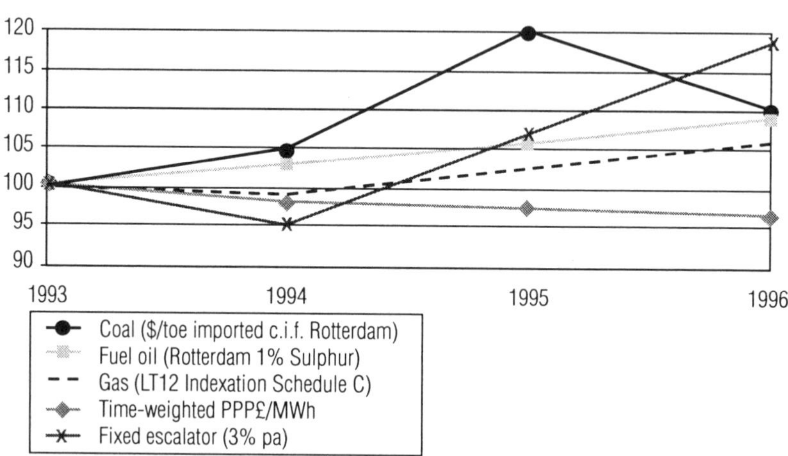

are linked to the dollar exchange rate. There is no fundamental reason why this should be so (other than to reduce the developer's risk profile), and it is important that utilities, perhaps with government support, attempt to negotiate their way out of this inequity. Breaking the linkage has been achieved in Brazil, where PPAs cannot be indexed to the dollar. While this will create significant risk for IPP returns, since it could lead to a misalignment between developers' revenues and their debt repayments, the risk would appear to be controllable. The management of currency risk is now a well-established science, and project developers, if encouraged to do so, can engage the expertise to help them to deal with such risk by means of a number of financial instruments.

Managing Price Risk

Because price risk is not yet a high profile issue, the Central American PPAs to date have failed to address it. The risk that the output of a project might become uncompetitive in the market can be managed in several ways.

First, the risk can be shared with the other parties involved in the scheme, such as the plant owner or the fuel supplier, both of whom can adjust their profit margins in order to maintain a competitive final price (fuel supply contracts therefore also need to be flexible and dynamic).

Second, the purchaser himself can manage risk more effectively by encouraging and participating in the creation of trading instruments and markets, and by developing trading skills within the company itself.

Third, a robust PPA should, in any case, contain internal mechanisms for dealing with price risk. Features such as indexation to end-user market prices, periodic contract reviews (i.e., "evergreen" contracts) and agreed re-opener clauses (if certain parameters move beyond defined limits) must be on the agenda for any contract negotiation.

Refinancing the Deal

In the past, by insisting upon virtually risk-free PPAs, project developers were able to realize handsome profits. There is a particularly attractive opportunity to enhance earnings (and, it has to be said, not unreasonably so) by refinancing the project once the construction risk has been successfully dealt with. While the developers undoubtedly deserve to be rewarded for their contribution to managing the risk, how much of the benefit should be directed toward customers ought to be recognized as a major point of contract negotiation. Unfortunately, this is often not the case.

Fuel Supply Agreement

Central American PPAs also pass the fuel supply risk on to the power purchaser, on the assumption that any excess costs can be passed through to the utility's monopoly market. This is not necessarily equitable, and if the competitive vision of the treaty is to be realized during the lifetime of these contracts, then such arrangements cannot be supported. Escalation in line with any parameter that does not reflect commercial behavior in the local market cannot be accepted. In a competitive market, commercial risk has to be shared among all the participants in a project and not just "dumped" on the purchaser.

Project Finance

As well as being perceived as politically risky, Latin American energy markets are only just starting to restructure, so financiers may well be reluctant to invest in a totally speculative plant unless there is a substantial risk premium. However, if the commitment to deregulation in the longer term is real, then the risks associated with 15-year PPAs have to be carefully managed. Perhaps five years is a more reasonable period over which to guarantee the project an earnings stream, but after that there must be a mechanism for reflecting market movements.

The task for power purchasers is to challenge the conventions of the financial markets and to demonstrate that the demands of a competitive market really do reflect the fact that without risk there can be no reward. In theory this is a straightforward task, but in reality such debates take a long time to reach resolution. In the interim, it may prove necessary to establish a regionally based agency that would complement the increased reliance on private sector capital by providing guarantees with respect to risks that the private sector will not bear and projects that it will not finance. This agency would act as a transitional source of finance and support until such time as private investors gained full confidence in the resilience of the restructured system.

The Hydro Factor

Central America has a significant existing and potential hydro resource. Hydro projects, however, present a number of unique problems for the independent project developer: they have a long construction period and a high capital requirement, face significant environmental risk, yield an uncertain energy profile because of hydrological risk, and have a long expected plant life. As a result of these features, positive cash flows cannot be expected until well into the life of the project (perhaps eight years or more), and financiers will argue that the shortest maturity of debt that can be supported is 30 years.

To deal with these issues, an independent hydro scheme needs to secure loan finance with a long grace period during construction and, to match the projected cash profile, either a front-end loaded tariff or, alternatively, a long maturity period. Furthermore, a significant proportion of equity finance will need to cover both construction cost risk and hydrological risk.

In fact, international experience shows that very few large hydro schemes have actually been financed, and in each case special arrangements (essentially the provision of government guarantees) had to be made to allow the projects to proceed. In North America, however, smaller schemes (<50 MW) have proved easier to finance, and this might be the most productive approach to take, since few IPP developers seem to be interested in pursuing hydro projects. The reasons for their reluctance range from long lead times and construction cost risk, to financing problems and environmental issues. However, perhaps the single most important factor is that hydro projects do not impact a developer's income stream for a long time.

Developers want to be relieved of risks involving construction costs, hydrology or the environment. They would like to have secure PPAs with financially sound purchasers and, finally, contract prices linked to the U.S. dollar. Given the preceding discussion, the prospects for privately financed hydro projects in a competitive market do not look too promising.

The conclusion, therefore, is that despite the availability of the potential hydrological resource, the future expansion of the Central American power system will probably be based on thermal plants, perhaps supplied by international gas pipelines.

Conclusions

The aspirations enshrined in the Central American Electricity Market Framework Treaty provide the criteria against which Central American power purchase agreements need to be appraised. Essentially, the appraisal needs to be approached from two directions. The first is a conceptual aspect to define the details of the new commercial environment, including the role of PPAs. The second is a practical aspect of deciding how the transition process to that new environment should be managed. PPAs therefore have to be reviewed not in terms of current market structures, but in terms of the future objectives that they should be instrumental in achieving.

Given the traditional, vertically integrated organization of the power industry in Central America, the PPAs currently in place are structured according to what is generally regarded as the standard model, with most of the project risk being passed on to the purchaser and ultimately on to the captive end-customer. While it is possible to argue that these PPAs could and should be negotiated more aggressively, with more of the risk picked up by the project developers, this would not fundamentally change the nature of the contracts.

When existing contracts are analyzed in terms of their ability to deliver the vision that the region's governments have signed on to, then it is clear that they are quite inadequate. Long-term technical PPAs that satisfy the investor's (but not the customer's) demands protect IPPs from market pressures, when exactly the opposite effect is required. The best solution to this problem is not to restructure PPAs, but to actually reconsider their very nature.

In light of the way other markets are developing in response to demands for greater efficiency in the electricity industry, the Central American countries need to move from the concept of the PPA as a contract for the delivery of energy toward the idea of financial instruments that guarantee the purchaser a fixed price for a fixed volume of energy, irrespective of the state of the generating plant.

Electricity has to be seen as a commodity, albeit with some special features, traded in a market where effective risk management is the key to success. Such a change requires institutions, skills, attitudes and therefore, quite probably, people. If this view of the new commercial environment is accepted, then what remains is the question of transitional arrangements.

To begin with, it has to be recognized that there are at present genuine political and institutional risks that will drive private capital away from Central American markets. While project developers have to be convinced that they must take on more commercial risk, during the period of transition it may be necessary to establish national agencies dedicated to providing financial guarantees to assuage concerns relating to institutional, structural and country risks.

The existence of such an agency is essential if independent hydro schemes are to become a viable proposition. Under present circumstances, the unique project risk that these schemes carry has to be mitigated through nonmarket mechanisms, although the commercial reality might be that the market considers thermal plant to be the best option for incremental plant (if the pipeline infrastructure is available.)

It has been noted that 15-year PPAs inhibit progress towards deregulation in Central America by creating long-term inflexibilities. Transitional contracts should therefore be of shorter duration—five years, for example—and feature re-openers or formally agreed upon procedures for revisiting the contract parameters.

In Great Britain, as the degree of market liberalization has gradually increased, IPP developers have shown themselves prepared to abandon traditional technical PPAs and move to the financial contracts for differences (CfD) structure. This change was achieved not through any government or regulatory intervention, but rather as a result of commercial negotiation between sellers and buyers. In many ways this is the most efficient means of managing the process of change, but unfortunately it is not always possible given existing constraints and imperfections.

One important way in which commercial risk is managed in competitive power markets is by ensuring that purchase and sales contract portfolios are well matched. In a completely free market, a utility has no guaranteed long-term customer base and therefore cannot afford to commit to long-term PPAs. However, as was done in Great Britain, it should be possible to phase in competition in Central America over a transitional period, so that for a limited time, independent power projects can be financed against a secure customer base, as long as the regulatory authorities can be convinced that the PPAs concerned were aggressively negotiated.

Once competition does become fully established and all customers are free to change their electricity supplier whenever they choose, there is no longer room for long-term PPAs in a purchaser's portfolio, unless project developers are prepared to assume full exposure to the market, which is, in effect, to operate a merchant plant.

In terms of energy sector reform, every country needs to go through its own learning process and develop contractual arrangements that suit its particular circumstances. The combination of national political commitment coupled with the opportunity to learn from the experiences of other markets suggests that the road to reform in Central America may be difficult, but is undoubtedly achievable.

Appendix 13.1

Case Study: The Experience of the United Kingdom

Reform policies of the British government of the late 1980s were based on the twin goals of promoting the development of a "shareholding democracy" and exposing the hitherto nationalized energy industries to the forces of competition. However, the longer-term goal of introducing competition had to be balanced by the need to create an attractive, predictable, low-risk investment environment in the short term (i.e., not too much competition initially).

Independent Power Projects (IPPs)

At the time of vesting in 1990, there was no real experience with developing generation projects outside the existing industry. Privatization was creating a new market with no track record, so there was no real understanding of how the pool might work, nor of what the risks involved in operating in the market would be. Since they had built up expertise in developing IPPs in the United States, a number of North American project developers[1] entered the market and proceeded to apply their experience to the British model.

The end result is that in the seven years since the British electricity supply industry was privatized, there has been a dramatic increase in the number of generators competing in the pool, with at least 21 new companies entering the market.

The majority of these new IPPs have been what could be called "traditional base-load projects;" that is, privately-financed combined-cycle gas turbine (CCGT) stations, backed by gas take-or-pay arrangements with fuel suppliers and long-term (15-year) power purchase agreements with the regional electricity companies that effectively guaranteed a minimum level of annual income. The PPAs were low-risk for the developers, operationally focused and based almost entirely on North American contract structures (i.e., compatible with a vertically integrated industry).

Essentially, the arrangement was that each generation project received agreed capacity and energy payments from the power purchasers and, in re-

[1]Companies such as Enron, AES, Mission Energy, CRS Sirrine, and Dominion Energy.

turn, paid them the revenue that it received from selling into the pool. Unless the plant was demonstrably unavailable (for example, by failing certain agreed-upon tests), the capacity payments would be paid by the power purchaser. Energy payments were paid for actual generation, which in turn was determined by the plant's position in the nationally defined merit order. Attached to each of the payments was an escalation clause which, in those early contracts, bore no relationship to market prices but was simply the result of bilateral negotiations between generator and purchaser.

It was assumed at the time that new IPPs would operate at base load. The fuel contracts struck with gas suppliers not only reflected the high price levels produced by linkage to oil prices, but in effect created a "take-or-pay" situation, since the gas had to be paid for whether or not it was actually burned. This, in turn, resulted in the IPPs offering their output to the pool at or around zero, on the basis that their fuel bill was effectively a fixed cost.

Having committed a proportion of their purchasing portfolios to long-term contracts over the last seven years (balanced, presumably, by their estimates of stable, long-term customer demand), any regional electric companies contemplating future involvement in generation will not have an appetite for "fixed price" deals of this sort.

The risks that have emerged over the last few years (regulatory intervention, increasing competition, falling fuel prices, etc.), and the fact that these risks will probably become even more acute in the future, suggest that the original model that nurtured competition in generation in the early days of the privatized electricity industry in Great Britain is probably now redundant. Committing to a long-term fixed price PPA in a highly fluid and unpredictable end-user market is commercially unacceptable.

However, there are a number of new "drivers" that will stimulate the continuing development of IPPs by those companies that wish to enhance their ability to compete successfully in the supply of electricity. These include:

- The prospect of gaining competitive advantage as a result of lower generation costs arising from improved technology. This would lead to reduced capital costs and increased efficiency; attractively priced gas supplies; and the availability of cheaper finance.
- The appetite of new entrants (both domestic and foreign) to take physical positions in the electricity market.
- Technological and commercial conditions favoring the specific development of mid-merit and peaking projects.
- Incentives to encourage the development of smaller-scale "niche" projects.

These factors will continue to attract new entrants to generation, specifically to compete with the incumbent generators (National Power and PowerGen) in the "mid-merit" market at load factors in the 30 to 65 percent range, particularly after 1998, when some of the existing coal-based CfDs expire.

Generation Costs

Significant reductions in CCGT generation costs have been achieved since the first IPPs were launched in the early 1990s, suggesting that a price of 2.2p/kWh is attainable for prospective projects compared with a headline base-load price (in 1996 money) of approximately 3.2p/kWh for early projects. This level of cost incorporates reductions in both the capacity and fuel elements of price.

(1996 price levels)	1991 IPP	1996 IPP
Turnkey cost (£/kW)	450	300
Efficiency (% LHV)	47	56
Gas price (p/therm)	21	15
Interest rate (Treasury + 1.25%)	10.75	9.25
Capacity price (£/kW/year)	118	91
Capacity price (p/kWh) (90% Load factor)	1.4	1.1
Variable price (p/kWh)	1.8	1.1
Total base load cost (p/kWh)	3.2	2.2

New Participants in the Generation Market

Nonregional electric companies. As a result of increasing difficulty in putting together joint venture IPPs based on the original model, in which power purchasers underwrite the revenue stream for a project by entering into long-term PPAs, projects have been financed with the power off-take being underwritten by each project owner in proportion to its ownership.

There are two significant consequences arising out of this structure. First, responsibility for power purchase is proportional to equity ownership, rather than being borne by the power purchaser (the regional electric company) alone. Second, only one company with an existing supply business is usually involved, with the other parties entering both the generation and supply businesses in England for the first time. (For example, the recently commissioned Humber Power Project has shown that it is possible to finance a project with a structure involving new types of participants.)

Gas suppliers. The current situation in the gas supply market has created the possibility of greater involvement in power projects by gas companies. This is because gas prices have collapsed as a result of oversupply, which cannot be managed simply by cutting back on gas production in the North Sea, since infrastructure is in place that cannot easily be redeployed; and because significant quantities of gas production are associated with oil production and cannot therefore be cut back without affecting it.

Gas companies, then, need to flow large quantities of gas from North Sea fields. One way to achieve this is by converting the gas to electricity through a "tolling" contract with an IPP, whereby the gas company pays a fixed annual fee for the right to use a power station to convert the gas at an agreed efficiency.

Such a structure is beginning to materialize in the United Kingdom. In view of the current surplus of gas, this structure is an attractive means for the gas supplier to utilize gas and minimize its price exposure to the gas market. From a project finance perspective, the tolling contract replaces both the gas purchase and power purchase agreements because the power station revenues are effectively underwritten by the gas company. This type of project could also attract companies not actually involved in gas production, but which have contracted to purchase long-term gas at prices above the current market level.

This structure produces a flexible arrangement which need not necessarily be constrained by the usual take-or-pay arrangements. The power station would only run when it is in the gas supplier's interest, in either mid-merit or base-load mode depending on the relative levels of gas and electricity prices.

Other players. Major industrial electricity users such as ICI also have the ability to underwrite the electricity purchases necessary to secure project financing, as have other large energy companies such as British Gas. In summary, there are a number of potential participants in new IPPs that could effectively fill the role of the utility in the traditional project structure. These include investors wishing to participate in generation and supply, gas suppliers entering into tolling arrangements, and major industrial electricity users and energy producers.

Development of Mid-Merit IPPs

Up until now, IPPs have been justified on the premise that they will be low-cost producers and will operate at base-load at a load factor of approximately 90 percent. Most projects will have take-or-pay obligations on gas purchases of around 85 percent, effectively requiring them to run at a minimum load factor of 85 percent.

The growing number of new participants in the base-load market has led to concerns of oversupply, particularly during times of lower demand such as on weekends and summer nights. This, in turn, has resulted in an increased interest in designing plants to compete specifically in the mid-merit market, running at load factors ranging between 30 to 65 percent, where National Power and PowerGen currently dominate.

Two complementary approaches are required to allow a project to operate in this mode. One is commercial flexibility to enable the project to reduce its load factor without incurring take-or-pay penalties under its fuel supply contract. The other is robust technology to allow frequent starts and stops and as high an efficiency for as low a capital cost as possible. As was mentioned earlier, the current state of the gas market provides just the right conditions for securing a flexible gas purchase contract at competitive prices.

With regard to the technology issue and the selection of plant, there are potentially two possibilities. One is that additional combined cycle capacity be added as an extension to an existing plant at an attractive incremental price. The other is that a high efficiency open-cycle plant be utilized.

The first option may be available at existing (and future) IPPs that have some provision for expansion. The second results from technological advances in the manufacture of aeroderivative gas turbines. These turbines are essentially the units that power the latest generation long-haul jets and can offer 50 MW output with approximately 40 percent efficiency. This efficiency does not compare with the 56 percent available from a 750 MW combined cycle unit, but the capital cost is lower and the construction time shorter. Furthermore, high efficiency becomes less significant with decreasing gas prices.

Niche Generators

Aside from changes in the costs, performance and structure of generation projects, there are a number of niche areas where incentives are emerging to encourage specific types of projects. Some of the initiatives are government led, while others flow out of the rules and regulations governing the electricity market. For example, the government has a stated policy of stimulating the development of renewable energy generation projects, with the aim of having 1,500 MW of new capacity commissioned by the year 2000. In the areas of combined heat and power (CHP) and embedded generation, economic incentives are being adjusted to encourage the relevant parties to optimize their use of the electricity system and to encourage new entrants on a smaller and more local scale (i.e., embedded within regional electric company distribution systems).

There are other opportunities available in terms of the supply of ancillary services to the national or local grid that are the product of local conditions, such as the provision of reactive power. At the distribution system level, the injection of generation can lead to considerable savings against investment in reinforcement, savings which could be shared with the generator. Finally, as the analysis below suggests, there are important opportunities emerging for the development of peaking projects.

Impact of IPPs on Electricity Prices

The impact of the new IPPs on market prices has been quite dramatic, but not perhaps in the way that might have been expected. It has been the pattern rather than the level of pool price that has been affected. That has been due more to the reaction of incumbent generators to the prospect of competition than to anything the new entrants did themselves.

Over the last two years, there has been a fundamental change in the pattern of pool prices. Increasingly (and with the regulator's encouragement), National Power and PowerGen have attempted to stretch the differential between the highest and lowest prices, resulting in the emergence of a significant differential between the time- and demand-weighted price of electricity.

Year	Demand-Weighted PPP £/MWh	Time-Weighted PPP £/MWh	Difference %
91/92	21.64	20.81	4
92/93	23.31	22.81	2
93/94	24.87	24.44	2
94/95	26.39	24.00	10
95/96	26.85	23.86	12
96/97	25.84	23.69	9

This trend has had two important consequences. First, the new base-load IPPs earn only a relatively modest time-weighted price, while a mid-merit and peaking plant is effectively remunerated at its more generous demand-weighted equivalent. Second, accurate forecasting of purchase costs has become more difficult than ever and, at the margin, there is now a forecasting risk premium (i.e., at peak times, the potential margin of error has increased and the cost of managing risk is therefore correspondingly higher).

Given the current pattern of pool prices, it is clear that a supply business most needs contract cover over the winter period. In order to manage peak price risk, a supplier can buy peak type hedges (at a price that reflects the forecasting risk premium), build in some kind of contingency, or remain exposed to the risk. However, estimating the size of a contingency is, by definition, no easy task. Furthermore, carrying a contingency or provision is not an easy luxury to afford in a competitive market, so supply companies will have to find some other means of factoring risk.

One option is to invest in a peaking plant as a (long-term) physical contingency. For the power purchaser, the key question to consider is what is the forecasting risk premium worth? How much is one prepared to pay, at the limit, for a peak generation facility/hedge for, say, five to 10 years?

If in the future pool prices remain at their current "stretched" levels, investment in non-base-load projects should provide the opportunity of an attractive return. But here, of course, lies the risk, because if peak prices are competed down as the result of new entry or as the result of generator bidding behavior, then the economic justification for the investment disappears.

Contract Structure

In general, the PPAs to date in the United Kingdom have been biased toward managing the project financiers' risks (guaranteeing a steady stream of income over time to meet the lenders' target cover ratios). In the new post-1998 competitive electricity market, this level of security will not be available to project developers. From now on, a power purchaser will be looking for nothing less than guaranteed price competitiveness from a PPA, not just competitiveness in terms of pool or contracts for differences (CfD) prices, but in terms of end-user prices. The starting price of any PPA will have to be one at which a supply company can be certain of selling to its customers, and the indexation will have to preserve that competitive edge over the life of the project.

Clearly, this will require that all the parties involved fundamentally reassess their perceptions of what is reasonable in terms of risk sharing. To provide the degree of price competitiveness that supply businesses will be seeking, a project developer will not only have to have confidence in the project but also in the fact that electricity prices will eventually settle into a discernible cycle, such that over the life of the project, the bad years will be canceled out by the good.

Appendix 13.2

Contracts For Differences

Contracts for differences (CfDs) have become established as effective hedging instruments in many markets. The basic principle is that two parties enter into an agreement over the forward price of a commodity. Take a consumer who knows that he will need 1,000 units of some commodity on a particular future date. One approach would be to contact a supplier and agree on a forward rate; however, it is frequently more convenient to transact a contract for differences.

As an example, the consumer might agree to a contract for differences on 1,000 units at $100 per unit. If the actual market price of the commodity on the date turns out to be more than $100/unit, the contract counterparty will pay the difference on 1,000 units; while if the actual price turns out to be less than $100, the consumer will be obliged to pay the difference on 1,000 units to the counterparty. Either way, the consumer has effectively locked in a purchase price for $100/unit on 1,000 units.

Note that in this simple case no payment is made up front when the contract is agreed upon; the only cash flow on the contract is the difference payment once the actual price is known.

Buyers and Sellers

The party that stands to benefit under the contract for differences if the actual price is greater than the agreed price is known as the "buyer." This matches with the fact that "buying" the contract for differences provides a hedge to someone who knows he will have to buy the physical commodity. Conversely, the other party is known as the "seller," since selling the contract provides a hedge to someone who knows he will wish to sell the physical commodity.

Hedging and Speculation

Of course, contracts for differences only provide a hedge against a corresponding exposure. Someone who buys a contract for differences will be hedged if he expects a requirement to buy the physical commodity; but if he has no such expectation, the contract will increase rather than reduce risk: the trader will be exposed to the commodity price, benefiting to the extent that the actual price exceeds the agreed price, but losing to the extent that it falls short.

Success of Contracts for Differences

Contracts for differences have proved highly successful in many markets. There are several reasons for this. First, they allow the trader to manage price risk independently of delivery of the physical commodity. Thus, a contract for differences might be agreed upon with a counterparty for whom physical delivery might not be practical, e.g., due to geographical distance. Of course, in the electricity market, forward agreements for physical delivery are impractical because of the nature of the commodity.

Second, when a producer and a consumer attempt to negotiate a forward agreement, each knows from the start who is to be the buyer and who the seller, so the producer will offer a high price, and the consumer will bid a low one. Unless both are keen to trade, agreement may be difficult. Markets for contracts for differences are generally more sophisticated, with brokers acting as intermediaries guaranteeing anonymity, and able to obtain prices from a wide range of potential counterparties. (Note that this is not the case for the electricity industry of England and Wales, where CfDs are negotiated bilaterally.)

Third, contracts for differences often provide a focus for liquidity, with keen prices and low transaction costs. This is partly because traders who have precise requirements for the type and grade of commodity for physical delivery may be happy to trade a standard benchmark contract for differences.

Consider a consumer who has a future requirement for grade A of a commodity, together with a producer who expects to sell grade C. Say grade A generally trades for $5 more than grade B, which in turn generally trades for $3 more than grade C. Provided that these price relationships are expected to hold, the consumer and the producer should be happy to agree to a contract for differences on grade B at, for example, $100. If the relationships hold, the consumer will have locked in a price of $105 for Grade A, and the producer, a price of $97 for grade C. Even if the price relationships do not hold exactly, the variations might be sufficiently small to be acceptable compared with the variations in price of the commodity overall. The use of benchmark instruments focuses liquidity and brings down transaction costs. The market then becomes more attractive to other traders, enhancing liquidity further.

Types of Hedge

The arrangement described above was a simple outright contract for differences (a "two-way" contract in the terminology of the electricity industry). Other structures are possible: the buyer of a cap ("one-way" contract) pays an up-front premium to the seller and in return receives a compensating payment if the actual market price exceeds an agreed price, known as the strike price; no payment is required if the market price is below the strike. Buying caps offers protection to the consumer against high prices without requiring him completely to forego the benefit of low prices.

A floor is a similar arrangement, suitable for purchase by a producer: in exchange for the up-front premium, the buyer of the floor receives a compensating payment if the market price is below the strike price.

Contracts for Differences in Electricity

Contracts for differences are ideally suited to the electricity market, where physical forward agreements are impractical, and the daily publication of pool prices makes settlement of contracts for differences straightforward.

To allow hedging of forward electricity prices, two types of contract for difference in electricity are available in England and Wales. First, at the time of privatization, long-term contracts for differences were negotiated bilaterally between generators and suppliers. Many of these contracts were caps (one-way agreements), but these have now been largely replaced by two-way hedges. Secondly, the market for electricity forward agreements (EFAs) was set up to allow electricity market participants to fine tune their cover, taking into account variations in demand together with changes in overall electricity market volumes. The first tranche of PPAs in the early 1990s did not adopt the CfD structure, although subsequently (post-1995) this did change and some IPPs were financed on this basis.

Electricity Forward Agreements

EFAs are bilateral outright (two-way) contracts for differences with weekly settlement based on the average pool price. An over-the-counter broker initiates transactions by matching potential buyers and sellers anonymously over the telephone. Once all details of the trade have been agreed upon, the identities of the two counterparties are revealed to each other. On acceptance of each other's name, the EFA contract exists between the two parties. The broker has no further involvement in the trade apart from the issue of a copy note confirming the verbal details.

The EFA market should be the natural hedging market not just for generators and suppliers, but for anyone else involved in the market, or indeed for other energy traders who wish to take on exposure to electricity. The market is open to anyone who wishes to trade (although, as in any over-the-counter market, completing a trade is dependent on finding a suitable counterparty prepared to take the trader's name).

Given that EFAs are purely bilateral deals arranged through a broker with no organized exchange, in principle it would be quite possible to trade any structure of deal required; there is no necessity for standardization. However, in many over-the-counter markets, although standardization is not essential, liquidity has tended naturally to focus on particular types of trade. Thus, a standard form of documentation generally emerges in a well-developed market, and trading interest typically centers on certain benchmark instruments, such as particular maturities and so forth, which are of general interest to the market participants.

Standard terms. For the EFA market, the electricity companies have agreed to trade on standard documentation, known as EFA standard terms, which set out the characteristics of the trade in general, the settlement arrangements, the events of default, and so forth.

Structure of contracts. A framework has also been constructed for the type of trade. This framework is sufficiently flexible to allow a full variety of structures for trading and hedging purposes, while maintaining simplicity. Each day is to be divided into six four-hour periods, as indicated in the adjacent table. Trades will cover one of these contract periods for either both days of a weekend (contract periods WE1 through WE6), or all the five weekdays of a week (WD1-WD6). WE1-6 and WD1-6 can be traded for a single week or a strip of weeks as long as is required; one might trade a four or five-week strip to cover a month, or a 13-week strip to cover a quarter, or even a 52-week strip to cover a year.

	Mon + Tues + Wed + Thur + Fri	Sat + Sun
23.00 - 03.00	WD1	WE1
03.00 - 07.00	WD2	WE2
07.00 - 11.00	WD3	WE3
11.00 - 15.00	WD4	WE4
15.00 - 19.00	WD5	WE5
19.00 - 23.00	WD6	WE6

Reference variables. While most EFA trading has been against PPP, it is possible to trade PSP, SMP, or spreads between them: the PPP/SMP spread is known as the capacity element, while the PSP/PPP spread is known as the uplift.

Settlement. EFAs are cash-settled weekly based on the average value for the appropriate variable (PPP, PSP, SMP, etc.), for the appropriate contract period (WD1-6 or WE1-6), and for the week. The fixings for the variables are estimated by the pool as part of the running of the physical electricity market, and are readily available. PPP and PSP settlements are published daily in the Companies and Markets Section of the *Financial Times.* The settlement day follows the arrangements for the pool, which is normally 28 days after the end of the week in question. Since settlement is weekly, a contract covering a range of weeks involves a series of cash flows.

Reasons for Hedging

- *For insurance.* Hedges smooth out short-term cash flow fluctuations and impose longer-term stability (at a cost, the insurance premium). A company that knows its future costs and revenues is better positioned to plan strategically.
- *To maintain profitability and competitive position.* Hedging need not be defensive. Risk management can be used positively to position a company for growth as well as defensively for protecting earnings and current market share.